6-HOUR GUIDE
TO PROTECTING
YOUR ASSETS
How to Protect Your Hard Earned Assets from Creditors and Claimants

MARTIN M. SHENKMAN

WILEY

JOHN WILEY & SONS, INC.

Published by John Wiley & Sons, Inc., Hoboken, New Jersey.
Published simultaneously in Canada.

For general information on our other products and services please contact our
Customer Care Department within the U.S. at (800) 762-2974, outside the United
States at (317) 572-3993 or fax (317) 572-4002.

Wiley also publishes its books in a variety of electronic formats. Some content that
appears in print may not be available in electronic books. For more information about
Wiley products, visit our Web site at www.wiley.com.

Library of Congress Cataloging-in-Publication Data:

Shenkman, Martin M.
    6-hour guide to protecting your assets : how to protect your hard earned assets
from creditors and claimants / Martin M. Shenkman.
        p. cm.
    Includes index.
    ISBN 0-471-43057-9 (pbk.)
    1. Executions (Law)—United States—Popular works.   2. Debtor and creditor—
United States—Popular works.   3. Estate planning—United States.   I. Title:
Six-hour guide to protecting your assets.   II. Title.
KF9025.Z9S52 2003
347.73'77—dc21

                                                                    2003041117

Printed in the United States of America.

10 9 8 7 6 5 4 3 2 1

This book is dedicated to my wife, Dr. Patti Klein,
whose protection I have total reliance on,
even if she forgot the three circles.

Acknowledgments

My thanks to Joseph A. Chapman of Passaic, New Jersey, and Nikhill A. Hanmantgad of Closter, New Jersey, for their Internet research of cases and stories included in this book, and to Dani Koestrich and Neil Goldberg for their help with the Web site www.laweasy.com that will continue to serve readers.

Contents

PART ONE

INTRODUCTION TO LAWSUIT PROTECTION

1 INTRODUCTION TO ASSET PROTECTION PLANNING

EVERYONE DOES ASSET PROTECTION AND EVERYONE NEEDS ASSET PROTECTION

Protecting yourself from lawsuits, claims, divorce, the IRS, and other risks is called *asset protection*. Everyone does it, even those with little money. Even if you've never heard the phrase *asset protection*, the odds are you've done some. Even if you sleep without a worry in the world, you need asset protection planning. Why? Because anyone can be sued or suffer a loss.

Automobile Insurance

If you drive a car you could be in an accident, so you buy automobile insurance. Most people probably wouldn't consider an auto insurance policy to be asset protection planning, but it is. If you get in an accident, the insurance company will help defend you and cover some or all of your legal fees. If you lose the case or a settlement is reached, the insurance company will pay for it. This spares you paying and, thus, saves or protects your assets.

Homeowners' Insurance

If you own a home, you probably have homeowners' insurance. If there is a fire or a flood, the insurance company pays. This protects the value of your assets and is a form of asset protection planning.

Business Owners' Insurance

If you own a business, you've probably done major asset protection planning, even if you didn't realize it (although if you're like most business owners, the planning wasn't implemented properly). If you set up a small or closely held business more than five years ago, you probably had a lawyer form a corporation to run the business. Your accountant probably had the corporation treated as an S Corporation for tax purposes (see Chapter 12). If you've set up a business more recently, it was probably set up as a limited liability company (see Chapter 11). The only reason either step was taken was to protect your personal assets in case of a lawsuit against your business. This book explains how to make sure this protection works. Even if you operate only a small home-based business, asset protection is important.

Caution: Don't assume that because your home business is small, you don't need protection. The amount of your sales or profits has nothing to do with the risks you face. The smallest home business could create a huge liability. A customer coming to your house could be severely injured by falling down the stairs going to your basement office. If your home-owners' insurance excludes business injuries from its coverage, the settlement of the lawsuit will come out of your personal savings. Asset protection may not require much more than your getting a $10 certificate for a home office from your town and a $250 rider (additional coverage) on your homeowners' insurance policy so that your home business is both legitimate and insured. For most home-based businesses, the additional step of forming a limited liability company (LLC) through which you operate the business is probably advisable. In that way, the customer's fall down the stairs, or any other claim, can reach only business assets if your insurance is inadequate. The victim shouldn't be able to touch your personal savings.

Professionals' Insurance

If you're a doctor, lawyer, accountant, or other professional, you probably carry malpractice and liability insurance. If you're sued, the insurance company will help defend you and cover claims up to the amount of insurance you purchased. But, as this book explains, malpractice and other forms of insurance are not foolproof, and you should do more to protect your savings and other assets—for many people, much more. Every malpractice policy has exceptions and exclusions. Every malpractice insurance application requires detailed information. If the facts vary from those that you reported, your coverage could be jeopardized. Malpractice carriers require that you report any potential claim. If you don't report quickly enough, your coverage for the claim could be jeopardized. If you report potential claims more frequently in an effort to comply with the policy requirements (even potential claims that never materialize), the carrier may assume you're a problem and cancel your coverage. The Rubik's cube of reporting to your carrier is just one of scores of reasons to have backup protection in place. Asset protection planning, explained in this book, is the cornerstone of that backup.

Employers' Insurance

State law requires that employers carry certain minimum insurance coverage. If an employee is injured, the state insurance program or other insurance arrangement will provide minimum benefits. The benefits may not be much, but they will help preserve the injured employee's bank account as long as those funds can be used to pay for his or her expenses.

At a different level, if you are an officer or director of a company, the rash of corporate, accounting, and other scams creates a huge risk for you even if you have behaved admirably. Expect a greater level of accountability for your actions and the actions of your corporation even if you were not directly involved. Directors and officers' (D&O) insurance is harder to get, and, like malpractice coverage, has more and more restrictions, exclusions, and caveats. Backup protection has become as important for officers and directors as it is for a high-risk surgeon.

Senior Citizens' Insurance

If you're a senior citizen getting on in years, you might be worried about nursing home costs. You give your assets away to your children so that if you are admitted to a nursing home; some of your assets will be preserved for your benefit or for your heirs. Perhaps you buy a long-term care insurance policy (see Chapter 7). That is asset protection planning. Consult with an elder-law attorney (not a general practitioner or merely an estate planner—get a specialist). Get a durable power of attorney in place with special provisions authorizing trusted family or friends to address planning in case you become sick or disabled and cannot do so on your own (see Chapter 2).

Preparing a Will and Estate Plan

In your will, you state that any assets bequeathed to your spouse are to be distributed into a bypass (applicable exclusion) trust to save estate taxes (this trust preserves the $1+ million you are entitled to give away without estate tax). You may have done this to save tax, but it is an asset protection plan as well. If your surviving spouse is sued, the assets in the trust formed under your will may be protected. If your surviving spouse remarries and the new marriage doesn't work out, the new partner won't be able to reach the assets in the trust. You may have focused on saving taxes, but you've also protected assets from claims and divorce.

The previous examples illustrate that everyone takes steps to protect assets from lawsuits and divorce. Even if you didn't focus on asset protection as a goal, it is clearly important to you, and you've likely already been doing it. This book helps you understand asset protection planning so that you can more consciously focus planning efforts on better achieving this important goal. It helps you understand the rules of protecting yourself from lawsuits, divorce, and other risks.

WHAT IS ASSET PROTECTION PLANNING?

Asset protection planning is the process of organizing and structuring your investments, business interests, and activities in a manner that minimizes, to the extent possible, the ability of malpractice claimants, creditors, an ex-spouse, or others to reach your assets to satisfy their claims.

Example: You have $200,000 in cash in a checking account. You're sued and the verdict was in the claimant's favor. The court awards your claimant a $100,000 judgment. The claimant establishes a claim against your checking account and receives the cash. You're now $100,000 poorer.

However, if you own a business and your wife is a homemaker, you can put all your savings in her name. Your claimant will have a harder time getting at the cash; it's not yours.

Now you get more sophisticated. Instead of keeping $200,000 in the bank, you invested it in a family limited partnership with other family members. As a result of your $200,000 investment, you own 30 percent of the family limited partnership. You are a limited partner, which means you have no control over partnership decisions. If the same claimant wins the same judgment, the only significant asset you have is an interest in a partnership—which you don't control. If the claimant gets your 30 percent partnership interest, they can't spend it. As a result, the claimant will likely negotiate a settlement to get some money and resolve the matter. The claimant may even settle for much less than the $100,000 awarded.

There is no law or other requirement that you have to own your assets and conduct your business in a manner that makes it easy for someone suing or divorcing you to get to your assets. The previous examples show that you and everyone you know have probably done some asset protection planning, even if they didn't call it that or didn't know it.

A guiding rule to protecting your assets from lawsuits and divorce is that any steps you take should be consistent with your overall financial, estate, and personal plan. If you don't have an overall plan, get one. Asset protection is only part of an overall plan. It should never be your entire plan. Protecting assets from claimants will be inadequate if investment planning, tax planning, and other vital goals are not met.

This book addresses many aspects of using trusts, partnerships, and limited liability companies to achieve your goal of protecting assets from lawsuits and divorce. It also explains many of the common steps, such as proper insurance coverage, conducting your affairs to minimize the likelihood of a suit, and so on. These steps, which almost everyone can benefit from, receive scant attention in the literature, which tends to focus on complex-sounding techniques such as a foreign trust formed in some island country you've never heard of and cannot find on a map. Foreign trusts are useful asset protection tools. However, they are not a substitute for taking basic steps first. Even if you use a foreign asset protection trust as the cornerstone of your planning, a host of other planning steps discussed in this book should be evaluated. Few people ever set up a foreign trust; however, there is still plenty of asset protection planning that can be done. This book shows you how to begin.

Note: See Shenkman, *The Complete Book of Trusts* (3rd ed.), John Wiley & Sons, Inc., 2002, for a detailed discussion of each of the trusts discussed in this book. See www.laweasy.com for sample forms and additional planning tools and ideas.

RULES ABOUT WHAT ASSET PROTECTION IS NOT

There are many rules about what not to do as part of protecting yourself against lawsuits and divorce:

1. Do not hide assets. All assets should be disclosed. Lying about what you own or putting cash in your mattress isn't asset protection planning. The most well-crafted and sophisticated foreign asset protection trust does not make your assets disappear. The assets are, in fact, reported on income tax filings with the IRS. An investigative accountant hired by a claimant or a private investigator can identify most attempts at hiding assets. Further, if you are sued, it is common for a *deposition,* or sworn questioning of you, to occur. If you lie about the existence or whereabouts of assets and are caught, the penalties are severe. That is not the way to protect your assets.

2. Calling the transfer of assets so that a creditor cannot reach them *estate planning,* or anything other than *asset protection planning* will not avoid the rules on fraudulent conveyance (see Chapter 8). Protecting your assets from claimants or divorce must be more than mere labeling.

3. You cannot transfer assets after claims already exist. Existing creditors are those with claims, whether their rights to payment are fixed, disputed, contingent, or other. Once you are named as a defendant in a lawsuit, all transfers thereafter are deemed fraudulent if you cannot satisfy the judgment. Asset protection is not about dissipating your assets from

existing creditors. The rules actually go further. You cannot transfer assets to avoid a claim you should have expected (see Chapter 8).

4. No asset protection plan is foolproof. Asset protection is not, therefore, about guarantees and absolutes. Remember the old adage: "Don't put all your eggs in one basket." Some professionals disagree with this and counsel you to put all your assets into a single family limited partnership or limited liability company, which, in turn, is largely owned by a foreign asset protection trust. Understand the pros and cons of the different options before you finalize your plan.

5. Asset protection planning is not about a magic bullet. There is no single step that should be relied on alone. No single step, trust, asset, insurance, or technique can protect you against every claim or suit. No malpractice policy or coverage limit is the ultimate answer. You cannot simply put assets in your spouse's name, assuming he or she is not at risk.

6. Asset protection is not only about paying a lawyer to implement a fancy plan. The most well-developed plans, accompanied by the best legal documents, are of only limited benefit unless you implement the plans. You have to adhere to the formalities and procedures required. You have to file tax returns and transfer assets as instructed. You have to observe and respect the formalities of the entities your attorney establishes.

7. Asset protection planning is never static. It's not a time capsule that you seal until opened. No plan that is not periodically reviewed and revised to consider changes in the laws, tax rules, or your circumstances can be effective.

Understanding what asset protection should not be will help you avoid many pitfalls. It will help you direct your efforts in a more productive manner.

WHAT ASSET PROTECTION PLANNING MUST INCLUDE

Where the transfer to a trust, limited partnership, limited liability company, or other entity is deemed fraudulent (done to prevent a legitimate claimant from collecting), the transfer can be set aside and the purported asset protection benefits reduced or eliminated. If the transfer is deemed fraudulent, you could be subject to additional penalties. Bad planning can be much worse than no planning. Therefore, careful planning is essential. Planning includes the proper selection of the structure for the transaction, appropriate timing, careful drafting of the appropriate documents, and implementation.

IDENTIFYING YOUR RISKS AND MONITORING YOUR PROTECTION

One of the first steps you need to take is to identify the risks you face. These risks can be created by the particular assets you own, the jobs you work, the investments you make, and just plain life. You need to identify any steps you have already taken to protect against these risks. You will probably be pleasantly surprised at the number of steps taken. You probably have insurance, have organized your business as a corporation, and so on. You need to identify as you work through this book the additional steps you could take and those that you decide to take. Finally, the net result identifies risks or assets that remain unprotected. You may consciously decide to accept certain risks because of the cost or difficulty of protecting against them. You may also be unwilling to give up the requisite amount of control necessary to protect a particular asset. The Lawsuit Risk Analysis Worksheet chart in the For Your Notebook section at the end of this chapter will help you accomplish this.

DON'T EXPECT THE SYSTEM TO HELP YOU

There is no shortage of absurd, even outrageous, lawsuit results, which should prove a clarion call for you to take asset protection action. Whether the results were modified on appeal (when a decision of one court is taken to a higher court for review) or the jury verdicts were scaled back by a judge, the conclusion is simple: Anyone with anything to lose should not rely on the legal system for protection from claims. It's not only the wealthy physician who needs to be concerned. Consider the following examples:

Restaurant Owner

- In May 2000, Amber Carson of Lancaster, Pennsylvania, was awarded $113,500 for the injuries suffered after slipping on a soda spilled in a restaurant. The jury was apparently undeterred by the fact that the soda was on the floor because Amber had thrown it at her boyfriend during an argument!
- In 2002, a New York City restaurant patron sued four fast-food franchises, claiming that they are liable for his obesity and heart attacks because of the unhealthy nature of the food.

Property Owner

- In October 1998, Terrence Dickson of Bristol, Pennsylvania, robbed a house and, while leaving via the side door, got locked in the garage. The house door locked behind him, preventing him from leaving the garage via that route. The garage door malfunctioned and he was trapped for eight days, sustaining himself on a case of Pepsi and a quantity of dog food the home-owners kept in the garage. A jury awarded him $500,000 for the anguish he suffered from the experience.
- Few law school students make it through their first year without pondering the case of a would-be thief who fell through an unguarded skylight on the roof of the building he hoped to rob. The would-be felon sued for injuries suffered from the fall and was victorious. Apparently, the jury felt the property owner owed a duty of care to a potential thief!

Business Owner

- Can anyone forget the infamous McDonald's hot coffee case? In 1994, 81-year-old Stella Lieback spilled a cup of McDonald's coffee on herself, resulting in third-degree burns. A New Mexico jury awarded her $2.9 million.
- Kathleen Robertson of Austin, Texas, was shopping in a furniture store and tripped over a toddler running through the store. She broke her ankle and was awarded $780,000 by a jury for her injuries. The store owners were probably very surprised by the verdict in light of the fact that it was Ms. Robertson's child who tripped her!

Pet Owner

- Jerry Williams of Little Rock, Arkansas, was awarded $14,500 for injuries suffered after being bitten by a neighbor's beagle. The jury wasn't bothered by the fact that Jerry had entered his neighbor's yard and incited the dog by shooting it with a pellet gun.

Wealthy Person

- Don't forget the notable quip of Willie Sutton, the famous bank robber, when he was asked why he robbed banks: "Because that's where the money is." For many Americans, the money is in your pocket, and the legal system provides at least a lottery's chance at plaintiffs' getting it. Consider the statistics. The median net worth of an American family is about $60,000. That includes home equity, retirement savings, savings, insurance cash value—everything. A net worth of about $275,000 places you in the wealthiest 10 percent of the population. About $2.5 million in net worth places you in the wealthiest 1 percent of the population. Different surveys reflect different data, but they all demonstrate that relative to the country as a whole, if you're reading this book, you're probably much wealthier than you imagined. Claimants and juries may all be influenced by that. Remember Willie Sutton!

ANCILLARY TOPICS NOT COVERED

Protecting your earnings and assets from income, estate, gift, and generation skipping transfer (GST) taxes can be viewed as an essential part of asset protection planning. While the phase in of the higher estate tax exclusion may eliminate the estate tax for many, the need to plan to assure avoidance of estate, gift, and GST taxes should not be overlooked. Even if estate and GST taxes are repealed, the gift tax and state death transfer taxes will remain. Many of the techniques used for asset protection planning (irrevocable life insurance trust, family limited partnership, etc.) have important tax benefits as well. Creditor protection planning without comprehensive tax planning is insufficient to constitute thorough asset protection planning. Because income tax planning is not essential to the focus of this book—protecting your assets from lawsuits and divorce, we do not focus on the tax planning aspects of asset protection planning.

Protecting assets from nursing home and other medical costs can also be considered asset protection planning. This type of planning is called *elder law* planning. For many senior citizens, this is the *most* important focus of protecting their assets but it should not be. Just like income tax planning, it is one important concept, but there are others.

SUMMARY

Everyone needs to engage in asset protection planning. How sophisticated and costly your planning becomes depends on the assets you have (how wealthy you are), your temperament (what you need to sleep at night), and your risks (whether you are a hermit painter or high-risk surgeon). This chapter provided an introduction and overview of the asset protection planning process. The rest of this book elaborates and provides you with the detailed rules you need to protect yourself against lawsuits and divorce.

FOR YOUR NOTEBOOK

Source of Risk (1)	Lawsuit Risks (2)	Insurance (3)	Trust/Entity Ownership (4)	Other Steps (5)	Divorce Risks (6)	Divorce Steps (7)	Action Steps (8)
Assets							
Cash/ securities							
House							
Investment land							
Business							
Jobs							
Director							
Profession							
Other							
Charity board							

LAWSUIT RISK ANALYSIS WORKSHEET

Set up your own risk matrix using the above as a model. Rules for planning:

1. Identify every source of liability, malpractice, or other risk by type of asset, job, and other categories. You might list the same or related risks in several categories and as several line items. For example, if you are a surgeon and own your own practice and office, list the practice and the real estate as assets (the steps to protect them differ). List your work as a surgeon in the Jobs category because additional protection is necessary for that aspect.

2. Identify possible lawsuit risks. Think broadly because different risks could help your advisors identify different planning steps. For example, if you have a retail store, you have risks relating to the landlord, patrons, and products.

3. Identify the risks that you can insure. See Chapter 7 and the detailed insurance summary template presented there. Insurance is your first line of defense for many risks. This should be supplemented in many cases by steps 4 and 5.

4. List the types of entities and describe how they can be used to protect your asset or risk. This is discussed in detail in Parts Four and Five of this book.

5. In addition to insurance and use of trusts and entities to protect assets, there may be other steps to take. For example, many obstetrician/gynecologists have opted in response to the malpractice insurance crises to provide only gynecological, not obstetric, services. Many do not want to make this decision, but it is a clear option for minimizing risk. You might sell or give away an asset to avoid the risks.

6. Identify divorce risks.

7. Identify divorce planning steps. These could include a prenuptial agreement, postnuptial agreement, careful maintenance of separate property to avoid commingling it with marital property, and so on (see Part Two).

8. List action steps to follow up on to protect yourself from lawsuits, divorce, and other risks.

2 BASIC RULES TO PROTECT ASSETS AGAINST LAWSUITS AND DIVORCE

Although asset protection planning must be tailored to your specific situation, there are general rules—guiding principles—that should be considered in most planning. This chapter provides an overview of those principles.

NEST EGG VERSUS COMPLETE PROTECTION

Some people attempt to protect every penny they have. They might try to transfer every asset they own to foreign asset protection trusts, family limited partnerships, or other protective arrangements. Their hope is the better that they protect everything, the better they will fare if sued. Unfortunately, the old adage holds true: "Hogs get fat, pigs get slaughtered." If you're a pig about protecting everything you own, you may jeopardize all of your planning. A less aggressive and more secure approach may be the nonintuitive approach of protecting significant assets, but much less than all. If you choose to be more conservative and, many experts say, wiser, you transfer only some portion of your assets to an offshore trust, family limited partnership (FLP), or other technique to secure those assets. This approach views asset protection planning as a nest egg concept. Protect a portion of your assets in the event of a lawsuit or other problem. Where the nest egg approach is used, asset protection planning is probably an appropriate objective for almost anyone with substantial means and even many people with more moderate wealth. Courts will be less likely to overturn your planning as a fraudulent conveyance (an attempt to inappropriately prevent your known claimants from reaching your assets) because substantial assets remain in your hands. Your claimants may reach those assets, but your nest egg is protected.

THE MORE YOU NEED IT, THE LESS IT MAY WORK

Like so many good things, the more you want it, the less likely you are to get it. Asset protection techniques are of less, if any, value when problems have already occurred. Where lawsuits or divorce are already pending (or happen so soon after your transfer of assets that suspicions are aroused), transfers could be set aside as fraudulent conveyances. The moral: Do it before it is really needed. Planning in advance out of fear of future creditors and claimants is acceptable. Planning to avoid the risks of possible future creditors, as opposed to probable future creditors, should not be problematic. The rule is plan now. Don't assume your insurance is foolproof or that claims won't exceed your coverage. Don't wait.

MORE THAN ASSET PROTECTION

Any step taken should be for purposes other than merely asset protection. Steps should be consistent with your overall personal plan, estate planning goals, diversification of assets, and so forth. One or, preferably, more business or other nonasset protection motives for every step you take give the transaction more credibility. Where transfers are part of an overall estate and personal financial plan and employ commonly used, nonasset protection motivated techniques, they are more likely to be respected. Nonasset protection motives may help deflect challenges that the transferor had fraudulent intent in making the transfer. If nothing else, reasonable motives for any planning steps you take will make those steps appear less offensive in the eyes of any judge or jury. As a bonus, because tax planning objectives are usually pursued as part of an overall strategy, the more realistic, reasonable, and varied the motives for any transaction, the more likely the IRS will respect the transaction as well.

Example: Real estate is transferred to a FLP. The limited partnership structure provides control over the management of the building, which is essential to prevent squabbles among the now numerous owners, because the general partner makes all management decisions and the limited partners are precluded from becoming involved. Children, as limited partners, cannot participate in management decisions, so the operations remain controlled by the senior person with the most substantial real estate expertise. As the children's competence is proved, a particular child may obtain certain rights and, perhaps, ownership interests in the corporate general partner, thus facilitating participation in active management. Thus, the FLP can provide a mechanism for transferring ownership interests to the next generation. The FLP structure may also serve as a technique to make gifts to children in lower income tax brackets, thus providing the family with overall income tax savings. All of these nonasset protection goals are legitimate and can provide important corroboration that the transactions were intended as structured. As such, they should be respected.

THE MORE, THE MERRIER

The greater the number of entities, the more components into which various interests and rights in your assets are divided, the more layers of entities and contractual relationships, and the more difficult your plan will be for a claimant to pierce. The option of transferring assets to a single limited partnership or limited liability company (LLC) to insulate assets should be carefully compared to the transfer of each individual asset, or perhaps each category of assets to a separate limited partnership or LLC to insulate each property, investment, or business from claims of your other properties, investments, or businesses. For example, a single partnership owning several assets can result in all assets being attacked where a liability or claim is made on one asset.

Example: A father owns a building and a widget manufacturing business. He wishes to restructure these two activities (building rental and widget manufacture) to facilitate a gift program for estate tax purposes, assure management of the property in a centralized and professional manner, and provide a measure of protection from future unknown creditors or claimants. The building is transferred to an FLP whose interests are to be owned by the family members. An FLP can have an S corporation as the general partner for greater protection (see Chapter 10). The children's interests in the limited partnership can be owned by trusts for their benefit, rather than by the children directly. This provides greater protection in the event a child ever divorces. The building can be owned by one limited partnership and the business by a second limited partnership. Alternatively, the business could be owned by an LLC or other entity. A prospective claimant would have to challenge each of the entities involved in the plan to reach all assets. This could involve substantial legal work. Assume the father formed an FLP with an S corporation general partner to own the building, an S corporation to own the manufacturing business, and a trust for each of his three children to own interests he gave them. This makes six separate entities, each of which may have a different person in charge, different legal documents governing operations, and some of which may be formed in different states. The complexity of understanding the structure and the legal costs of naming each a party to a suit and reviewing all applicable documentation will prove a deterrent to a claimant or divorcing spouse. In addition, the other limitations and restrictions on a creditor's ability to attach limited partnership interests, or membership interests in an LLC, would hinder the creditor in collecting on any judgment.

The later chapters of this book explain in detail each of the entities and techniques used in the previous example. The rule for protecting yourself remains simple: Don't rely on one technique, and don't put all your eggs in one basket.

What can you do if you already have several substantial assets in a single entity? Your attorney may be able to divide the entity into multiple FLPs or LLCs. The division of a single partnership into multiple partnerships, for example, may minimize this dangerous situation, thus providing important asset protection benefits.

Caution: Dividing an existing FLP or LLC into multiple FLPs or LLCs may be good asset protection planning, but, as with every step, competent legal assistance is essential. Almost every step or technique to safeguard your assets from lawsuits or divorce has ancillary consequences that must be addressed. Dividing a partnership, for example, raises the issue as to whether there will be a termination of the partnership for tax purposes. Termination can have a number of potentially adverse tax consequences; for example, the partnership tax year ends. When the partners and the partnership have different tax years, a bunching of taxable income into one year can result. When the cash distributed by the partnership in the event of termination exceeds the partner's tax basis in the partnership, gain will be recognized. A number of other consequences can also occur. The partnership will not be deemed to have terminated if the successor partnerships are considered to be a continuation of the prior partnership. This occurs if the members of the successor partnership have interests of more than 50 percent in the capital and profits of the prior partnership. In most cases, because there is no significant change in ownership accompanying the restructure, this requirement should readily be met.

IF YOU CAN'T DO IT RIGHT, DON'T DO IT

The best-laid plan is useless if the formalities and details are not adhered to. You cannot hire a lawyer to prepare a plan to protect your assets from claimants or divorce and assume that once the paperwork is completed, your responsibilities end. There will always be follow-up required. If you don't respect the details of your own plan, don't expect a court (or the IRS) to either.

Example: Wally Worried sets up a corporation to protect his home and savings from a suit against his business. He pays a lawyer to form the corporation. Once the lawyer is paid, Wally assumes his worries are over, so he sleeps well at night and concentrates on building sales. Wally, unfortunately, ignores any of the formalities of operating a corporation. With no corporate minutes (legal record confirming actions of the directors), no stock formally issued, and the form of a corporation largely ignored, Wally is unlikely to withstand a challenge of a claimant seeking to pierce the corporate veil (see Chapter 12) and reach his home and savings to satisfy a claim. If you think Wally Worried is unusual in ignoring formalities, think again. The vast majority of closely held businesses lack many of the essential formalities, documents, and steps that Wally's corporation does.

GOOD FAITH EFFORT

If something doesn't "smell right," it may not be right. If a judge or court thinks you've attempted to inappropriately hide assets you knew about (or perhaps should have known about) from a claimant, they are more likely to decide against you. If you are considering asset protection steps, make a good faith effort to identify and then estimate all outstanding claims against you. Then be sure to reserve, unprotected, in your name, adequate assets to reasonably meet those claims and any expected costs, as well as your necessary living expenses.

Planning Tip: Prepare a personal budget to demonstrate that your income is sufficient to support your lifestyle. Have a qualified accountant compile a personal financial statement in accordance with applicable accounting standards to demonstrate solvency (your assets exceed any claims) before and after any transfers.

Caution: Don't make any statements, or take any actions, that indicate an intent to defraud your creditors. Use reputable professionals whose reputation give you credibility, not a presumption that your planning was aggressive or worse.

ARM'S LENGTH

If a stranger wouldn't pay the price or conclude the transaction the way you want to, you shouldn't either. In legal jargon, your transactions and planning should be done on an *arm's length basis*—as if you and your own entities were unrelated people. If your children set up an LLC to own a warehouse, which it then rents to your business, the rent you pay could be set unusually high so you could transfer assets to your children via the high rent. Neither a court nor the IRS will be impressed. If you divorce, be assured that your ex-spouse's attorney will have the rent figures scrutinized. Extra care must be taken when any arm's length transaction is structured. Where the rights and interests in an asset are divided, each component of the transaction should stand independently and be consummated on terms that can be demonstrated to be arm's length.

Example: Real estate is transferred by gift to various trusts for minor children. The rent the business pays to the trusts is set by the trusts' retaining and paying a qualified local real estate broker for a written appraisal of a fair rental price. A preferable approach may be to have the rent appraisal determined by a certified appraiser. Further, the trustees of the trust save the real estate sections from several local real estate and general circulation newspapers to demonstrate the state of the market at the time the transaction was consummated.

RULES TO HELP YOU UNDERSTAND THE LEGAL SYSTEM

The ostrich approach doesn't work. You can't ignore a lawsuit, claim, or legal notice and expect everything to work out happily in the end. While it is helpful to have some general knowledge of how the legal system works to understand how you can protect your assets and how to respond to a claim, the bottom line is simple. If you have any concern, if you receive any type of notice or formal letter, get professional help. The old adage, "It's better to be safe than sorry," certainly applies to asset protection planning.

The first step in the process is that something happens to create a claim. This may be something obvious, such as you hitting another car while you are driving, someone tripping on your walk, you certifing financial statements and missing a key problem, you leaving a sponge in a patient, or extracting the wrong tooth. Often, however, the act giving rise to the claim is something you had no knowledge of. Frequently, the first time you learn of the situation is when you get a lawyer's letter or are served with documents commencing a lawsuit.

Depending on the circumstances, the first step in the legal process may be a letter from a lawyer demanding that you correct a problem (e.g., pay past due rent, pay a loan in default). In other situations, the claimant's lawyer may begin the process more formally by starting a lawsuit (action). This is generally accompanied by your being presented with (served) the formal legal documents indicating a suit has begun. This can be done by a person physically handing you legal documents or, in other situations, mailing them to your legal address (your home or employment). These papers could include a *summons,* which is an order that you appear in court, and a *complaint,* which lists the claims asserted by the person suing you. You need to immediately notify your insurer and hire a lawyer to respond by filing a formal reply with the court (answer). If you fail to do this in a timely fashion, the court automatically treats the claimant as victorious. After all, if you didn't think it worth responding to the lawsuit, you must think that there was nothing you could do to prove the claim wrong. The court then enters what is called a *default judgment.* You threw in the towel. If you have any arguments whatsoever, you should never let a claim be resolved through a default judgment.

In some instances, you may know you're wrong but be willing to cut a deal with the claimant to avoid the lengthy and expensive process of a lawsuit. It can benefit you and the claimant to do this. Most claimants are willing to accept something less than they asked for in the complaint if they know they have a deal and can avoid the potentially large costs and long time delays of winding the claim through the legal system. You and the claimant may contractually agree on how to resolve the issue, what you will pay, and what other actions you both agree to. This document is called a *settlement agreement.*

The next step in the process is the preparation for a trial, which attempts to determine whether the claims are correct. Before the trial, both sides—the claimant (called the *plaintiff*) and you (the *defendant*)—try to find out facts to support each side of the dispute. This may include serving written *interrogatories* (formal written questions that must be answered) on the other side. They often run on for hundreds of pages. There may be *depositions*—formal meetings, usually documented (transcribed) by a court reporter in which each attorney asks the other side, and other people who may know about the case, questions. The questioning is done under oath; therefore, a false statement can have serious consequences. People other than you and the claimant (third parties) may be ordered to appear for questioning (*subpoena*). Once the preliminaries are completed, the issue (case) goes to trial.

When the trial is concluded, if the claimant loses, you're done (assuming that you don't pursue the claimant). If the claimant wins, the story may still not end. You may appeal the verdict. This means asking a higher court to question some aspects of the conclusions reached by the first court. If you don't appeal the loss, after the trial the claimant's lawyer will have the court enter a judgment in the claimant's favor. This is a formal procedure that acknowledges the amount you owe the claimant. The now victorious claimant will next try to collect your assets to satisfy the judgment. If you simply pay what is due, the process is over. Insurance may cover some, but too often not all, that you owe. If not, the claimant may file a summary of the court's ruling (abstract of the judgment) in the governmental records (county clerk) in each county where you own real estate or other assets.

If the assets are located out of state, the judgment of the court that gave the ruling must be entered in that other state. The foreign state judgment is said to be "domesticated" in the state where assets are located. This may be little more than a formality between one state and another within the United States. However, if you have assets in a foreign country, the process of having the U.S. court's judgment honored may be laborious or impossible. A complete new trial may be required. That foreign country's laws may preclude a victory for the claimant. This is a key aspect to the protective benefits afforded by the use of a foreign asset protection trust.

The claimant will try to obtain your assets in whatever manner necessary. This can include filing a *lien,* which is recorded in the public record (and may first require that the judgment be domesticated); no one can buy your real estate or personal assets (e.g., medical equipment, fork-lift) until the lien is satisfied. Because the liens apply only to assets owned by the persons named, your claimant will try to name every entity that you own that owns assets. The claimant may have the sheriff levy on a house or other asset in your name. Your wages may be partially earmarked (*garnished*) to be paid to the claimant. Accounts receivable from your business may be attached.

While the legal process may sound disconcerting to you, as a potential defendant with income and assets at risk, understanding it is important. A default judgment should almost never be permitted. Holding all of your assets in one entity or form makes it easier for the claimant to reach them. Holding assets in one jurisdiction makes it easier for the claimant to reach them. Time delays and costs of the process can encourage a claimant to settle. Planning to take maximum advantage of these workings of the system is an important, and legal, part of what asset protection is about.

RULES ABOUT LEGAL DOCUMENTS YOU SIGN

Know What You Are Signing

If you don't understand it, don't sign it. Any legal documents you use should be appropriately tailored to your situation, and you should understand the broad strokes (details can be left to your lawyer) of the document. Using *boilerplate* or standard documents that are not tailored to your situation can undermine the best of plans. If you don't understand the general concepts and key provisions of every legal document, you won't be able to implement the planning, and your efforts will more likely be unsuccessful.

Closely Held Corporation Documents

For a corporation to be respected as an independent legal entity (so that claims against the corporation cannot reach your personal assets), the formalities of the corporation must be observed. This means that you should operate the corporation in accordance with the legal documents, the bylaws, shareholders' agreement, and various contracts that govern the corporation. If you don't understand these documents, you can't possibly operate in accordance with them. If the bylaws require that there be a certain number of directors and specified officers, follow these criteria. If the shareholders' agreement requires that certain documentation be provided at set time periods to various shareholders (e.g., reports on sales each quarter), comply with these requirements.

Power of Attorney—Your Most Important Legal Document Can Save or Destroy Your Plan

The most common estate planning document, and one of the most common legal documents, is a *durable power of attorney*. This is a document in which you designate an agent to handle your legal, tax, and financial matters in the event of your illness and disability. A power of attorney can be a critical document.

A key use of a durable power of attorney is to facilitate a continuation of your ability to give gifts in the event of disability. Each person is permitted to give away $11,000 (indexed for inflation) each year to any number of people, as well as make direct payments for tuition and medical expenses. If you have a taxable estate, these gifts can make tremendous headway in minimizing, or even eliminating, that tax cost. If you're concerned about lawsuits, your agent may be able to use these gift powers to safeguard assets if you are disabled. If this use is appealing, your power of attorney should include a provision expressly permitting such gifts. Many standard forms don't include the right to make gifts for tuition and medical and, thus, inadvertently limit the gift-making capacity.

Example: Mother began a regular gift program where each year she and her husband join in making gifts of stock to each of their five adopted children, their children's spouses, and their eight grandchildren. The gifts are each $22,000 in value, the maximum amount that can be given away each year without any gift tax, for a total of $396,000 [(5 + 5 + 8) × $11,000 × 2]. Mother falls ill in December and is unable to sign the necessary documents to make a transfer for the year, so the couple makes no gifts in that year. The couple could incur an unnecessary additional estate tax cost of as much as $198,000 (assuming a 50 percent maximum rate) because this gift was not made. Had Mother prepared an appropriate power of attorney, her agent may have been able to handle the paperwork necessary to make the gifts and eliminate this unnecessary estate tax burden. The figure would be higher if gifts of tuition and medical were also made.

The gift provision in a power of attorney is also susceptible to abuse. If you are seeking to safeguard your assets, this abuse must be considered.

Example: An elderly widow's nearest living relative was a nephew she saw a few times a year around the holidays. She named the nephew as agent under a general power of attorney. The nephew, realizing that his elderly aunt had limited mobility and limited awareness, began to actively use her funds for his benefit. By the time he was discovered and the powers revoked, he had nearly wiped out his aunt's estate. By then, his aunt was too elderly and infirm to pursue the matter and had insufficient funds to hire an attorney. The nephew was never taken to task for his actions. A funded revocable living trust with an institutional cotrustee would have been a preferable approach.

Most people tend to view a power of attorney as a cheap, boilerplate form. However, the risks are substantial. Abuses are becoming excessive. Powers of attorney should be treated with the same caution and importance as your will. If abuse is possible, perhaps you should use a revocable living trust instead (a more formal document and arrangement). You might also expressly exclude the agent from having the right to make gifts. Alternatively, you may limit the agent's right to make gifts to a minimum of annual exclusion, presently $11,000, or even a smaller amount.

Divorce has become common in today's society and presents additional issues for powers of attorney. As soon as marital trouble is brewing, consider canceling any power of attorney for your spouse. This is as essential as canceling credit cards and other vehicles for creating debt. Record the termination by having your attorney file the cancellation in the county clerk's office (often referred to as the public records). Have your attorney send letters to any appropriate people stating that the power has been canceled. The key step, however, is to destroy all originals of the previous documents.

With an aging population, Medicaid or elder law planning is increasingly common. In the event you become disabled before the implementation of planning to safeguard your assets from nursing home and other medical costs, a durable power is essential to facilitate the transfer of assets. This is done through a broad gift power, which must be included for Medicaid issues. If there is no express gift power in the power of attorney, the gifts won't be recognized as having triggered the commencement of the look-back period (the time during which Medicaid can attach your assets). However, such a broad gift power is tantamount to a will substitute because of its broad and unlimited scope permitting your agent to transfer all of your assets.

Documentation Must Be Thorough

The documentation for any transaction intended to protect assets from creditors, or between related parties, must be thorough and complete.

Example: If a family member is retained as a consultant, an independent consulting agreement with arm's length terms should be negotiated and signed. The agreement should be a full-fledged agreement with all the provisions that an agreement between related parties would include. It should not be a one-page "quickie." Loans between related parties should be documented with written loan agreements (notes) prepared in the same manner as independent parties would require. This means include all of the protection and provisions an unrelated party would require (e.g., only reasonable grace periods, acceleration clause, reasonable interest rate and payment schedule, default provisions). If the collateral is real estate, a mortgage should be recorded. If the collateral is personal property, the appropriate Uniform Commercial Code statements securing the lien should be filed as they would for an unrelated person.

RULES TO DOCUMENT THE REASONABLENESS OF YOUR PLANNING STEPS

Any plan to protect your assets from lawsuits or divorce should include steps to document the facts and circumstances surrounding the transactions. Review the following with your advisors, and prepare a file of all relevant documents to prove the facts and circumstances surrounding any asset protection steps you take.

Background

Describe your background and give your reasons for seeking asset protection techniques. Explain how your background and specific liability concerns affect the planning. Include your resume to help corroborate your competency, skills, ability to earn a livelihood, and other important factors. Your file should include an express statement that you understand what a fraudulent conveyance is and that you will not participate in one (see Chapter 8).

Reference Letters

Obtain reference letters from your accountant, banker, attorneys, and other professional advisors. These can attest to your character, integrity, business acumen, and so forth.

Business Practices

List your business practices and explain how they affect your liability exposure. For example, having proper insurance coverage for your business (or businesses) is essential. Have your business insurance consultant prepare a summary chart of all coverage. If you have an outside accountant who has prepared an internal controls analysis (the procedures used by your business to ensure accuracy of reporting information, safeguarding of business assets, etc.), include a copy.

For divorce planning, analyze and document (with the assistance and direction of a matrimonial attorney) whether your business practices could taint the character of any separate or immune assets as marital. If you had a business before you married or you inherited a business, your work efforts or poor record keeping could result in that separate asset (which your ex-spouse should not have access to as part of a property settlement) being characterized as marital property. Specify whether your soon-to-be-ex-spouse listed on your business books gets a salary and perquisites. If so, what effect will it have on the division of your business?

Investigations, Searches

Document any investigations by any branch of the government or other issues that may affect your liability situation.

You should obtain lien, judgment, and claim searches. These can often be obtained online. You might be surprised to discover issues you did not even know about. Each such issue should be addressed with your advisors. If there is a lien or claim that you can settle before proceeding with any planning, that may be advisable.

Order a credit report from all the major credit reporting agencies. If there are any problems with credit noted, endeavor to clear them; if you cannot, request that the credit reporting agency reflect your explanation in your credit report.

Criminal Status, Convictions

Document whether you have had any prior convictions for any crimes.

Bankruptcy Filings

Document and elaborate in writing any prior bankruptcy filings you, or any entity you've controlled (e.g., a business), have made.

Tax Filings

Determine whether you have filed all tax returns and paid taxes on time. This is vitally important because one of the most common exceptions to many asset protection steps is for the IRS to be paid its due. If you haven't filed all returns or paid all taxes, have an accountant complete the returns and calculate any taxes due so that you can "clean up" these issues before planning. If you are a *responsible person* (a technical term your business accountant can best help define) for a business, verify that the business paid all taxes and filed all returns. This is especially important for payroll and sales taxes the business collects (called *trust fund* taxes because you are really holding monies collected from the customer for the government in the case of sales taxes and from employees in the case of payroll taxes).

Divorce Risks

If you're planning for divorce, or were previously divorced, be certain that all child support and alimony payments are current. Have an attorney review your property settlement or other divorce or marital agreements to help you verify that you are in compliance with all requirements. This is important because alimony and child support are another common exception to the benefits of many asset protection techniques.

Prove Your Worth

Do a solvency analysis. Demonstrate and document that after any transfers or changes you are contemplating, you have adequate financial resources to meet any commitments you have, including living expenses for you and your family. This step might include having an accountant prepare a personal financial balance sheet in accordance with applicable accounting standards. Subtract all liabilities including threats, contingent liabilities, and so on. Defense counsel may give you an estimate of reasonable settlement costs so that they can be included. Other common liabilities include an estimate of income taxes payable, current credit card debt, and estimates of liabilities under guarantee agreements you may have signed (e.g., you guaranteed your child's home mortgage).

Include any possible claim in your analysis. Your advisors may recommend that you even make an additional calculation of your net worth (assets less liabilities) further reduced by assets that are already protected under state or federal law. These are exemptions such as qualified retirement plan assets that a claimant cannot reach, life insurance arrangements, homestead exemption (in some states, claimants cannot reach your house value; see Chapter 3), and so on. Your solvency analysis might also include preparing a budget to demonstrate that your annual income or cash flow is sufficient to meet expenses.

Business Financial Records

If you are an officer or director of a company, obtain financial statements for that company to include in your file. Conduct some of the same procedures for each company and business as you did on yourself personally. Obtain a Dun & Bradstreet report on the company. Documenting the lack of claims, suits, and liens on the company and corroborating its real value help demonstrate your care in not violating the fraudulent conveyance rules discussed in Chapter 8. It helps demonstrate why you have undertaken planning; it helps your advisors tailor your planning to meet your needs.

The previous items and any others your advisors believe to be pertinent to your situation should be included in a file supporting your asset protection planning. You and your key advisors should retain copies of this file.

SUMMARY

Safeguarding yourself from lawsuits and divorce requires that some basic rules of documentation and procedure be followed. There are many steps of basic asset protection you should consider taking, including obtaining adequate insurance (but never relying on it as absolute protection), executing powers of attorney, transferring assets to partnerships, limited liability companies, and family limited partnerships. Your transactions should be conducted on an arm's length basis and your situation thoroughly documented. In addition, a general knowledge of the legal system is necessary to understand the process of lawsuits so that you can take the appropriate protective steps, retain professional advice, and protect yourself and your assets.

3 RULES FOR HOW TO OWN (TITLE) YOUR ASSETS TO MAXIMIZE SAFETY

The title and structure of asset ownership is a critical, and an often misunderstood or overlooked, component of planning to protect your assets from lawsuits and divorce. *Title* is who and how the asset is owned. The simplest and most common example is a bank account. Whose name is on the account? Is there another person listed on the account name? How do these various people own the account, or more correctly, what interests in the account does each have?

Example: Dr. Jenny Jones is an obstetrician. She is very worried about the state of malpractice insurance coverage. Coverage has been cut back and is nearly unaffordable. She transfers the ownership, title, of all her assets to her husband, George. The marriage starts to falter over the next few years as Jenny becomes increasingly engrossed in her practice. Eventually, George files for divorce. Although the state they live in provides for equitable distribution of assets, George has an important strategic edge for the time being because he has control over all of the assets. Jenny's simplistic asset protection plan was not particularly successful. Worse, what if George was sued?

The ownership structure of assets can affect your ability to make gifts to remove assets from the reach of claimants, the likelihood of creditors reaching the assets, and the rights of a surviving spouse exercising a right of election (claiming the minimum amount state law mandates a surviving spouse can claim) against those assets. See www.laweasy.com for details.

Example: Dr. Jones, the obstetrician in our previous example, owns two assets—a house and a brokerage account. Under her state's laws, the house is classified as a specialized type of asset, a *homestead exemption,* which creditors cannot reach. Pension assets are also protected (see Chapter 9). Instead of transferring all assets to George, Jenny retains the house, which is protected, pays off the mortgage with some of their cash, transfers all investment assets to George, and sets up an individual retirement account (IRA), which has protection under state law. If the same scenario plays out years later in a divorce, Dr. Jones will have a better strategic position than in the prior example. Regardless of the resolution of the marital situation, if a malpractice suit or other claim affects Jenny or George, the family is in a better position to resist the claims and ravages of an unfavorable settlement. If the marriage ends in divorce, both Jenny and George will benefit if there are more marital assets because of the protective steps taken. The impact of these steps on their divorce is analyzed in Chapters 4 and 15.

Title is also far more complex than simply choosing among joint tenants, tenancy in common, and tenancy by the entirety (all these terms are explained later). Title, in the broadest sense in which it must be analyzed to properly address estate planning issues, must include the allocation of investment assets (i.e., what assets should be owned), the entity or entities that should own the assets, and the many ways which you can alter title (spousal right of election, disclaimer, etc.).

Example: After obstetrician Jenny seeks professional guidance, she decides not to transfer substantial investment assets to George and leave her house unprotected other than the homestead exemption. Jenny and George together seek professional guidance. The house is transferred to a special type of house trust, a *qualified personal residence trust* (QPRT; see Chapter 16). The securities are transferred to a family limited partnership (FLP; see Chapter 10). Most of the limited partnership interests in the FLP are then given to a foreign asset protection trust (see Chapter 18). Jenny hires a pension consultant to set up a qualified retirement plan for her medical practice. This permits her to contribute far more than she can to an IRA account, and qualified plans have protection under federal law that IRAs do not (see Chapter 9).

The following discussion reviews many of the common titles in which you may hold assets. Integral to this analysis is the structure of the asset itself. Is the asset owned directly in the title format set forth in this discussion, or is there some type of intervening entity, which triggers its own asset protection implications?

IDENTIFYING ASSET TITLE AND OWNERSHIP

The first step in the asset protection planning process is to identify
the manner in which your various assets are held. This task is usually far more difficult than it sounds because most people do not
know the correct ownership of many of their assets. In addition,
the knowledge required to properly plan is substantially more than
merely knowing the title on your house. Consider the following:

1. Review all relevant documents (deeds, stock certificates, brokerage account statements, etc.) to determine the exact ownership of the assets involved. Don't assume; verify each item.
   Consider the governing language in the account title (i.e., the
   terms other than the names). If there was a contract signed
   when the account was opened, the terms of that contract need
   to be considered. Be sure insurance is in the same name as title.

2. Determine your income tax cost basis (in simple terms, your investment, less depreciation, plus improvements) in the property. This depends, in part, on the manner in which the
   property was acquired: gift (carry-over basis), inheritance
   (step-up basis at date of death or the alternate valuation date),
   or purchase (acquisition cost). Income tax consequences should
   be considered when you do your planning to protect assets as
   well. Tax consequences might determine which assets you use
   for certain planning techniques.

   > **Example:** Sally Senior is planning to gift assets to minimize the value
   > that may be exposed to claimants, Medicaid in particular, and estate
   > taxes. She should gift assets with the least amount of appreciation (i.e.,
   > whose cost is closest to its current value) because under the current tax
   > system, assets she owns on her death will have their cost basis increased
   > to their fair value, thus eliminating any capital gains tax advantage her
   > heirs would have when they sell the assets. Ignoring this tax fact can
   > still enable her other goals to be achieved but ultimately at a cost of 20
   > percent or more of the value to her heirs.

3. Where there are co-owners, determine the contribution (investment) of each co-owner. Identify contributions made at different times. The timing could be critical to properly allocating
   the contributions and appreciation to determine ownership and
   tax consequences. In addition, timing is critical if a husband

and wife acquired property while married and in a community property state (see later discussion). This can be tricky, and the guidance of a tax accountant is advisable.

4. Determine legal consequences of your ownership interest in each asset with the help of an attorney. This could include a review of applicable local law as well as the application or contract documents for the bank, brokerage firm, or other legal entity involved with the establishing of the asset.

5. Analyze your overall personal, tax, investment, and liquidity situations to determine the optimal, or at least a preferable, method of ownership. In considering your circumstances, identify whether you and your spouse are both U.S. citizens because this can affect your ability to change the ownership (retitle) assets. There are significant restrictions on how much you can give each year to a spouse who is not a citizen. In addition, special will provision may be necessary. Overlooking this point could trigger a substantial gift or estate tax cost that could be worse than the other claims you may have been trying to protect against.

6. Consider the costs and difficulties of restructuring the ownership interest. Where real estate is involved, transfer and recording fees may be incurred. Environmental review may be necessary to approve a transfer. Changing title may require a consent of all tenants under leases, mortgages on any loans to the owners, a new title policy, and so on.

7. Determine your motives. Transferring an asset from your name alone to joint ownership with your spouse or another person causes a loss of some element of control. What if the survivor lacks management skills? Perhaps a trust is better than joint ownership.

HOW TITLE TO ASSETS AFFECTS ESTATE TAX PLANNING IN A TRADITIONAL FAMILY UNIT

Basic financial information is critical to estate planning. Estate planning may have focused primarily on minimizing estate taxes. However, a byproduct of that planning was always some type of protection against lawsuits and divorce. As the impact of the estate tax wanes (or is perhaps even eliminated), the asset protection benefits that had been only a byproduct will become primary for more people.

Caution: Too many people, and even many professionals, viewed estate planning only as a method of saving tax. This erroneous attitude results in many people forgoing the asset protection benefits that planning can offer. Don't assume that the increase in the estate tax applicable exclusion (the amount you can give away without tax) means the end of planning. Planning should continue, with similar trusts used, not to achieve estate tax savings, but rather to achieve income tax benefits, safeguard assets if your surviving spouse remarries, protect assets in the event your surviving spouse is sued, and so on.

If you are married, you may wish to take advantage of the current $1 million (increasing to $1.5 million in 2004 and further in later years) estate tax exclusion available to each of you and your spouse to minimize estate taxes. Ownership of assets generally should be divided between you and your spouse so that the estate of the first spouse to die will have sufficient assets to use this benefit. The traditional approach is for the will of the first spouse to die to transfer approximately this amount into a special trust to benefit the surviving spouse, without being taxed in his or her estate. Hence, this trust is often called a *bypass* trust because it bypasses the surviving spouse's estate. The surviving spouse is generally provided for by this trust, but the trust assets are not pulled into the survivor's taxable estate. This technique is one of the most commonly used estate tax planning strategies. Joint ownership of all assets could defeat this type of planning. Importantly, if you are very concerned about being sued, the traditional approach of dividing assets one-half in your name and one-half in your spouse's name may be foolhardy. Other alternatives, such as an *inter vivos* QTIP trust, are explored in Chapter 16.

SOLE OWNERSHIP

It seems almost so obvious that it needn't be said, but one way to own property is in one person's name alone. Is this asset protection planning? Well, maybe.

If you're a painter and your wife is a lawyer, owning assets solely in your name is a means of protecting your assets. This was illustrated in the previous examples with Dr. Jones. It probably won't be the best approach, but it's cheap and simple and perhaps better than nothing. The other variation of this approach illustrated for Dr. Jones is to leave ownership of only specially protected assets in your name if you're subject to lawsuit risks (exempt assets are discussed in Chapter 9).

There is another aspect to owning assets in your name alone. If you owned assets before your marriage, or inherited or received assets as a gift before or during your marriage, under many state laws those assets won't be considered marital assets to be divided in the event of a divorce. If instead of keeping these separate (immune) assets in solely your name, you put them in a joint account or your spouse is actively involved in the management of those assets, the property may become tainted as marital assets. This might mean you lose 50 percent of the assets in a divorce. In this context, keeping the assets in your name alone is a plan to protect them from divorce—not the best plan, but still a benefit.

JOINTLY HELD PROPERTY

What Is Joint Property?

Joint tenants is a possessory interest in the same property where all cotenants own a whole or unified interest in the entire property. Each joint tenant has the right, subject to the rights only of the other joint tenants, to possess the entire property interest. The traditional common law definition of a joint tenancy requires the presence of the four unities:

1. *Unity of interest:* Each joint tenant must have an identical interest).
2. *Unity of title:* The same will, deed, or other document must confer title to all joint tenants.
3. *Unity of possession:* Each has the right to possess the entire property interest.
4. *Unity of time:* The rights of each joint tenant must vest at the same time.

Rules for Protecting Assets Using Joint Ownership

From an asset protection perspective, it can provide some benefit in certain situations, but as a protective step, joint ownership may not be ideal at all. The liability exposure problem of joint ownership is that the property held as joint tenants is subject to the risk of all joint owners.

Example: You and your two college buddies, Joe and Sam, buy a summer home at the shore. The deed lists the three of you as joint tenants with the right of survivorship. Joe is sued for more than his malpractice insurance, and the victorious claimant puts a lien on your house.

Joint tenants status does, however, provide some modest protection in that the property owned jointly is less valuable to a claimant seeking to get paid than if you owned the property entirely yourself.

Example: Joe's claimant puts a lien on your summer home. Although the claimant is entitled to Joe's interests in the home, he cannot sell it because who would buy one-third of a home to share with you and Sam? Depending on state law, Joe's claimant might go back to court to have the house divided up so he can sell his interest. This type of action is called a *partition* proceeding. However, the cost of this proceeding might serve as a sufficient deterrent that Joe's claimant might well prefer to settle with Joe for a lesser amount than is due to end the matter.

If you have a relatively modest level of risk, perhaps you've retired, owning assets jointly with your daughter, the surgeon, may expose your assets to her malpractice claimants. Better approaches should be considered.

If you are seeking the asset protection benefits of joint ownership, caution should be exercised to assure that the interest created is in fact a joint tenancy. In some states, for example, one owner cannot convey to himself or herself and a second person as joint tenants. Instead, a third person or intermediary must accept conveyance and reconvey to the two joint owners to establish the four unities. Check with an attorney in your estate any time you want to change the title to significant assets.

Estate and Related Planning Considerations of Joint Property

When an account is taken in title of joint tenants with rights of survivorship, the account title itself constitutes a beneficiary designation. If an account is established "John Doe, payable on death to Nephew Doe," or "John Doe, ITF (in trust for) Nephew Doe," the beneficiary designation is similarly accomplished by the mere titling of the account. From an estate planning perspective, this type of arrangement determines the beneficiary and avoids probate. However, several issues must be considered.

How likely is it that your dispositive scheme can really be accomplished? In many cases, it will not. If asset protection for your heirs (the designated joint owner) is an objective, joint ownership will clearly undermine your planning.

People mistakenly believe that if they designate, for example, half their accounts in joint names for each of their two children, each child will receive one-half of the estate. It is often far more likely to accomplish this distribution scheme through having all assets held in the decedent's name alone and distributable to the two heirs under the will. Problems are often overlooked. Different accounts may grow at different rates. Further, funds may be accessed in one, but not all, accounts to meet your expenses. If you're concerned about the protection of your heir, joint ownership is not effective because the heir will inherit the asset outright on your death (if you are the other joint owner). A far better approach for your heir's protection is to transfer the asset into a trust for the heir, instead of outright via joint ownership (see Chapter 16).

Joint Property—What Language to Use

If you want to own an asset jointly, use the following title: "Sam Smith and Joe Jones, as joint tenants with right of survivorship." On death of the first joint tenant, the asset automatically becomes owned by the second. Even if the account is simply listed as "Sam Smith and Susan Smith," a presumption exists that the tenancy is a joint tenancy with right of survivorship. However, there is no reason to take a chance; clarity is always preferred. A common issue with respect to joint tenancy is the determination of the nature of the ownership interest where the title is unclear. Therefore, the preferable approach is to play it safe. If joint ownership with right of survivorship is desired, the account title should so specify. This is especially important if one of the purposes of establishing the joint ownership is to protect the property from the creditors of one of the joint owners.

Distinguished from Other Forms of Ownership

Joint tenancy should be distinguished from tenancy in common, where each person owns an undivided interest in the property. Although in both types of ownership, you and a second person can own equal interests in property, the legal consequences are substantially different. On the death of a joint tenant, the survivor obtains ownership of the entire property. On the death of a tenancy in common, the deceased person governs where ownership of his or her interest in the property goes.

Joint ownership can be distinguished from tenancy by the entirety where asset protection planning is an important goal to be considered. Tenancy by the entirety cannot convey or encumber their interest in the property held as tenancy by the entirety. However, a mere joint tenant can encumber his or her interest in the joint tenancy property. The key asset protection aspect of this form of ownership is that having a joint tenant makes the property less valuable and, hence, less desirable to the creditor/claimant.

Income Tax Consequences of Joint Ownership

If an asset is transferred to joint ownership, the income earned on that property can be divided between the joint owners. If the donor/depositor joint owner (e.g., the parent) is in a higher tax bracket than the donee joint owner (e.g., the child), a tax savings may be realized (assuming inapplicability of the kiddie tax, which taxes income of a child under age 14 at the parent's rate). When the property subject to the joint ownership is sold, the profits on the sale may be allocated to the joint owners in proportion to their ownership interests.

If the property transferred to joint ownership has a mortgage or other liability in excess of the donor's tax basis, the transfer could be characterized as a part-sale (to the extent that the liability exceeds basis) and part-gift (for the balance) to the extent of the interest given up.

Example: Parent transfers $100,000 asset to the child. The income tax basis of the asset is $10,000. The property is subject to a mortgage of $50,000. Thus, the income tax basis in the property is exceeded by the mortgage in the amount of $40,000. A taxable gain of $20,000 should be realized by the parent [$\frac{1}{2} \times (\$50,000 - \$10,000)$].

These rules do not apply in the case of savings bonds and joint bank accounts.

Estate and Gift Tax Consequences of Joint Ownership

Joint ownership can create some notable tax problems, which are important to be aware of before you title any significant assets in joint names. The general tax rule is that on the death of a joint tenant, the entire value of the joint property is included in the estate of the first joint tenant to die. If, however, the executor can prove that the surviving joint tenant contributed some portion to the property, some portion of the value can be excluded from the estate of the first joint tenant. The consideration furnished by the surviving joint tenant will not be counted if it was provided to the surviving joint tenant by the deceased joint tenant. If contribution is demonstrated, it is not only the amount contributed that is removed from the decedent's (first joint tenant to die) gross estate, but a proportionate amount of any appreciation in the property could be argued to be included in determining the contribution by the surviving joint tenant. Income earned on the property given to the joint asset counts toward contribution.

Example: John Smith and Sam Jones purchased a beach house years ago for $55,000, as joint tenants with the right of survivorship. On John's death, the entire $400,000 fair value of the beach house will presumptively be included in his estate. However, if John's executor can demonstrate that Sam contributed $30,000 of the original purchase price, a proportional amount of the value of the beach house won't be taxed in John's estate. If the executor is successful, $218,182 will be excluded from John's estate [$\$30,000/\$55,000 \times \$400,000$].

If the joint tenants are husband and wife, the presumption is that one-half of the value of the jointly held property is included in the estate of the first to die.

Creating a joint tenancy can also have important gift tax consequences. If the joint tenants each own half of the property, but only one joint tenant contributed to the purchase of the property, the creation of the joint tenancy will create a gift equal to one-half of the value of the property from the contributing joint tenant to the noncontributing joint tenant. The unlimited marital deduction, the $11,000 annual gift tax exclusion, or the $1 million applicable exclusion (increasing in future years) may eliminate any tax. Joint owners generally report equal amounts of income on their respective tax returns.

The decision may be made that it would be preferable to terminate a joint tenancy. There could be tax consequences to this if you and the other joint tenant receive different percentages than you own. For example, if you and a friend owned real estate equally, but on the division of the joint tenancy you let your friend take a 75 percent ownership interest, this could constitute a gift by you to the friend equal to 25 percent of the value of the property. A similar result could occur where the joint tenants have very different ages. For example, if you're 85 and your joint tenant is 25, there could be a tax cost to an equal division of the property because your life expectancy is so much less. According to actuarial calculations, you would be entitled to much less than a 50 percent share.

Severing a Joint Tenancy

If a joint tenancy is terminated (severed), any protection afforded would be destroyed. A joint tenancy may be terminated by:

1. Partition, the dividing up and distributing joint property for the purpose of terminating a joint tenancy, selling part or all of the property, and so on.
2. Mortgaging the property. In some states, where one joint tenant grants a mortgage on the jointly held property, this severs the joint tenancy because the mortgagee will be permitted to foreclose only on the divided one-half interest of the joint tenant who granted the mortgage.
3. Leasing the property (in some states).

4. Conveying the property to a third party. This severs the joint tenancy by destroying the requisite four entities previously described. For example, if the property is held by two joint tenants, "Bob and Sam as joint tenants," Bob's transfer of his interest to Joe would result in "Joe and Sam as tenants in common."

Severing a joint tenancy could trigger tax consequences. If the joint property is converted into tenancy in common, however, there should be no income tax consequences. Gift tax consequences could be triggered, depending on how the property is severed. If there was no completed gift on the transfer of the property to the joint tenancy, and on severing, the joint property reverts back to the contributor, there should be no gift tax consequences. If, however, the property is transferred even in part to the other joint tenant, the transaction could trigger a gift tax cost to the extent the value of such portion exceeds the annual exclusion amount.

COMMUNITY PROPERTY CONSIDERATION

Generally, all property acquired by a husband and wife during their marriage while they are domiciled in one of the community property states belongs to each of the marriage partners—share and share alike. They share not only in the physical property acquired but also in the income from the property and any salaries, wages, and other compensation for services. At the same time, each may have separate property. They may also hold property between them in joint tenancy and generally may adjust between themselves their community and separate property (i.e., use a transmutation agreement).

Note: You cannot ignore community property rules just because you now live in a noncommunity property state.

Couples can state before marriage via a prenuptial agreement that they will not be bound by the community property laws of their state of domicile. Generally, community property assets retain that character even after the parties have moved to a noncommunity property state, unless the parties are able to adjust their rights between themselves. This is important in your actions with respect to the assets held.

Real estate generally retains the original form of ownership assigned to it. Real estate in a community property state acquired by either spouse while married may be treated as community property without regard to the domicile or residence of the spouses. It is the law of the location (situs) of the real estate that determines whether the income from it is community property.

Property acquired before marriage retains the form of ownership it had when acquired—separate, joint, or other. Property acquired during the marriage by gift or inheritance by one of the parties, such as gifts received by one spouse from his or her parents, retains the character in which it was acquired. Property purchased with community property is community property, and property purchased with separate property is separate property. Property purchased with commingled community and separate property, so that the two cannot be separated, is community property.

Community property is included in the estate of the first to die only to the extent of the decedent's interest, generally, half of its value—and that half is subject to probate. Transfers of community property between spouses qualify for the marital deduction.

If a couple lived in a community property state before marriage and was married in a noncommunity property state, community property laws should not be applicable because the couple was not husband and wife at the time they were living in a community property state. There is no prenuptial agreement. Texas, for example, adopted the English common law and the Spanish civil law of the community system of property rights of the spouses.

A spouse's separate property consists of:

1. Property owned by the spouse before marriage.
2. Property acquired by the spouse during marriage by gift, devise, or descent.
3. The recovery for personal injury sustained by the spouse during marriage, except the recovery for loss of earning ability during marriage.

Community property is the property, other than separate property, acquired by either spouse during the marriage. The presumption of holding community property exists if property is held by either spouse during or on dissolution of the marriage.

A spouse may record separate property in the county where the couple resides and where real estate is situated. A spouse has the sole management, control, and disposition of his or her separate property. Each spouse has the sole management, control, and disposition of the community property that he or she would have owned if unmarried. If mixed community property that is subject to the sole management, control, and disposition of one spouse with community property is subject to the sole management, control, and disposition of the other spouse, the combined or mixed community property is subject to the joint management, control, and disposition of the spouses.

On the death of one spouse, all property belonging to the community estate of the husband and wife vests in the surviving spouse if there are no children of the deceased spouse or descendants of the children. If there are children or children of the deceased spouse or descendants of these children, the surviving spouse is entitled to one-half of the community property and the other one-half of the community property vests in the children or their descendants.

In some community property states (the rules differ, so you need an attorney in the state in question), a creditor of either spouse may reach community property assets. From an asset protection perspective, one spouse should generally not be liable for claims of the other spouse. However, in a community property state, this rule doesn't necessarily apply, which can create problems. You may not be able to give your community property interest in an asset, via an interspousal gift, to your spouse to avoid your future claimants. Assets accumulated during marriage, for example, earnings from your business, are generally treated as community property, which is subject to contracts and other creditors of either spouse, even if they are deposited in your spouse's bank account. Merely depositing in a spouse's account won't change the character of the monies from community property. Another risk is that your claimant may try to partition community property into separate property so that the creditor can obtain a lien on the asset.

Planning Tip: There is a technique that you might use to convert your community property into separate property of the spouse with the least liability exposure. You enter into a contract in which you give up your community property rights in certain property and thereby convert those assets into your spouse's separate property. This agreement may be called a *transmutation agreement*. In this manner, assuming that the change in ownership is not construed as intended to defraud your claimants, you may be able to insulate those assets from your claimants and creditors. This type of agreement may even be able to cover property you and your spouse acquire in the future. Your lawyer may advise you to file the agreement or a summary of it (record it) in the county clerk or other government office to put the public on notice that the change was made.

TENANCY BY THE ENTIRETY

When property is owned jointly by a husband and wife, it can become a special form of joint ownership called *tenancy by the entirety*. This concept arose from the common law concept of treating husband and wife as a single person. The same four entities required for joint tenancy (described previously) are also required here. The surviving spouse has the right to the property by operation of law on the death of the other tenancy by the entirety spouse.

Tenancy by the entirety can be distinguished from joint tenancy in that the methods used to sever or terminate a joint tenancy do not apply. The spouse, however, can terminate a joint tenancy by agreement or divorce. Thus, neither tenant alone can force the termination of the tenancy by the entirety or the partition of the property. For this reason, this type of ownership structure has significant value in the context of asset protection planning where only one spouse is a target for creditors or malpractice claimants. In 23 states, this ownership between spouses is permitted. In these states, your creditor cannot reach an asset held in tenancy by the entirety between you and your spouse. In these states, using tenancy by the entirety can be a helpful asset protection technique. This is an alternative to the approach of transferring all assets into the ownership of the spouse with less risk. In our previous example, Dr. Jones' initial reaction was to put all assets in her husband's name. Depending on her state's laws, she could have instead retitled the house into tenancy by the entirety, kept an ownership interest in her name, but made that ownership interest so difficult for a malpractice claimant to levy on that a better settlement could be reached.

A number of caveats should be considered:

- Some states permit tenancy by the entirety only for real property, such as the marital residence.
- If assets other than real estate can be held as tenancy by the entirety, you should do so only on the advice of a local attorney

because other complications may arise in trying to characterize a brokerage account, for example, in this manner. Income
from the account may not have the same protection as the
principal. If either spouse can unilaterally withdraw funds, the
protection of tenancy by the entirety for that account may be
ineffective.

- Some states permit each spouse to convey or encumber their
  one-half interest in the property.

- The IRS may be able to assert a tax lien on your interest in a
  property even if it is held as tenancy by the entirety. No sur-
  prise here; the government writes the laws and the government wants to get paid.

- A joint creditor of both you and your spouse can get the entire
  property regardless of the tenancy by the entirety protection.

Example: Tenancy by the entirety can trip up a lot of people. A husband begins an auto repair business. A bank loan is obtained to purchase equipment. The bank asks both husband and wife to sign the
loan documents. Years later, after both have forgotten about the wife's
signing, the business goes bad. The fact that the house is owned as
tenancy by the entirety won't provide any protection. Had wife not
signed the bank loan, the house may have been protected.

It can be useful from an asset protection perspective. If separate property is transferred into a tenancy by the entirety ownership, the value of the property to a prospective creditor is reduced
substantially.

As noted in Chapter 1, asset protection planning must be part of
an overall coordinated plan. One problem that tenancy by the entirety creates in planning is that in many estate plans, a basic step is
to split assets between the husband and wife to fund a bypass trust
by converting jointly owned assets into separately owned assets, or
tenancy in common (see later discussion). If this estate tax planning
approach is used, the tenancy by the entirety protection is lost. Thus,
you have to coordinate your estate planning and asset protection
planning. You might choose to keep your house owned as tenancy
by the entirety while you are working to maximize asset protection
benefits; then when you retire, you could change the ownership to
achieve a better estate tax result. The intervening years could be protected from estate tax by purchasing a term life insurance policy.

Planning with tenancy by the entirety can be coordinated with state exempt property rules (see Chapter 9). For example, if your state provides an exemption that protects certain property, such as your house, you can retain that property in your name without using a tenancy by the entirety form of ownership. If you or your spouse owns real estate in another state that has tenancy by the entirety protection, the law of the state where the property is should apply. In that state, you may use the tenancy by the entirety approach to protect that property. Thus, you can coordinate the type of protection used for different assets and in different states.

TENANCY IN COMMON

In a tenancy in common, two or more persons share ownership in a property at the same time, but each party has a separate undivided interest in the property (as contrasted with joint tenancy where each has an equal interest in the whole). A key consequence of this difference is that a tenancy in common, unlike a joint ownership, can bequeath property anywhere he or she wishes, whereas the joint tenant property passes to the surviving tenant by operation of law. This is critical from an estate planning perspective. It is not, however, particularly beneficial from an asset protection perspective. Converting the ownership interest to tenancy in common (by deeding the house from "John Doe and Jane Doe, his wife" or "John Doe and Jane Doe, as joint tenants with right of survivorship" to "John Doe and Jane Doe, as tenancy in common") is sufficient to permit the spouse the ability to fund the bypass trust for estate planning purposes.

Note: While converting a house owned as tenancy by the entirety into a tenancy in common arrangement, the parties can fund a bypass (applicable exclusion) trust using that asset under the will of the first spouse to die; the change in title may also expose the property and make it vulnerable to attack by the creditors of either spouse. While a creditor of one tenancy by the entirety can generally not attach that spouse's one-half interest in the property, a creditor of a tenancy in common can attach the tenant/creditor's interest in the property.

Perhaps a modest advantage of tenancy in common is that no co-owner can act as an agent of another co-owner, creating legal liability for that other co-owner. The key asset protection benefit is that if you own a rental property alone, your creditor can realize its full value if he or she successfully sues you. If, instead, you transfer the rental property into a tenancy in common ownership, your creditor would be able to realize only a fractional interest, for example, your 50 percent ownership. This is worth less than 50 percent of the whole. However, you can often achieve a better result with other techniques, such as a limited liability company (see Chapter 11).

BENEFICIARY DESIGNATIONS FOR BANK ACCOUNTS

The status of bank account titles can be troublesome. Many people, especially senior citizens, establish a joint account to facilitate management of that asset (e.g., to enable a younger family member to assist by paying bills). Unaware of the use of a revocable living trust or durable power of attorney, they often opt for the method suggested by a bank clerk. In other instances, the intent of such an account is to pass assets on the death of the transferor (i.e., for the account to serve as a will substitute). In yet other instances, the intent of establishing a joint account is to make a gift (e.g., parent wishes to give a child money but may believe it advisable to keep a parent's name on the account to facilitate making future gifts or helping the child make investments). Difficulties arise because the person establishing the account (only sometimes really being a "donor") could have such a broad range of intents, and those giving advice often do not understand the legal and tax implications of the various available account titles.

For the following discussion, assume that *Parent Taxpayer* is the person establishing the account and placing funds in the account. *Junior Taxpayer* is the child of Parent Taxpayer. The consequences of each account title may expose your assets to lawsuits or divorce (yours or your child or other heirs). Understanding these consequences is significant.

Junior Taxpayer

If Parent Taxpayer opens an account solely in the name of Junior Taxpayer, the funding of the account should constitute a completed gift for gift tax purposes. Junior owns and controls the account. If Junior is sued, the money will be lost. If Parent is sued, it's probably irrelevant because the money is Junior's, unless the claimant can successfully demonstrate that Parent transferred the assets knowing a claim existed (see Chapter 8). A more sophisticated approach of Parent giving the bank account to a trust for Junior would be far more protective for Junior (see Chapter 16). If Junior gets divorced, if he has carefully maintained the gift account as a separate asset, it should not be included in the marital assets for purposes of a property division.

Parent Taxpayer in Trust for Junior Taxpayer

In these instances, Parent Taxpayer may wish the funds to be transferred to Junior's control only on Parent's death. Thus, Parent Taxpayer likely has the right to revoke, in whole or part, the account at any time simply by withdrawing funds from the account. This type of account should likely not constitute a completed gift for gift tax purposes until such time as funds are spent on Junior Taxpayer's benefit or Parent Taxpayer dies, resulting in a transfer to Junior Taxpayer of the balance of the account. Unlike the joint account discussed next, a completed gift should not occur where Junior Taxpayer withdraws funds because the nature of this account should not permit Junior the powers to withdraw without Parent's approval or act. In almost all situations, Parent possesses the exclusive right to control or withdraw funds.

This type of account is often called a *Totten Trust*. The account name derives from a landmark case, which held that the fact that the depositor could withdraw funds at any time, thereby revoking the gift, did not serve to revoke the arrangement and thereby deny the survivor (Junior Taxpayer) from receiving the balance on Parent Taxpayer's death.

From an asset protection perspective, this type of account would provide no benefit to Parent because the funds remain totally within Parent's control. If Junior is sued or divorced, the assets have not been transferred to Junior, so Junior's claimant or ex-spouse should not have access to them. However, having Junior's name on the account may create a presumption that Junior has some interest, which could be strategically, if not legally, detrimental to negotiating a settlement.

Parent Taxpayer and Junior Taxpayer, Jointly, with Right of Survivorship

In this type of account, funds can generally be withdrawn by either joint tenant. This is perhaps the most common structure for a joint bank account. Parent Taxpayer likely has the right to revoke, in whole or part, the account at any time simply by withdrawing funds from the account. This type of account should likely not constitute a completed gift until such time as Junior Taxpayer withdraws funds, funds are spent on Junior Taxpayer's benefit, or Parent Taxpayer dies, resulting in a transfer to Junior Taxpayer of the balance of the account.

The Uniform Probate Code provides that while both joint tenants are alive, the presumption is that the account balance is owned in the proportion of the contributions of each joint tenant to the account. In the previous examples, this would result in Parent Taxpayer's owning the entire balance of the account until death.

On the death of Parent Taxpayer, Junior Taxpayer succeeds to the entire property interest. The deceased Parent Tenant has no right to transfer the joint account by will or otherwise. Thus, this type of ownership has been used as a will substitute.

From an asset protection perspective, this type of account would provide no benefit to Parent because the funds remain within Parent's ability to withdraw. If Junior is sued or divorced, the assets can be withdrawn by Junior and, therefore, are at risk to Junior's claimants or ex-spouse. Thus, the assets that were subject only to risk to Parent's problems are not at risk for both. This type of account creates more risk and provides no benefit whatsoever.

Parent Taxpayer and Junior Taxpayer

This type of account is likely an unartful attempt to establish the type of account referred to previously, namely, a joint account with right of survivorship: "Parent Taxpayer and Junior Taxpayer, Jointly, With Right of Survivorship." Courts have held that the fact that the depositor (Parent) could control the right of withdrawal from the account did not invalidate the survivorship feature that was intended. Thus, this creates all the risks of the previous account, as well as the uncertainty as to what the account title really means.

Parent Taxpayer, Payable on Death to Junior Taxpayer

This type of account, called a *POD* for short, is not a completed gift. The account balance should be included on Parent's estate tax return and should be transferred outside probate directly to Junior at such time. While probate is avoided, Parent's divorce or creditors are not. If, following Parent's death Junior is alive, Junior will own the assets outright with no protection from Parent's claimants. A trust would be a better approach.

Issues Affecting Various Types of Bank Accounts

Controversies can arise when, on the death of the depositor, Parent Taxpayer, both the estate of Parent and the survivor (Junior Taxpayer) claim the funds.

Where a creditor of one, but not both, joint account holder seeks to reach the assets, the question arises as to what protection exists. If one owner has the exclusive and complete right to withdraw funds from the account, the funds in that account are more likely to be reached by a creditor. If the two tenants own the property as joint tenants, a creditor of one joint tenant often does not have rights against the interest of the other joint tenant. If the joint tenant who owes the debt dies first, the surviving joint tenant may be able to take the entire asset free and clear of any creditor claims.

If the IRS exerts a lien over an account, it will levy on the entire account even if only one of the joint owners is liable.

Similar concepts have been applied to assets other than bank accounts, such as securities.

SAFE DEPOSIT BOX

The title of a safe deposit box does not necessarily determine the title and ownership of the contents of the safe deposit box. Rather, the title to each item in the safe deposit box determines the ownership of that individual item. If you have gold bullion in your husband's safe deposit box and he's sued and loses, his claimants can get those assets. An approach that many people use is to have an entity, such as a limited liability company, own the safe deposit box.

Then, the entity will be deemed owner of nontitled assets in the box, such as jewelry, bearer bonds, and so forth. If a corporation owns a safe deposit box containing a valuable silver collection, the IRS could argue that the distribution of the silver to a shareholder is a taxable dividend—a rather unpleasant and costly tax mistake.

SUMMARY

The manner in which you own assets, from simple bank accounts to checking accounts, can have a dramatic impact on those assets if you are sued or divorced. This chapter reviewed many common types of assets and accounts and the legal and related issues affecting them. Simply opening a bank or brokerage account based on the advice of the teller or broker could jeopardize your wealth. Even for such simple and common transactions, obtaining legal guidance is essential for your security.

FOR YOUR NOTEBOOK

WORKSHEET TO ANALYZE ASSET OWNERSHIP

ASSETS AND HOW THEY ARE OWNED					
Asset Type and Description	Yourself	Spouse/ Partner[a]	Jointly Owned[b]	Beneficiary Designation	Entity or Trust[c]
Totals					

[a] Marital status can have a significant impact on the safety of the asset and the available ownership classes.

[b] Abbreviations to use: JTWROS for joint tenants with rights of survivorship; TbyE for tenancy by the entirety; TinC for tenancy in common; and COMM for community property.

[c] Indicate the type of entity (LLC, S Corp, C Corp, FLP, GP, etc.) and your ownership and management interests. This is likely to be sufficiently unique and complicated, so the best approach is to use a footnote explaining each item.

PART TWO

DIVORCE
PROTECTION RULES

4 HOW TO PROTECT YOURSELF AGAINST DIVORCE

With a 50 percent divorce rate (with a higher rate for second and later marriages), and because as much as 50 percent-plus of your assets could be distributed in a property settlement, careful planning for matrimonial implications is a critical part of asset protection planning. Matrimonial-sensitive asset protection planning is complex, requiring the consideration of difficult personal issues, matrimonial law, estate planning considerations, and tax issues (income tax as well as gift, estate, and GST tax). Protecting your assets from malpractice or other claimants is vital, but so is divorce protection.

Example:　Dr. Smith is in a high-risk medical specialty. His malpractice carrier has lowered its maximum coverage limits, raised his premiums, and expanded the exclusions. He's worried. His colleague tells him over lunch that he's responded to the malpractice worries by transferring all his assets to his wife. Dr. Smith's marriage, however, is far from stable. Transferring assets to his wife could put him at a substantial disadvantage if their marriage cannot be saved. Ignoring this risk could be dangerous. However, ignoring malpractice risks could be worse. The two somewhat conflicting goals must be reconciled with a plan. Most books and literature on asset protection ignore the key risk of divorce—not exactly an informative approach.

Caution:　Most asset protection planning is done in consultation with an estate planner. If you consult an estate planner with your spouse to address estate, asset protection, and financial planning, the attorney cannot help you address divorce protection with you and your spouse both as clients. It is a clear conflict of interest. You might need to consult with your own matrimonial and estate planning attorneys to understand the matrimonial implications that the joint estate planner recommends.

Throughout the process, bear in mind that the rules differ dramatically from state to state. Also, the dynamics of the matrimonial process can be as important as the technicalities of the law. The fact that a particular legal rule seems clear doesn't mean that in the context of your future divorce, the judge won't begin to view your actions as excessive or inappropriate. These risks must be assessed with a matrimonial attorney as part of your estate and asset protection planning team.

SAFEGUARDING PREMARITAL ASSETS

Assets that you received as gifts or inheritances are separate property, which should not be reached by your ex-spouse under most state laws. However, for this result to be achieved to the best degree your state's laws permit, you must carefully maintain the separate identity of these assets and not transmute them into marital property. Keep any gifts or inheritances in separate accounts. If the amounts are not very large, set up a special brokerage or bank account to hold solely these separate assets. If the amounts involved are larger, consider setting up a revocable living trust as an accounting entity to keep property separate. The best approach, however, is to plan further in advance to have your parents secure these assets before you receive them (see Chapter 5).

Rules to Keep Your Spouse Away from Separate Property

If you have separate property and your ex-spouse contributed to its appreciation (e.g., spouse helped you pick the stocks, ran the computer program that helped you select the asset allocation), that appreciation becomes marital. Worse, in some states, your spouse's activities in the management of what was once your separate property might taint the entire asset as marital.

Example: You have to be careful how you handle separate assets. In one case, the husband, Joe, used separate trust fund assets to directly pay from the trust for a host of personal expenses, from vacations to a new sports car for his wife. Later, the husband transferred cash from his business to the trust to replace the money previously spent. The amount of marital expenses funded from the trust and the frequent commingling of marital assets (i.e., business earnings) with the separate property in the husband's trust resulted in the court finding that the trust assets had been so commingled and the independence of the separate property so totally disregarded that the entire trust was treated as a marital asset.

Example: John and Jane have been married for several years. John is a computer consultant, and Jane is a real estate broker. When John's parents died, John inherited their home. Jane fixed it up, redecorated it, marketed it, and sold it. Her efforts turned a run-down property into a quaint and charming home. The deed remained solely in John's name. The proceeds remained in a bank account in John's name until Jane found, in her brokerage work, a distressed property she could buy and flip to another purchaser quickly. This happened several times. Meanwhile, the marriage began to falter and Jane filed for divorce. Jane's attorney will likely argue that the substantial contribution that Jane made to John's inheritance, the almost complete control Jane had over the property, and the commingling of Jane's earnings (from improving the first house, profits on flipping successive properties, and the brokerage commissions she waived) have transmuted the entire value into marital property. Whether Jane succeeds depends on many factors—laws in John and Jane's state, the judge's perception of the equities in the case, the persuasiveness of each attorney, and so on. The lesson, however, is clear: Avoid active contribution by your spouse to property that would otherwise be separate.

If you have separate property, save the documents demonstrating that you received it as separate property. If you can, ask your parents or your aunt or whoever else gave you gifts to provide you with copies of the cancelled checks, deeds, or other documents used to make the gifts. If the amounts were more substantial, obtain copies of the gift tax returns from your parents or whoever made the gifts. For inheritances, try to obtain a copy of the federal estate tax return that demonstrates what you received. If the estate was smaller than the amount required to file a federal estate tax return, obtain a copy of a state tax filing. Many states have inheritance or other taxes that are assessed at levels much lower than the federal estate tax. Thus, even if a federal estate tax return wasn't filed, a state return may have been. If these are not available, try to obtain a copy of the will and any releases signed when assets werc distributed. These items can all help to confirm the separate nature of the assets.

If your marriage was relatively short lived, some assets you earned and owned before the divorce may be held outside of the settlement. Review this with your attorney because laws differ from state to state and depend heavily on the facts involved.

Minimize or Eliminate Your Spouse's Involvement with Your Business

In a recent divorce case of considerable notoriety, the CEO of a major corporation concluded a divorce with his wife of many years. She argued, very persuasively as the settlement demonstrated, that she had been very involved in his business. She hosted many dinner parties for her husband and his colleagues. She traveled regularly with him on his business trips throughout the United States and the world. If divorce is likely, minimize or eliminate any involvement your spouse has in your business to reduce such claims.

Be Certain of a Nest Egg in Your Name

Many professionals (doctors, accountants, etc.) transfer most or all of their assets to their spouses to avoid malpractice and other claims. This is not an ideal approach because, in the event of a divorce, even in states where "equitable distribution" should equitably distribute assets, there may be a lengthy period of time before you are able to access them. A preferable approach would be to retain some assets in your name. If you are still concerned about malpractice or other risks, consider forming a domestic asset protection trust to hold some of your assets (see Chapter 17). This will enable you to transfer assets where your creditors cannot reach them (assuming there is no fraudulent conveyance in the transfer), but you can remain a discretionary beneficiary of the trust. Also, use irrevocable trusts, S corporations, family limited partnerships, and other techniques to minimize the risk of a creditor or malpractice claimant reaching your assets without ceding complete control to your spouse (see Chapters 10 through 13).

PRENUPTIAL AGREEMENTS

What Is a Prenuptial Agreement and How Can It Protect Your Wealth?

A contract between you and your future spouse (prenuptial agreement) can be used for three important, but very divergent, asset protection motives:

1. If you have significant wealth, a prenuptial agreement can be vital to maintaining the separate nature of certain assets to ensure that if your planned marriage ends in divorce, your spouse won't have any claims on those assets. It can also be used to set limits on financial and other aspects of your potential divorce. This is the familiar use of prenuptial agreements and is explained in detail later.

2. If you are at risk for malpractice or other claims and your future spouse is not, you can use a prenuptial agreement to recharacterize property that is solely yours to be property solely of your new spouse to protect it from your claimants.

Example: Frank and Fran plan to marry. Fran is a well-known ambulance-chasing litigator. She's always aggressive and on the edge in her practice. This modus operandi has served her well, and she has amassed quite a bit of wealth. Frank is an accomplished pianist whose greatest liability risk is playing a bad note. Frank and Fran make great music together, and Fran is fully trusting of Frank. Frank and Fran can use a prenuptial agreement to document the transfer to Frank of substantial portions of Fran's wealth and the fact that Fran will have no claim on the assets so transferred. Fran must still be certain that these transfers to Frank are not done to hinder, delay, or defraud a creditor, or they will be set aside.

---

3. If you're remarrying, a prenuptial agreement can help you protect yourself from your new spouse's angry ex-spouse.

Example: Sally and Sam Secondtime are getting married. Sally's first husband, Atilla the Bum, remains unemployed, vindictive, and nasty. Sam has made plenty of room in his attic for Sally's baggage but isn't thrilled at having his hard-earned assets ever questioned by Atilla. Sally and Sam can enter into a prenuptial agreement and maintain their assets and lifestyle to keep Atilla at bay.

This less common use of prenuptial agreements is discussed later in this chapter.

In addition, the Uniform Premarital Agreement Act was adopted in some form by many states; it defines the prerequisites of a valid prenuptial agreement, one of which is financial disclosure.

Rules to Make Your Prenuptial Agreement Work

Regardless of which of these objectives is driving your prenuptial agreement, you have to play by the rules if you want the agreement to be respected in the event of a legal challenge. These rules include:

- You and your spouse-to-be must be represented by different lawyers. Not only does this ensure maximum legal fees, but it is really essential for the agreement to be respected. A prenuptial agreement will be respected in the event of a later divorce or lawsuit only if it was fair at the time it was signed, voluntarily entered into, and knowingly signed by both of you. If you hired a tough shark to pressure your spouse-to-be into signing an agreement, don't expect much success in proving its fairness or that your future spouse understood it. If both of you are represented by independent attorneys, the presumption is that each of your attorneys explained the agreement to you and could represent your interests in negotiating a fair agreement. Don't try to save money by doing the agreement yourself or having one lawyer. Be certain each lawyer's name is listed in the agreement and that each lawyer signs the agreement proving representation.

- One of the concerns with these agreements is that the economically powerful spouse anticipates making more money in the future and wants to protect the growth of those assets in the future. Meanwhile, the dependant spouse, in contrast, who may have to take care of small children, is seen as not being in an arm's-length position to negotiate the agreement. The agreement itself and the surrounding circumstances should demonstrate that this is not the case.

- Both you and your future spouse should sign the agreement and have your signatures notarized. Consider signing four originals—one for each of you and one for each of your attorneys.

- Both of you must have reasonably understood the agreement and had reasonable knowledge of the legal consequences of the agreement. The best way to demonstrate this is for each of you to be represented by a qualified attorney knowledgeable in the area. If you hire one of the country's top matrimonial experts and your spouse-to-be is represented by a general practice attorney past retirement age, whose practice consists primarily of house closings, don't expect a judge to be impressed with your spouse's knowledge of the agreement.

- The agreement should be negotiated and signed without undue influence and duress. If you make your spouse-to-be sign while on the steps of the wedding chapel with the entire family inside waiting, don't expect anyone to buy the validity of the agreement. Have it signed as far in advance of the wedding as possible. Be certain that each of you receives a draft and reviews the draft with your respective attorney; then revisions are made as a result of those meetings.

Planning Tip: To prove that you were each represented, have the attorney who drafts the agreement save an electronic copy of each draft of the agreement. You should obtain electronic copies and save each version on your computer. Also save the review copies showing the comments and changes resulting from the discussion with your attorney.

- If you have a prenuptial agreement, be certain that all the appropriate exhibits and financial disclosures were attached. Many prenuptial agreements include only statements as to the wealth of both parties. Others include a quick balance sheet or summary you've each prepared or data you provided that the lawyer simply typed up. While these may suffice, always err on the side of more disclosure. Consider attaching actual bank and brokerage statements, tax returns, detailed financial statements, and other relevant documents.

Planning Tip: Don't be cheap. Pay your accountant to assemble a financial statement that complies with accounting industry guidelines and formalities. The financials the accountant prepared are preceded by a cover letter (report) stating that they were prepared in accordance with the American Institute of CPAs' Statement of Position (SOP) 82-1 "Accounting and Financial Reporting for Personal Financial Statements" and other pronouncements. This is also the recommended approach when documenting your net worth for an asset protection plan.

- It may be advisable to periodically update the exhibits for future events, such as a large inheritance. Ask your attorney.

- If you have any concerns as to validity, changed circumstances, or other issues, address them up front as quickly as possible with your attorney. While this may be too late at the stage you're reading this book, getting your records together to show that you made full disclosure at that time and that your spouse was represented by counsel and other actions that will help uphold a prenuptial agreement can still be taken.

- If asset protection from lawsuits is a motive, ask your attorney whether some type of memorandum of the agreement should be filed (recorded) in the public records, such as with the county clerk's office.

- Some experts recommend that the signing meeting be video-taped to demonstrate that both of you were represented by an attorney, questioned as to an understanding of the agreement, and so on.

- Be certain to have a tax accountant or tax attorney review the income, gift, estate, and other tax consequences of the agreement. Don't focus on the divorce or lawsuit protections of the agreement to the exclusion of the tax concerns.

Community Property States and Prenuptial Agreements

Prenuptial agreements require care, especially in a community property state.

Example: A husband kept his separate property trust in his name alone. He never deposited any community property money into the account, or so he thought. As it turns out, he had periodically loaned money from his trust account to the family to buy a house, take trips, and so on. When his community property account had surplus cash, he repaid the money to the separate property trust. Even though he thought these transfers were simply loan repayments, the court characterized them as community property. He had to analyze years of statements and treat each repayment and the earnings attributable to it as community property.

Rules on What to Include in Your Prenuptial Agreement

The most important rule is to have your lawyer include in your prenuptial agreement the provisions that are specifically tailored to meet your unique circumstances. Every marriage is different, so every prenuptial agreement should be unique. The following checklist is a partial listing of some provisions that might warrant consideration:

- Delineate the rights that each of you will have to the assets (estate) of the other in the event of death or incapacity of either of you.
- Establish the rights of each partner in the event of an annulment, separation, or dissolution of the marriage, including the rights to support, palimony, alimony, equitable distribution, and any other relevant matters.
- State (and, preferably, demonstrate with detailed statements and attached exhibits) that each of you has been allowed complete inquiry as to the extent and approximate value of all of the income, property, and assets of the other.
- Indicate that each of you has had the opportunity to obtain independent legal, financial, insurance, and accounting advice from the professional advisors of his or her choosing before the signing (execution) of the agreement and that each of you has been fully advised as to rights both under the agreement and in the absence of any agreement.
- If you both intend to use all income from either of you, and from separate and joint assets, to jointly fund expenses once you're married, the agreement should say so. If you plan to use all income jointly but keep assets separate, the agreement should address the practical implications of how you will implement the agreement. For example, if your wife-to-be has substantial inherited assets and the income will be used to fund joint marital expenses but the assets will remain hers, the agreement might state the name of the account that remains hers, and a mechanism could be established with the brokerage firm to transfer income as earned on that account to a joint checking account at the same firm. This could simplify record keeping and help ensure that premarital/immune assets

(at least the principal portion and any income intended to stay separate) retain such character. Including this level of detail in the agreement can help fulfill the financial arrangements you both have agreed to.

- If some premarital assets are to be kept separate, the agreement might provide that if both of you choose to purchase any property that should be treated as marital property, the funds used in such a purchase should be noted in a letter, signed by both of you (acknowledged), and the property so acquired shall be owned and held by both of you jointly in the proportions each has contributed to the acquisition and maintenance of the property. Typically, such an agreement provides that on termination of the marriage, each party is entitled to such undivided interest in the property.

- If you have significant premarital assets, you might wish to include a provision that each party will, during his or her lifetime, keep and retain sole ownership of your respective assets, including any increase or decrease in the value of that property, whether you own the property at the date of the agreement or it is thereafter acquired by either party in his or her separate name or in the name of an entity in which that party has an interest. This is especially important if protection from lawsuits is important for you because lawsuit protection is generally achieved with an array of entities (family limited partnerships, corporations, etc.) and trusts (marital trusts, asset protection trusts, etc.). Thus, your separate property may be held in a complex form that few prenuptial agreements address adequately.

- Family limited partnerships (FLPs) and limited liability companies (LLCs) are commonly used to hold investment and other assets, including separate assets. It may be advantageous for the couple to gift or sell a percentage of such assets, or even of a real estate property, to secure lack of marketability discounts for estate and gift tax purposes, provide general creditor protection by creating another owner whose consent to a transfer may be required, and so on. The pursuit of these valid nonmatrimonial planning objectives should not be used in the event of a later divorce to challenge a greater portion of the property so given. This should be addressed in some detail in the prenuptial agreement. Unfortunately, because matrimonial and asset protection planning applies to a small, wealthy, and generally sophisticated component of the population, few planners are familiar with this level of planning. If your agreement and planning do not address these vital issues, insist that your existing advisors add an additional specialist to your advisory team.

- You and your future spouse should agree to each of your individual income and individual expenses and indemnify and hold the other harmless from any and all liability, expenses, penalties, and costs arising out of, or connected with, any income tax returns.

- If your future spouse was married previously, there may be concern about the ex-spouse's coming back to court to request increased support or to challenge other aspects of the prior divorce. If this is a concern, your financial and legal arrangements in your new marriage should consider the possible protective benefits of planning to keep each of your assets, tax returns, and other legal and financial matters insulated from the ex-spouse. Your agreement should address these issues by mandating that assets be kept separate. You should consider submitting independent and separate financial, tax, and other data and records to different accountants for tax preparation. If it has been determined that there is substantial income tax benefit to filing a joint income tax return, you should still endeavor to keep all data separate so that if the ex-spouse sues, the data will be sufficiently independent that the attorney can argue that the ex-spouse should not have access to your data. If these precautions are not taken at the outset, the commingling of tax and other data, even if assets are largely kept separate, may result in the ex-spouse's convincing a court to allow access to your joint income tax return.

POSTNUPTIAL AGREEMENTS

Postnuptial Agreements to Address Marital Issues

Too often, couples that should have signed prenuptial agreements don't get around to it before the wedding date. Sometimes changes in their financial, personal, liability, or circumstances after the marriage make some type of agreement necessary. The rule about contracts signed after the marriage (postnuptial agreements) is simple. Do a prenuptial agreement if you can. It's always better to have had the agreement in place before the marriage. There is a much greater likelihood of negotiating the provisions you wish and having the ultimately signed agreement respected by a court if it is done in advance of the marriage, instead of during the marriage.

Postnuptial Agreements to Address Lawsuit Protection Issues

A major reason to consider a postnuptial agreement is to shelter and protect the assets of the wealthier spouse. In this manner, the wealthier spouse makes asset transfers to the poorer spouse, often in trust for further liability suit protection, and the postnuptial agreement documents the transfers. Importantly, the postnuptial agreement is designed to ensure that the ownership and nature of the property is changed from the wealthier spouse subject to greater risk, to the poorer spouse with less risk. The wealthier spouse may want some assurances of what will happen if the marriage ends. The postnuptial agreement can provide that.

Postnuptial Agreements to Address Inadequacies of a Prenuptial Agreement

Often, years after a prenuptial agreement is signed, circumstances change or errors or oversights are found. It's impossible to identify every issue in any marital agreement. Not only are the financial, tax, and legal issues complex, but personal issues and emotions (so common before marriage) make it difficult to see every issue or best identify how to address it. In some cases, more sophisticated counsel consulted on a tax or estate planning issue at a later date may identify additional, ancillary, or better approaches. In these cases, the postnuptial agreement is really a modification and clarification of the prenuptial agreement. Consult with a matrimonial expert in your state as to the strength of such a modification. Even if your state laws are unfavorable toward postnuptial agreements generally, modifications and clarifications of an existing prenuptial agreement may be viewed more favorably.

AGREEMENTS TO PROTECT NONMARRIED PARTNERS

There are about 550,000 people estimated to be living together who are not married. This figure has grown 72 percent in the past decade, and the trend is increasing. This includes not only same-sex partners but many elderly who may choose for financial or personal reasons not to marry. A fundamental rule to plan for you and your nonmarried partner to minimize your risks if the nonmarital relationship terminates is to obtain a contractual arrangement governing the legal, economic, and perhaps other aspects of your relationship. Because you are not married, a prenuptial or postnuptial agreement is not relevant; instead, a type of agreement called a *living together* agreement is used.

Caution: The law governing these arrangements and the documents is new and unproven. Therefore, great care must be exercised. Ideally, this type of planning should be coupled with trust and other planning discussed in this book to help safeguard your assets.

A living together agreement is very important to protect your interests precisely for the same reason that its validity is subject to question. You and your partner living together without the formality of a marriage do not have many of the legal certainties, or protections, married couples have. Married couples have common law rights of dower and curtesy, the statutory right of election against an estate, the estate and gift tax marital deduction, and forms of joint ownership (tenancy by the entirety). The law is less certain as to how the rights between nonmarried partners will be determined in the event of separation or death. Even in a relationship where you have cohabited with a single partner for decades, state law may provide you no right if the relationship ends. If you are the nonmonied partner, this may leave you with nothing financially, even if you had contributed to the assets your partner owns and had assumed that they were half yours. If you are the wealthier partner, the absence of law governing your relationship makes the end result a financial gamble. An agreement is always wise.

Planning Tip: Be alert to disparate economic or other influences that might leverage one party against the other in assessing the reasonableness of a living together agreement. This might include the presence of domestic violence between you and your partner, disparate negotiating positions, substance abuse, children, and so on. Be certain that your professionals address these issues to preempt, to the extent feasible, future claims.

One of the problems with living together agreements is that many state courts have held that contract law principles (the rules governing the relationships between independent persons or businesses entering into a contract) may not be applicable to family law matters. If contract law won't apply and your relationship with your partner is not a marriage, what law does apply? This uncertainty is precisely why you should retain a family law attorney who has experience with living together agreements.

Living together agreements also differ from prenuptial or postnuptial agreements in that a living together agreement may state that you expressly do not intend to marry. Alternatively, it may indicate that you do wish to marry.

The living together agreement should indicate, in some detail, the economic, legal, and other ties you and your partner intend to have, both during and after dissolution of your relationship.

The payment of periodic funds for the support of a former nonmarried partner (palimony) is recognized in some, but not all, states. Such payments could be based on concepts similar to those of common law marriage. If your state's laws do not provide any protection for the nonmonied former partner, the best bet is to assert a claim on the basis that the unmarried partner has a theoretical legal right to financial support, if the existence of a living together agreement to provide that support can be established. An oral agreement might suffice, but you should never count on an oral agreement except as a method of last resort.

Items to Address in a Living Together Agreement

As with any marital contract, your living together agreement should address the issues appropriate to your facts and circumstances. The following list can be reviewed with your attorney to highlight some ideas to consider:

- The agreement should specify what you and your partner's wills and trusts will include and who inherits what assets on the death of each. You might even include a contractual stipulation as to how your wills distribute property to ensure that neither of you can change the arrangements without the other's consent. The estate tax marital deduction available to every married couple is not available for the transfers of assets between nonmarried partners. Therefore, more sophisticated estate tax minimization techniques should be addressed.

- If you or your partner, separately or together, acquires real or valuable personal property, a host of decisions should be addressed in your agreement; for example, who pays which expenses associated with the property, who keeps the property if the relationship terminates, how the property should be titled (e.g., you and your partner as joint tenants; see Chapter 2).

- Life insurance should be addressed, assuming that you and your partner have sufficient economic rights (an *insurable interest*) that the insurance company will recognize to sell you each a policy. Your agreement should address amounts, coverages, and viatical settlement provisions in the event of terminal illness. An insurance trust (see Chapter 16) is even more important for nonmarried couples to minimize estate tax in the absence of a marital deduction and to protect the insurance proceeds from claims by a disgruntled family member who disapproved of your relationship.

- Disability insurance should also be addressed. Whether one or both you and your partner work, what happens if only one, or even neither of you, is able to work? For many nonmarried couples, addressing sharing of expenses is common in a living together agreement. The issue of who can pay if one is disabled is critical, and insurance is often the only practical answer.

- Living wills and health care proxies must be completed, and the relationship must be addressed. Without this authorization, a partner, even a lifelong partner, may be denied visitation access by a hospital.

- Employee medical and other benefits are not automatically afforded to a partner, so these issues should be addressed in your planning and in your agreement. This might require that

private savings, retirement, insurance, and other arrangements
be obtained.

- If you and your partner may have or adopt a child, a host of issues concerning the child are important to address in the
  agreement. Unlike a surviving spouse, you as the surviving
  partner will not automatically be named guardian of the child.
  You want to avoid bitter litigation over parenting rights and
  custody.

- Income taxes present a host of problems and complexities,
  many of which should be addressed in the agreement, others
  are addressed in your planning. When you are married, you
  can file a joint tax return and may have liability on a joint return. As a nonmarried couple, you may avoid the joint liability issue but you may also face a greater income tax cost.
  Caution is still necessary because joint economic undertakings
  (e.g., owning property together) may create joint liability even
  without a joint income tax return. Your agreement should
  specify who pays what taxes, how an audit should be handled,
  and what happens in the event the relationship terminates.

PROTECT YOURSELF THROUGH AND AFTER A
DIVORCE PROCESS

The devastating financial impact of divorce can be somewhat mit-
igated and your assets preserved, or at least better directed, with
planning. The following is a sampling of some of the matters you
might wish to address with your matrimonial and asset protection advisors.

Using College Savings Plans to Safeguard
Assets from Divorce

The tax laws permit you to save money for college expenses for
children or other persons. These savings have tremendous tax advantages, which has led to their growing popularity. These tax
advantages, contained in Section 529 of the Internal Revenue
Code, are called *Section 529 plans*. Some states even provide state

income tax benefits for contributions made to these plans. Money in the plans grows tax free, and when it is withdrawn to pay for qualified education costs, there is no tax cost. These income tax benefits make Section 529 plans advantageous for many. In addition, you can gift $11,000 per year (and even front-load five years of $11,000 contributions, or $55,000, into a single year) without any negative gift tax implications. These plans have important implications to divorce planning, whichever side of the divorce you're on. They can also be an opportunity for abuse.

Section 529 plans can be established for "family members," which includes sons, daughters, grandchildren, brothers, sisters, nephews, nieces, and certain in-laws as well as spouses of such persons. Did your spouse set up Section 529 plans in contemplation of the divorce for his or her own family members? Should you set up plans for your children or other family members?

Example: Frank and Fran are divorcing and have a daughter, Sue, age 5. Fourteen months before the divorce, Frank funded $55,000 of marital funds into a Section 529 savings plan for Sue after meeting with a financial planner. About two months before the divorce, Fran also contributed $55,000 of marital savings to a Section 529 plan for Sue by signing documents Frank stuck in front of her and insisted she sign. Frank and Fran divorce. What happens to the $110,000 invested in Section 529 plans?

This example raises a host of questions that highlight possible dissipation of your assets by your spouse or may present planning opportunities for you as long as you stay on the right side of the law. Was the transfer by Frank of $55,000 really for Sue's benefit, or was it a predivorce transfer to reduce marital assets? If it was an attempt to reduce marital assets, can it be reversed or the asset considered in the equitable distribution equation as to who receives what assets? What about the transfer by Fran to the Section 529 plan? Was it a legitimate education plan? After all, Sue will incur significant education costs and Section 529 plans make sense. Or perhaps was Fran's transfer a contrived method by Frank to reduce marital assets? Could Frank's transfer be legitimate but Fran's not?

How far and under what circumstances might a prospective divorce litigant reasonably set up Section 529 plans and make transfers in advance of a divorce filing? Front-loading five years of payments into a Section 529 is sufficiently common that the mere front-loading is not necessarily a factor really indicating abuse. The absence of prior contributions is not necessarily a factor indicating abuse.

The threshold issue might really be whether the forensic accountant can spot the Section 529 plan contributions. What if in the previous example, Frank had contributed $11,000 to Section 529 plans for his siblings and their issue more than a year before the divorce? Following the consummation of the divorce, Frank, as account owner, exercises his right to take back all of those funds. The contributions are not reported on a gift tax return. The income tax return may reflect nothing. Short of a forensic analysis of all bank, brokerage, and other accounts for years preceding the divorce, there may not be any method to identify Frank's machinations to hide assets. In smaller estates where hiring a forensic accountant might be cost prohibitive, no one may discover the abuse and hidden funds.

Standard of Living Establishes Maintenance Levels

The standard of living established during the marriage is what helps to set the target range for maintenance for your ex-spouse. This needs to be considered when you plan any asset protection steps. If you transfer substantial assets into your spouse's name to protect them from your malpractice claimants, your spouse may use some of those funds for an enhanced lifestyle, which may only serve to increase the alimony you may have to pay in the event of a divorce. If you use the technique discussed in Chapter 16 of setting up a marital trust (qualified terminable interest property [QTIP] trust), you'll have created a periodic income stream for your spouse that may also enhance lifestyle expenditures and impact an ultimate divorce settlement.

Get Your Experts Lined Up

A key to successfully navigating the divorce process is having a good team of experts. You can't navigate the legal mine fields without a good matrimonial attorney. A forensic accountant may be essential to ferreting out assets your spouse hides, interpreting expense data, and cautioning you about tax return problems. Getting these professionals involved before you move out is advisable. Once you've moved, you may not have access to data the accountant wants. You may have sacrificed important legal rights. If asset protection is important for either or both spouses, you should include estate and asset protection attorneys on your team to analyze and interpret the array of trusts, entities, and other techniques used in the process. Explaining the implications of these arrangements to the court often proves challenging, especially because the provisions and techniques are so much more complex than the arrangements typically seen. Importantly, if one or both you and your soon-to-be-ex-spouse need asset protection planning, undermining prior planning as part of the divorce process could jeopardize the very assets being disputed.

Innocent Spouse Relief

When a former couple is assessed a substantial tax assessment, including penalty and interest charges, following divorce, for a prior year when a joint tax return was filed, one spouse often claims that he or she should be able to avoid the additional charges because they were not aware of the tax problem. The opportunities to do so, however, are severely limited. In these instances, the innocent spouse exception to joint liability may be one of the only opportunities to avoid tax liability. Innocent spouse relief has long been an important tax consideration in divorce planning. The concept of the innocent spouse rules is simply that situations occur where it is inequitable to hold a spouse liable for a tax liability relating to a joint return simply on the basis that the spouse signed the return.

Note: See www.laweasy.com for sample forms.

SUMMARY

Protecting your assets from lawsuits can be a vital part of assuring that your wealth remains intact for your benefit. Divorce can prove to be a major threat to your wealth. The interplay of the complex and adversarial divorce system and the complex and vital asset protection planning you have or should undertake make for a wide range of controversial and difficult issues. This chapter highlights many of these issues.

5 HOW TO PROTECT YOUR HEIRS' ASSETS FROM DIVORCE

You're bequeathing assets to children or other heirs; how can you protect these assets from the risks of divorce? This is a question almost every parent or other person planning their estate asks. The answer affects how every will, trust, and estate plan should be formulated. If you are involving your children in a family business, the issue takes on even greater importance because of the need to prevent a family business from becoming embroiled in an acrimonious divorce battle. This chapter explores some of the ways you can protect your children and other heirs.

ENCOURAGE YOUR CHILD TO SIGN A PRENUPTIAL AGREEMENT

The single most important step to protect your children's gift or inherited assets from the ravages of their possible future divorce is for them to sign a prenuptial agreement before they marry. The discussion of how you can use a prenuptial agreement to protect yourself, or a postnuptial (antenuptial) agreement if you missed the prenuptial, are discussed in Chapter 4 and apply similarly to your children. But there is much more you can do as a parent.

What if your love-struck about-to-get-married child won't listen to reason? Try encouraging and discussing the issue. Help your child understand that a prenuptial agreement doesn't have to be unfair, unreasonable, or antimarriage. The prenuptial agreement can be restricted to addressing issues they are comfortable with if they don't wish to address the full range of legal, financial, and personal issues typically addressed. A limited agreement, even if confined to addressing a few specific bequests or other assets, may still be better than nothing.

Some parents take a far more aggressive approach of bequeathing all assets to their child in trust and provide in the trust that if the child marries without a prenuptial agreement (or is then married but doesn't get a postnuptial agreement), no distributions can be made to the child from the trust. While this approach may force the child to sign a prenuptial agreement, it is not exactly consistent with fostering a great relationship. If you opt for this approach, be sure to have an attorney verify that the provision will be valid.

PROTECTING THE FAMILY BUSINESS

One of the most important assets you have to protect for the sake of your heirs is an interest in a family or other closely held business. This is especially important when different family members are involved and if several people rely on the business for their livelihood (not to mention your relying on it for your retirement).

Planning Tip: Often, children are reluctant to sign a prenuptial agreement expressly excluding the business interests because they view a prenuptial agreement as a statement of mistrust, which is an anathema to their forthcoming marriage. To the contrary, every child (or other heir to the family business) needs to take this protective step for the entire family's sake. Often, if the context is everyone in the family taking the same precautionary step to protect the family unit as a whole, the context changes from something your child is "doing to" his or her beloved, to something a family is doing to protect everyone, including your child.

Limited Prenuptial Solely for Business Issues

In many cases, the soon-to-be-married couple is not willing to sign a comprehensive prenuptial agreement, however advisable from a legal, tax, and financial standpoint. In some of these situations, when a family business is involved, the family may be concerned about protecting the stock in the family business from attack in a divorce. If this concern is sufficiently strong, the family may insist that the soon-to-be-married family member who owns stock (or partnership or other family business interests) sign at least a limited agreement to protect the family business. This limited type of prenuptial agreement, illustrated in the "For Your Notebook" section following this chapter, presents another approach to the complex issue of protecting a business and child.

Rules to Protect the Family Business Require More Than Prenuptial Agreements

Other steps are important to take to protect the family business. There should be a comprehensive agreement among all of the owners:

- Shareholders' agreement for shareholders in a corporation.
- Partnership agreement for partners in a partnership.
- Operating agreement for members in a limited liability company.

This agreement should clearly delineate the restrictions on transfer, control issues, and so on. Some attorneys even have the new spouse, the son-in-law or daughter-in-law, execute a copy of the entities agreement (e.g., shareholders' agreement for a corporation) in the limited capacity of stating they agree to the non-transfer provisions.

Planning Tip: Discuss this issue with both your corporate and matrimonial attorneys; they each bring a different knowledge and expertise to the process.

Consider with your corporate attorney what provisions should be in the entity's documents as well. Consider the use of trusts for transfers rather than outright transfers. For example, if gifts of stock in a family business are to be made, consider making the gifts into trusts for the benefit of the donee, rather than directly to the donee. If spouses are to receive the economic benefit of shares, consider using *inter vivos* marital trusts (such as an *inter vivos* qualified terminable interest property [QTIP] trust; see Chapter 16).

KEEPING THE SON-IN-LAW OR DAUGHTER-IN-LAW IN CHECK

In some instances, it is not your child who is active in the business, but rather your child's spouse. There are a host of steps you can take to protect your child's interest in the business in these instances. Consider the following:

- Get your child to sign a prenuptial agreement.
- Have your child, not the son-in-law or daughter-in-law, own the stock. If not possible, the next alternative may be to ensure that your child at least has control.
- Include buy-sell restrictions as well as restrictions on transfer. If you have several children owning the business, you could have each child commit in the shareholders' agreement that their estates will sell any stock they own on their death to the other children. This can keep the stock in the family line.
- If a son-in-law or daughter-in-law is an employee, document and have them acknowledge in writing the fair and reasonable nature of their compensation.
- Don't think that you can cheat the IRS and then change the facts when your child divorces. Some family businesses get rather aggressive at deducting cars, entertainment, and a host of expenses on the business. If your child divorces, don't expect the divorce court to be swayed that the son-in-law or daughter-in-law working in the business really didn't earn certain benefits—that they were just done for tax purposes.
- Have control provisions in the shareholders' agreement to protect your child. These may include placing your child on the board of directors, naming your child an officer, giving your child veto power over certain decisions, restricting certain decisions that the working son-in-law or daughter-in-law can make, and other provisions your corporate attorney may advise you of.

- Consider what happens if your son-in-law or daughter-in-law is disabled and cannot work in the business. What happens to your child's earnings? This can be especially complicated if you have several children and in-laws working in the business.

USING TRUSTS FOR GIFTS AND INHERITANCE

The key to planning to protect from divorce a child's inheritance or gifts you make to the child while you are alive is to give the gifts or bequests to a trust for the benefit of your child, not to your child directly. This ensures that the assets in the trust are never commingled with your child's marital assets and thus insulates those assets from a claim that they have been commingled with (transmuted into) marital assets. Chapters 15, 16, and 17 provide considerable detail on using trusts to protect assets in divorce. These concepts can be similarly applied to how you can use trusts in your planning to protect your children (or other heirs) from the risks of divorce.

Note: Most steps taken to protect assets from your children's divorce are consistent with asset protection steps for them generally.

Planning Tip: If the estate tax is repealed (or the applicable exclusion amount increased to the point where it really doesn't concern you), you might be inclined to forgo using trusts in your estate and other planning for your children. Big mistake. If the estate tax disappeared tomorrow (which still isn't a guarantee, and Congress can reenact it), trusts remain essential to protect assets from your children's potential lawsuits and divorce.

SUMMARY

Every parent is concerned about the personal and emotional damage a child's divorce can have on the child and even on the entire family. This chapter provided guidance on how you can minimize the financial risks and detriments for your child in the event of divorce.

FOR YOUR NOTEBOOK

SAMPLE PRENUPTIAL AGREEMENT TO PROTECT STOCK IN FAMILY BUSINESS

Note: In many cases, the soon-to-be-married couple will not agree to sign a comprehensive prenuptial agreement, however advisable from a legal, tax, and financial standpoint. In some of these situations, when a family business is involved, the family may be concerned about protecting the stock in the family business from attack in a divorce. If this concern is sufficiently strong, the family may insist that the soon-to-be-married family member who owns stock (or partnership or other family business interests) sign at least a limited agreement to protect the family business. This sample prenuptial agreement illustrates one approach to this complex issue. Other steps are also important to take to protect the family business. There should be a comprehensive shareholders' (partnership or operating) agreement among all of the owners. This agreement should clearly delineate restrictions on transfer, control issues, and so on. Some attorneys even have the new spouse, the son-in-law or daughter-in-law, execute a copy of the entities agreement (e.g., shareholders' agreement for a corporation) in the limited capacity of stating they agree to the nontransfer provisions. Discuss this issue with both your corporate and matrimonial attorneys.

Note: Consider with your corporate attorney what provisions should be in the entity's documents as well. Consider the use of trusts for transfers rather than outright transfers. For example, if gifts of stock in a family business are to be made, consider making the gifts into trusts for the benefit of the donee, rather than directly to the donee. If spouses are to receive the economic benefit of shares, consider using *inter vivos* marital trusts (such as an *inter vivos* qualified terminable interest property [QTIP] trust).

This Prenuptial Agreement made on DAY, MONTH, YEAR between CHILDOWNER, residing at CHILDOWNER-ADDRESS, and NEW-SPOUSE, residing at NEWSPOUSE-ADDRESS.

RECITALS

WHEREAS, CHILDOWNER and NEWSPOUSE intend to be married in the near future. They have entered into this Agreement with respect to certain assets of CHILDOWNER.

In consideration of the foregoing, and of the provisions of this Agreement, and for good and valuable consideration, receipt and adequacy of which is hereby acknowledged, the parties agree as follows:

1. *Definitions*

    For purposes of this Agreement, the following definitions shall apply:

    a. CORPNAME means Corporation, a STATENAME Corporation, with its principal place of business at CORPADDRESS, which operates a business DESCRIBEBUSINESS (the Corporation or Business).

    b. CHILDOWNER's Present Shares—The shares of CORPNAME's stock presently owned by CHILDOWNER, including any shares in CORPNAME's stock which might be issued to CHILDOWNER as a dividend on, in exchange for, or with respect to CHILDOWNER's Present Shares.

    c. CHILDOWNER's Future Shares—Any shares in CORPNAME which CHILDOWNER may acquire in the future by gift or inheritance, or otherwise, including any shares in CORPNAME's stock which might be issued to CHILDOWNER as a dividend on, in exchange for, or with respect to such shares.

    d. CHILDOWNER'S Shares—CHILDOWNER's Present Shares and CHILDOWNER's Future Shares.

    e. Board means the Board of Directors of CORPNAME and any successor Board.

    Note: If other family members are involved, consider how they should be affected. If the objective is to safeguard the business for a particular family, having only some but not all sign agreements will not suffice.

    f. Minority Shareholders means CHILDOWNER and GRAND-CHILDNAME (both of whom are children of CHILDOWNER) and OTHERFAMILYNAME and (all of whom are children of RELATIVENAME).

2. *Representations*

    CHILDOWNER represents to NEWSPOUSE as follows:

    a. CHILDOWNER presently is the owner of XNUMBER shares of common stock of CORPNAME. (CHILDOWNER's Present Shares). There are presently issued and outstanding NUMBER shares of common stock of CORPNAME, and no shares of any other class of stock. Accordingly, CHILDOWNER's Present Shares constitute __ percent of CORPNAME's issued and outstanding shares. For purposes of this Agreement, various share holdings of shareholders expressed as a percentage have been rounded to the nearest hundredth of a percent.

b. CHILDOWNER and FORMERSPOUSE each own NUM-BERSHARES shares of common stock in CORPNAME, so that their aggregate Shares represent PERCENT (__ percent) of CORPNAME's issued and outstanding shares. The Minority Shareholders other than childowner, either individually or by way of holdings under the STATENAME Uniform Gifts to Minor's Act, are the owners of PERCENT (__ percent) of CORPNAME Shares.

c. CHILDOWNER and PARENT each own NUMBER shares of common stock in CORPNAME, so that their aggregate Shares represent PERCENT (__ percent) of CORPNAME's issued and outstanding shares. The Minority shareholders other than CHILDOWNER, either individually or by way of holdings under the STATE-NAME Uniform Gifts to Minor's Act, are the owners of percent of CORPNAME shares.

d. CHILDOWNER's shares as well as the shares of all other CORPNAME shareholders are subject to a Shareholders Agreement dated as of DATE and amended AMENDEDDATE. Said Agreement as so amended is referred to in this Agreement as the Shareholders' Agreement. The Shareholder's Agreement, among other things, prohibits transfers of CORPNAME's shares except under certain circumstances, and provides for the purchase by CORPNAME of CHILDOWNER's shares under certain circumstances. Included as one of the circumstances is the death of CHILDOWNER.

e. CHILDHOLDER's shares are also the subject matter of an agreement dated as of AGREEMENTDATE between all of the Shareholders of CORPNAME, including CHILDOWNER, FORMERSPOUSE, and CORPNAME. That agreement is referred to as the Shareholder Agreement. Among other things, the Shareholder Agreement provides for the following:

(1) Restriction of transferability of all of CORPNAME's stock owned by Minority Shareholders, including CHILDOWNER's; and

(2) Acquisition of all of the shares of CORPNAME, its nominee, or other shareholders of CORPNAME, under certain

circumstances, which circumstances include the death of a Minority Shareholder.

f. By virtue of the provisions of the Minority Shareholder Agreement, CHILDOWNER's shares are not transferable except under certain limited circumstances, and are transferable only to PERMISSIBLEENTITY, its nominee, or other shareholders of CORPNAME. In the event of CHILDOWNER's death, or the occurrence of certain other events, CHILDOWNER or his estate, must transfer CHILDOWNER's Shares in accordance with the Shareholders Agreement and/or the Minority Shareholder Agreement.

g. By reason of the fact that CORPNAME is a closely held corporation, all of whose shares are owned by PARENT, PARENT, and the Minority Shareholders, no market exists to establish their value. The shareholders' Agreement does not establish a value of any of CORPNAME's shares including CHILDOWNER's except in the event of a sale of shares, triggered by the death of either PARENT or PARENT. The value of CHILDOWNER's Present Shares, in the event of the death of PARENT in accordance with the Shareholders' Agreement, is approximately DOLLARS. The Minority Shareholder Agreement does not independently establish the value of CHILDOWNER's Shares. It does establish a value of (CHILDOWNER's Shares which is related to the value of such shares in accordance with the Shareholders' Agreement.

h. The Board has determined that it would be detrimental to the best interests of CORPNAME if spouses of Minority Shareholders had the right to inquire into CORPNAME's books and records in the event of matrimonial litigation. The Board has also determined that it would be detrimental to the best interests of CORPNAME if the spouses of any Minority Shareholders have the opportunity to acquire any interest in the shares of CORPNAME's stock owned by a Minority Shareholder by way of equitable distribution in the event of matrimonial litigation or otherwise.

i. As a result of the determination of the Board referred to in Paragraph G of this Section, the Board has required, as a condition to a Minority Shareholder being permitted to retain his CORPNAME shares upon marriage, that the prospective spouse of the minority Shareholder enter into an agreement containing the terms of this Agreement, prior to his or her marriage to the Minority Shareholder.

3. *Agreements by NEWSPOUSE*

   a. In the event of any matrimonial litigation involving the parties, NEWSPOUSE waives any right which she might otherwise have to inquire into the financial affairs and business affairs of CORPNAME. This waiver shall be contingent upon receipt of evidence that at the date of commencement of any marital litigation, a binding shareholders' agreement is in full force and effect between CORPNAME and all of its shareholders covering the disposition and value of shares held by a minority shareholder.

   b. In the event of any matrimonial litigation between the parties, NEWSPOUSE waives any right which he or she otherwise might assert to seek distribution to him or her of any of CHILDOWNER'S Shares, but such waiver shall in no way affect NEWSPOUSE's rights to see equitable distribution of the value of CHILDOWNER's shares.

   c. In the event that CHILDOWNER or CHILDOWNER's Estate (in the event of his or her death) becomes obligated to transfer CHILDOWNER's Shares, in accordance with the Shareholders' Agreement or the Minority Shareholder Agreement, as either may presently exist, or as the same may subsequently be amended, NEWSPOUSE agrees that he or she will not interfere with, or seek to enjoin in any manner, performance by CHILDOWNER or his or her estate of their respective obligations under either the Shareholders' Agreement or Minority Shareholder Agreement. The provisions of this Article will be effective notwithstanding any rights which NEWSPOUSE may have to CHILDOWNER's estate, in the event of his or her death, by way of Will, intestacy, surviving spouse elective share, or otherwise. CHILDOWNER agrees that any such rights will not be asserted by him or her so as to seek an interest in or with respect to CHILDOWNER's Shares. NEWSPOUSE does not relinquish any such rights with respect to any proceeds to which CHILDOWNER's estate will become entitled as the purchase price of CHILDOWNER's Shares, in accordance with the Shareholders' Agreement or Minority Shareholder Agreement.

4. *Representation by Counsel*

   a. NEWSPOUSE acknowledges that NEWSPOUSE has conferred with counsel ATTORNEYNAME1 with respect to this

Agreement, and that such counsel has fully explained this Agreement to NEWSPOUSE, that NEWSPOUSE person has signed this Agreement voluntarily after having received such advice deemed necessary from counsel.

b. CHILDOWNER acknowledges that CHILDOWNER has conferred with counsel, ATTORNEYNAME2, with respect to this Agreement and that CHILDOWNER attorney has fully explained this Agreement to CHILDOWNER and that CHILDOWNER has signed this Agreement voluntarily after having received such advice deemed necessary from counsel.

5. *Construction and Miscellaneous*

a. The rights and obligations of the parties hereto, as set forth in this Agreement, shall be governed by the laws of the State of STATENAME.

b. This agreement is not intended to be an all-encompassing premarriage agreement. The effect of this Agreement is limited to CHILDOWNER's Shares. By reason of the foregoing, CHILDOWNER agrees that it is not necessary that NEWSPOUSE make any disclosures to her as to the value and extent of his assets, with the exception of his shares of CORPNAME stock.

c. This Agreement shall be binding upon and inure to the benefit of the parties and their respective heirs, personal representatives, and assigns.

d. This Agreement represents the entire agreement between the parties and supersedes any prior discussions, understandings, or agreements. This Agreement may be amended only by a written agreement signed by both parties.

In Witness Whereof, the parties have signed this Agreement as of the date set forth hereinabove.

Witness:

_____   _____

                                      CHILDOWNER

_____   _____

                                      NEWSPOUSE

PART THREE

GENERAL LAWSUIT PROTECTION RULES

6 RULES TO LIVE SMART AND SAFE

WHY LIVING SMART IS THE BEST ASSET PROTECTION

The best asset protection plan is not to get sued in the first place. Setting up a sophisticated array of family limited partnerships, limited liability companies, and irrevocable asset protection trusts is a great way to insulate assets from lawsuits. However, it is far better to minimize the likelihood of the lawsuit in the first place. Why test your asset protection structure? No plan is impervious. There are certainly legal costs, anxiety, and risks to any suit, so plan to avoid lawsuits, not just to protect your assets from them. However confident you are in your advisors and plan, why incur the expense of the battle?

There is no doubt that some lawsuits are unfair, claims that are so ridiculous no one could anticipate them, and jury verdicts that are astronomical in comparison to what should reasonably be paid. But in spite of all the evils that antilawyer groups shout, our legal system is generally rational and does seek to mete out justice, and more often than not, it does. Therefore, taking steps to minimize risks will help you. Many, perhaps even most, lawsuits can be anticipated and avoided by carefully living your life, conducting your business, and handling your affairs. This chapter sets up some rules for doing just that. The fact that the system isn't perfect, and problems do arise and verdicts can sometimes be huge, is the reason you should still engage in the asset protection concepts in this book. Endeavoring to minimize suits is just half the job.

GENERAL RULES ON HOW TO LIVE WITHOUT BEING SUED

Use common sense and caution. Sounds simple? It is. But most people just don't bother. There are steps to help protect you from a lawsuit. Although this chapter can address only a few common areas, the lessons learned, with a bit of imagination and research, can be applied to almost any situation you face.

Use Common Sense and Reasonable Caution

Everyone is at risk for being sued, so be careful in how you conduct your business and activities. Use common sense:

- If you own a home or business, leaving a garden hose lying on the lawn so that any passerby could trip is asking for a lawsuit.
- Have fire extinguishers in easy view and reach, even if local law doesn't require it.
- Use a gun locker for your gun even though kids don't come into your house.
- Serving improperly prepared food to your family or patrons of your restaurant is asking for a lawsuit. Be sure you know minimum temperatures and times for which food should be cooked to kill bacteria. Cutting boards and utensils need to be cleaned after cutting meats, and so on. If you don't follow obviously well-known, almost common sense, food preparation rules, you're asking to be sued.
- Talk on the cell phone while while you drive your car is extremely foolhardy.
- Does it make sense to have a three-foot high picket fence when your attack dog can clear six feet with a hangover?

Applying common sense safety measures should become part of your routines and lifestyle.

Don't Assume You Are Immune to Suit

Don't assume family won't sue. They do. Don't assume your employee of 40 years won't sue. Your best buddy from college? She'd probably sue you, too. Anyone can sue anyone for any reason. There is no "base" where you can't get tagged. The best approach is to exercise reasonable caution and take preventative measures, regardless of who may be involved.

Example: You and your long-time friend buy a rental home together. You don't bother with the legal formalities because you trust each other. You handle all the work; your friend just keeps taking half the checks. You get progressively more annoyed at the inequity, but you're friends so you march on. A tenant gets hurt and sues. Your "friend" now claims that the two of you agreed that you would assume responsibility for the daily management, so it is your responsibility. Whatever the outcome, the legal battle between the two of you is likely to be ugly and costly. A simple agreement between the two of you may have avoided your partner's lack of contribution (or at least enabled you to get paid something extra for your efforts) and would have eliminated your partner's argument over your presumed responsibility. Importantly, addressing the legal formalities would probably have resulted in an attorney setting up a limited liability company for your purchase, which would insulate both your and your friend's personal assets from the tenant's claim. All too often, the fact that someone's partner is a friend or family member results in everyone's ignoring the protective steps they would insist on if they were involved with a stranger. Don't make that mistake.

Get Practical Information on How to Minimize Lawsuits

To live smart, you need information on practical steps you can take to avoid suits and claims. There are a number of great sources to tap.

If there is a risk you face, there is probably an insurance company that sells insurance to protect you. You don't need to insure against every risk, and you can't. But, if you analyze the insurable risks you face, the coverages that are available, and their costs, you can make informed decisions as to what to protect with insurance and what risks you might wish to bear yourself (self-insure; see Chapter 7). What this process can afford you is a better understanding of the risks you face. Most importantly, for tips on how to live smart, most insurance companies can provide you with articles helping you understand ways to minimize the risks they are insuring.

For professional work, investments, businesses, and many other activities, there may be a trade organization that can provide you with practical information on minimizing lawsuits for your particular situation.

Note: If you own a car, the American Automobile Association (AAA) is a great organization to help alert you to safety features. If you're a home-owner, *Consumer Reports* will alert you to many safety issues to be aware of. If you're an anesthesiologist, the publications of the American Society of Anesthesiologists and your state society provide regular tips on mini-mizing the likelihood of a malpractice claim. If you own a shopping cen-ter, the International Council of Shopping Centers has myriad publications, seminars, and other resources to guide you. Every profession and almost every line of business and investment has a trade group. If you're not a member, join. The periodic newsletters, seminars, and other resources they can make available can be invaluable in your protecting yourself.

HOMEOWNERS' RULES TO LIVE SMART

If you own a home, you face the risk of a lawsuit from anyone who visits your property. Don't let debris accumulate on the property where a passerby may trip or be injured. If something is broken, fix it.

Example: In 1999, Kathleen McDermott of Lynn, Massachusetts, was looking at a home she wanted to buy. She fell off a step onto the back deck of the home and broke her hip. She sued the seller, claiming that the seller failed to keep her property in "reasonably safe condition" for the use of visitors.

Here are some common and obvious exposures that you, as a homeowner, can remedy to minimize the likelihood of being sued:

- *Cracked or uneven sidewalks:* These are tremendous tripping hazards that result in lawsuits. Find out if you or the town is responsible.
- *Lights:* Be certain that the outside of your home is reasonably illuminated to minimize the likelihood of someone slipping or tripping. As a side benefit, exterior lighting is one of the best ways to avoid burglary.
- *Snow and ice:* Shovel snow as quickly as possible after a snow-fall, and salt or sand walkways to minimize the risk of some-one slipping.
- *Fire:* Install smoke alarms. Keep fire extinguishers in accessi-ble locations.

- *Stairs/steps:* Install railings, handgrips, and other safety devices. For steps leading up your front porch, install an iron railing for visitors. Handrails in the shower or bath may prevent Aunt Nellie from slipping and suing when she visits for Christmas. (If you think Aunt Nellie won't sue, read the introduction to this chapter again.)

- *Parties and events:* Your eight-year-old has a sleepover party, and you drive to the nearest 24-hour drugstore for another bottle of aspirin. A child gets hurt. No one was present to supervise the children while you were gone. The injured child's parents sue. Or, you're on vacation and your teenage son, who is supposed to be staying with grandma, instead has a wild "my parents are away" party. Drinking and drugs abound. There is a car accident. The injured sue you for negligence for not properly supervising your underage son. These are common stories, all obvious, but all continue to happen.

Caution: Too often, people assume that the only lawsuits to worry about are malpractice or other sophisticated claims. Wrong. The common stuff that you ignore is often what creates the devastating claims.

- *Pets:* Secure any pets so they cannot injure a visitor. Post a warning sign. If you have a dog run for your pit bull, be sure the water meter is on the outside of the run!

- *Toys:* Be cautious with children's toys. Is the tree house you improvised really safe? Will it attract neighborhood children while you are not there to supervise?

- *Swimming pools:* If you have a swimming pool, get it properly fenced in.

- *Home business:* If you have a home-based business, as tens of millions of Americans do, be sure that you comply with all safety codes and regulations of your town. Be sure to obtain specific insurance for the business—don't assume that your homeowners' policy covers it.

RENTAL PROPERTY OWNERS' RULES TO LIVE SMART

Owning a rental property is one of the most common investments, but one fraught with risks if not properly handled:

- See a business lawyer before you purchase the property; have an entity, perhaps a limited liability company, set up to purchase the property initially. Don't buy the property yourself and later transfer it to an entity. This puts you in the public record as an owner (chain of title) in the event of a suit. If the entity owns the property from inception, your personal assets are better protected from claims made concerning the property.

- Get adequate insurance. Don't assume your homeowners' insurance covers a rental property. Don't assume that your umbrella liability insurance does either.

- Review all the issues previously noted for homeowners. Most apply to you.

- Install a central monitored smoke and fire detection system. Make fire extinguishers accessible.

- Ensure that snow is shoveled promptly, spills that could cause slips are wiped up quickly, and so on.

- When making repairs or additions, favor fire retardant materials. Sheetrock that is ⅜" thick will give tenants or patrons more time to escape a fire than ½" sheetrock.

- Install an automatic external defibrillator to use in case a patron should have ventricular fibrillation.

- Know your tenants. A simple credit check or Internet search may reveal problems that might make a particular tenant inadvisable.

- Always have a written lease prepared by an attorney.

EMPLOYERS' RULES TO LIVE SMART

Many issues can affect business owners:

- When hiring an employee, confine the questions you ask to questions pertaining to the job. Never treat one applicant (or employee after hiring) different from another based on race, color, gender, religious beliefs, national origin, or age. Don't make statements about the position that you cannot meet. You cannot mischaracterize the compensation, kind of work, conditions, and so on. Use a written job application. Get a written resume. Check an applicant's references.

- If you fire an employee, consult an attorney about how to proceed. Inform the employee of the problems with his or her performance and document that the employee has been informed and given an opportunity to correct the problems. Consider obtaining a written termination agreement and release (commitment from the employee not to sue). Be cautious in explaining the reasons for the termination to other employees or future employers calling for a reference. Consider limiting your comments to inquiring future employers to confirming the employment dates. You do not want to defame the terminated employee. You also don't want to give ex-employees a good reference if they don't deserve it. You could be sued by the new employer who hires based on your reference.

Example: In a California case in 1997, a former employer gave a prospective employer a positive reference for the terminated employee—a teacher. After being hired, the employee molested a student and the former employer was successfully sued.

Be certain to give terminated employees notice of their right to continue medical coverage under federal law (COBRA). Conduct an exit interview and listen to the employee's comments:

- Minimize risks of being sued for harassment. Have an anti-harassment and antidiscrimination policy. Require all employees to report any incidences that arise. Document every complaint. Ask an employment attorney to guide you as to how to investigate each complaint you receive. Do not engage in, or tolerate others' engaging in, pejorative talk.
- Make the workplace physically safe. See the previous suggestions for real estate owners and apply as many as you can. Install a first aid kit. Consider an alarm system. Set security procedures for those staying after hours.

PROFESSIONALS' RULES TO LIVE SMART

There are so many different professions, and each has its many nuances for minimizing claims. There are, however, some general guidelines that can help any professional. For simplicity, we use the term *clients* for the people you serve, whether they are patients, clients, or customers:

- *Don't assume that the only matter you can get sued for is malpractice.* Be certain that your office or other premises are physically safe, that you have adequate insurance protection, and that you've addressed all the issues previously noted that affect any business.

- *Know the standard of care for your profession and in your area.* Are your colleagues taking steps that you are not taking? The standards by which you are judged are determined by statutory law, rules of court, rules of professional conduct, accepted or acceptable practice, retainer agreements, client-defined objectives, your specialization, and other factors. This requires that you possess the knowledge ordinarily possessed and exercise the skill ordinarily used by others engaged in the general practice of your particular profession. The law does not require that you guarantee a favorable result for your client.

- *Treat all clients with respect.* Many suits result from annoyance with the arrogance, and often nastiness, of the professional involved.

- *If a client has a problem, address it.* Don't ignore or dismiss a problem, assuming the client will simply disappear. In many cases, the mere acknowledgment that something was done inappropriately may suffice to satisfy a client. Good client communication is an effective way to minimize malpractice claims. However, when apologizing or acknowledging a problem, exercise sufficient care to avoid documenting the basis for a later lawsuit.

Caution: If you're not sure how to phrase an apology letter to avoid documenting an actionable claim for your client, consult a malpractice attorney. Paying a malpractice attorney to review a simple letter is far cheaper than defending a claim.

- *Be sure that the client's expectations are clear, reasonable, and can be met.* While this varies by profession, a verbal or written explanation of what services you provide and what services you cannot provide is important. Many professionals use written fee, retainer, engagement, or other agreements.

These are excellent tools, but too often they are so generic or so complex and legally dense that few clients understand them.

- *Maintain detailed records of the services provided and cautions given to your client.* For many professionals, this is addressed in their billing system. If a particular matter concerns you or a particular client is proving difficult, write a more detailed memorandum for the client files.

- *You don't have to accept every person as a client who wants to retain you.* If a client starts off difficult or unreasonable, it usually get worse, not better. While it may be hard to walk away from a fee, it's usually cheaper (and much less aggravating) to fire clients when they first become difficult or unreasonable than after you've become more involved in assisting them.

- *Look for signs of problem clients and terminate them, or, better yet, don't let them hire you.* A client who cannot work within your normal methods of operating is more likely to become a problem. A client who has fired several prior professionals is often not a client you want. A client who wants to tape record your meetings is cause for concern. A client who tells you how to do your job often proves nettlesome.

- *Properly supervise your staff.* You are responsible for their actions.

- *Cooperate in the defense of your case.* Don't assume that it is your malpractice carrier's or lawyer's job, not yours. Your full involvement of time, effort, and thought is essential. Never dismiss a claim or treat it lightly.

PHYSICIANS' RULES TO LIVE SMART

While the advice differs somewhat by medical specialty (and you should review the literature from your malpractice carrier and medical societies), the following generalized advice can be used as a starting point:

- Treat patients with respect.
- Apologize to a patient if the patient is upset.

- Inform the patient of all issues and risks, and if an error occurs, inform the patient of the error, apologize for the error, and explain the steps being taken to address it.
- Never tamper with a patient chart. If you noted something in the patient chart that is incorrect, cross it out and write the correct comments following. Also indicate the date and time of the correction and the reason. Never change the chart.

Example: A patient with a history indicating coronary heart disease (smoker, overweight, family history, etc.) was examined by his physician in California. Doctor noted in the chart that the patient had mild chest tenderness and right chest wall pain. The patient, on the doctor's approval, took a vacation to London where he died of a heart attack (acute myocardial infarction). At trial, the family's attorney discovered that the patient chart had pen impressions, which, on examination, revealed the words *tightness* and *pressure* that did not appear in the final chart. This gave the impression that the physician may have changed the chart to cover his trail. Whatever the facts, the physician faced the impossible task of convincing the jury that nothing inappropriate had occurred.

Once a record is lost or tampered with, the plaintiff's (the person suing you) attorney will argue conspiracy or cover-up:

- Be sure all patient records are complete. Remember that the expert witnesses, who will examine your patient charts, all have the benefit of hindsight.
- Properly supervise nursing staff.
- Review prior medical records and address any history that could indicate problems.
- Properly and reasonably follow up on all ordered medical tests.
- Cooperate in the defense of your case.

Caution: Exercising all reasonable professional care, unfortunately, is not enough to prevent a suit. Arizona ophthalmologist Dr. Robert Snyder was sued and a $4 million verdict awarded even though his LASIK surgery procedure was successfully completed. The patient, Stephen Post, an airline pilot, had 20/20 uncorrected vision following the procedure but suffered impaired night vision. This was a known risk of the procedure, listed in the informed consent and signed by Mr. Post.

TRUSTEES', EXECUTORS', AND GUARDIANS' RULES TO LIVE SMART

It is common and, as the population ages, it will become even more common for your friends or family to name you an executor or trustee. As an executor, you will be responsible for administering an estate, collecting assets, paying bills, investing estate funds, and making distributions to heirs. As a trustee, you will be responsible for investing trust funds and making distributions to the trust beneficiaries. While it may be a compliment that you are named, it is also an invitation to suit. Serving as a trustee or executor means you are acting in a fiduciary capacity, a position of trust, for the beneficiaries depending on you. This responsibility must be taken seriously and requires attention to investment and legal details.

Read the Document; Know the Law

Before you take a job, you read the job description and ask the employer about the details. Before accepting the formal appointment as a trustee or executor, read the will or trust agreement. They are the rulebook and job description you are bound to. Because these documents are generally complex legal documents and there are key rules contained in state law that the will and trust documents may not mention, you need an estate planning attorney to interpret the job description and rulebook for you. Take notes about your responsibilities, get an understanding of what your obligations are under both the legal documents and state law, and develop a checklist of steps you must take to fulfill your duties. Your failure to abide by these rules can expose you to a lawsuit.

Example: You're named trustee of a trust for your nephew. You distribute most of the money to your nephew to pay for college, which was your sister's wish. Your nephew reaches age 25, the trust ends, and the remaining monies are to be distributed to your deceased sister's friends. They aren't at all happy that most of the funds were already distributed or, in their view, dissipated. What is your obligation to them? Does the trust really say to distribute funds liberally for your nephew's education without regard to what is left? Can these friends (remainder beneficiaries) sue you?

Failing to follow the actual terms of the will or trust (not what you "knew" your sister wanted) is a major cause of lawsuits against fiduciaries.

Asset Allocation—Key to Preserving and Enhancing the Estate

Asset allocation is an essential component to the administration of any trust or estate. Asset allocation can address many important estate and trust objectives. A proper investment plan minimizes the risk that investment assets are exposed to, thus giving greater security to the estate or trust (and to you from being sued).

Example: You're a trustee of your son's college trust. You invested solely in tech stocks in 1998. You may have looked like a hero for a while, but the trust was depleted 70 percent in value from 2000 to 2002 until you sold and bought bonds in a panic. You might think you've still done a reasonable job, but what about your ex-wife? Might she sue you for the college costs that now won't be covered? May your son sue you for having dissipated funds so that he has to work his way through college?

If you're a trustee or executor, have an investment professional give you a written plan that reasonably relates the risk of the investments to the objectives being pursued.

What is asset allocation? It is the process of identifying the asset classes in which the trust or estate will invest and then allocating the assets held in trust or in the estate to those asset classes through an analysis of rates of return and risk tolerance. The basis of this is modern portfolio theory. The trust or estate document should (but most really don't) provide guidance to the financial planner or money manager as to how much risk you as a fiduciary should be willing to endure to achieve the return you desire.

Modern portfolio theory, in very general terms, assumes that the investment markets are efficient. Therefore, the decision as to which asset categories trust or estate capital is allocated to is more critical than picking specific assets (e.g., stocks) in any particular category. Selecting asset categories that have negative correlation (i.e., when one rises, the other tends to fall) can minimize risk while achieving the desired level of return. The relationship of asset categories can be indicated by their correlation. A correlation of +1.0

indicates assets whose values move in perfect tandem. A correlation of −1.0 indicates assets whose values move in opposite directions. The technical term used to describe the relationship between asset categories is *covariance*. Covariance is a measure of the likelihood of the assets to move in the same direction and the momentum of their likely movements.

Studies have demonstrated that 90-plus percent of the risk of a portfolio can be explained by the allocation of assets. Where a portfolio is diversified among asset categories, approximately 90 percent of the risk can be viewed as market risk, while only 10 percent or less of the risk of that portfolio will be a specific risk of a particular stock.

Through an analysis of covariance of particular assets and expected return of those assets, a portfolio can be constructed, which theoretically minimizes the risk faced by the investor attempting to achieve any particular level of return. By optimizing this relationship, in theory, an investor could earn greater returns than on his or her present portfolio while reducing risk.

What does this mean to you as a trustee or executor? If the assets you're responsible for are invested in a haphazard manner, with no plan and asset allocation model, if the investment performance is poor, you are likely to lose a lawsuit challenging you. Instead, retain, in your capacity as trustee or executor, a financial planner or money manager to develop a plan. Consideration of modern portfolio theory concepts is vital to your protection.

SUMMARY

Everyone should be concerned about lawsuits. Often, the best and cheapest defense is simply living smart and safe. Whatever businesses, investments, or other activities you're involved in, conducting them with some prudence can go a long way toward minimizing the likelihood of someone's suing you, or if they do, of their succeeding. This chapter reviewed some general principals of how to live smart and presented examples of how to live smart in the context of a number of different business, professional, and personal activities. Even if the specific situations don't apply to you, the general lessons do. Live smart and safe, so you never have to test the insurance you buy, or the asset protection steps you take.

FOR YOUR NOTEBOOK

INVESTMENT ANALYSIS WORKSHEET

Asset Category[a]	Asset Description	Share/ Bond/ etc.	Cost Basis	Fair Market Value	Percent of Total Portfolio	Target Asset Allocation Percent for Category	Adjustment Required	Comment
Growth equity								
International equity								
Corporate bonds								
Municipal bonds								
Government bonds								
Precious metals								
Real estate								
Alternative investments								
Hedge funds								

[a] Attach a written investment policy statement demonstrating the reasons for the target allocation. Specifically address: time frame, cash flow needs, risk tolerance, tax considerations, and other factors.

7 INSURANCE RULES ARE A KEY TO ASSET PROTECTION

Insurance provides three vital types of protection for your assets. Liability insurance is a key to protecting all of your assets if you are sued. Insurance protects the assets themselves (e.g., fire insurance) and your income stream, which you use to accumulate assets (e.g., disability insurance). Finally, life insurance can provide a method of creating an asset that itself is protected. This chapter presents the rules for these three steps.

Protecting yourself from lawsuits is critical to your financial well-being. Even if you take all the steps in this book to protect your assets, if you are sued, it's always better to have an insurance company at your side for the suit or other loss and at the end if you lose and have to pay. Purchasing the right insurance coverage is the key to this protection. If you have proper protection, your asset protection plan may never have to be tested. You cannot safeguard your assets if you don't have insurance to protect your home and business from fire and other obvious risks. This is all part of asset protection planning even though it is rather mundane. However, it is *never* enough.

Make sure that you have insurance protection for risks that might affect you or have a significant adverse impact. If the likely cost of a loss is small, the fact that you might face a loss is not significant. While this might sound obvious, most people buy insurance without applying this bit of common sense. For example, if you can save hundreds of dollars each year on your automobile or homeowners' insurance by increasing your deductible a few thousand dollars, isn't it worth the risk?

START WITH A SUMMARY

If you haven't obtained a recent summary of all your insurance coverage, do so immediately. If you have one primary insurance agent, the agent can provide the summary. If not, assemble the data yourself. Then review all your coverages. Do they seem adequate? Are there risks missing? Note them in the margin and review these issues, along with the entire summary, with an insurance agent. Also consider getting a second opinion.

Type of Coverage	Insurer/ Policy Number	Matters Covered	Matters Excluded	Policy Limits/ Deductible	Annual Premium	Overlay or Gap in Coverage	Comments/ Issues/ Insurer's Record

Insurance is never a complete protection. Every policy has a deductible, which is the amount you have to absorb if there is a claim. As you take a comprehensive look at your insurance coverage, you're likely to see that an increase in the deductibles on many policies will save you premium dollars that can be better used buying additional coverage for more significant risks. Every policy has exclusions that could leave you open for a large loss. Your insurance summary chart and, in particular, the column "Overlap or Gap In Coverage" will help you identify risks that are not insured so you can evaluate additional insurance coverage to protect against these risks or perhaps determine that other lawsuit protection steps are necessary. While the risk of an insurance company's defaulting and not paying the promised coverage is rare, it should still be considered in your analysis. Review the financial status of each insurance company you are using and its claims history to see if changes should be made. These gaps and risks are the reason that you must still take the further lawsuit protection steps discussed in this book. Insurance is your first line of defense against most risks and liability claims, but it should never be your only defense. Don't assume a malpractice suit will be limited to the amount of your insurance coverage. Most claims start much higher, and many settle for more than the coverage limits. Don't assume a law limiting "pain and suffering" will protect your assets. These decisions, as most in this book, are best made with a team approach. Your insurance consultant and asset protection/corporate attorney and accountant or financial advisor should all be "in the loop" on insurance decisions because they impact your other planning.

RULES FOR PERSONAL PROPERTY AND CASUALTY INSURANCE

Although often considered the stepchild of financial planning and asset protection, frequently nothing could be more important than properly structured liability, property, and casualty insurance. You should review with an independent insurance consultant the level of coverage in place.

Coordination of Coverage

Insurance coverage must be updated as your risks change. Your liability exposure will increase if you go back to work as a professional after a maternity or other hiatus. As the composition of your assets changes, insurance must be updated. If your savings are initially marketable securities but then you purchase rental real estate and a business, your entire liability picture has changed. If your assets grow in value, coverage limits need to be reevaluated. Throughout this process, you must be sure that the various insurance coverages remain coordinated. Often, umbrella liability, auto, and home, as well as ancillary, coverage are interrelated, and if you don't expressly coordinate coverage, gaps or other problems can easily occur.

Many insurance policies name additional insureds. These should be reviewed to remove any named insureds that are no longer appropriate to list. For example, a mortgage lender that loaned funds to your ex-spouse or for a property or business that has been sold may still be named in your policy and should be deleted. More importantly, you may have to add new named insureds to your insurance policy. This could include, for example, the trustees of a trust to which you transferred ownership interests in assets covered or the managers of a limited liability company to which you transferred real estate or other assets.

Homeowners' Insurance

Your home is likely to be a major asset and should be protected by proper insurance coverage. Also, don't forget the tips for how to live smart in your home (Chapter 6), and be sure the ownership of your home gives you optimal protection (Chapter 3). Homeowners' insurance protects the value of your home against loss from fire, theft, and other risks, all part of a comprehensive asset protection plan. Homeowners' insurance is also the primary source of liability protection from suits relating to your residence.

Homeowners' insurance includes various types of coverage, and you should make sure all are reasonable in light of the value of your home and other assets covered. The *dwelling* coverage protects the house itself. *Other structures* covers insurance on a garage or other structure. *Personal property* covers the contents of your home. In most cases, you probably need to review this carefully and add additional coverage, as discussed later in the Scheduled Property section. Many policies also include *loss of use,* which covers the cost of living expenses if you cannot occupy your home because of damage. You probably want an *all risks* policy, which covers all types of loss, not just specific losses or risks specified in the policy (called *specified perils*). There is a wide range of variations on these policies, all of which are beyond the scope of this book, but which you should review, understand, and plan for. You must also pay careful attention to how the policy describes costs that will be paid. You want replacement cost or something approaching it at least for the dwelling, so that you receive sufficient insurance proceeds to pay for rebuilding what was lost.

If you have a home-based business, don't assume that your regular homeowners' insurance covers it or, if it does, that the coverage is adequate. Many policies limit coverage to a modest amount, for example, $2,500. Ask your insurance agent about obtaining an endorsement to your existing homeowners' policy that adds additional coverage for a fee, or determine whether you need a separate business policy.

Even if you don't own a home, you still need coverage. If you rent, a landlord's insurance coverage won't cover your personal

Rules for Ownership and Beneficiary Designations on Life Insurance Policies

When you're seeking to protect your assets, owning your own life insurance may be a sufficient protection if, under your state law, life insurance is a protected asset. However, if you can obtain additional protection by properly arranging the ownership of your policy, the extra protection should be carefully considered. The rule for insurance ownership is one word: trusts. In most cases, an irrevocable (cannot be changed) life insurance trust (ILIT) is the answer. Importantly, as discussed in Chapter 5, having life insurance owned by a trust also protects your beneficiaries' interests in the life insurance proceeds from their claimants or divorce.

Because life insurance is often the largest asset in an estate, and even where not the largest asset, it may still be one of the most important because it provides liquidity to pay estate taxes and other death costs. Careful determination of the appropriate beneficiary is critical to properly implementing an estate plan:

- *The insured:* If you own the policy, you can access the cash value, subject to the terms of the policy, but if state law protects the insurance policy from your creditors, the cash value, up to your state's limit, may remain safe. As noted previously, the risk is that if you can readily get at the cash value, might your claimant?

- *Spouse:* You could have your spouse own the policy directly. If you need funds, he or she could borrow on the policy or even cancel the policy and make funds available to meet marital expenses. This approach has a host of problems. You may divorce your spouse. Your spouse may be sued. There are myriad cases of wealthy doctors transferring all assets to a nonworking spouse, who then is in an uninsured car accident, which decimates the estate. You may not be able to control your spouse's decisions.

- *Insurance trust:* The insurance trust is probably a safer option than having you or your spouse own a policy directly. Neither your creditors, nor your spouses, nor your heirs (if the proceeds stay in trust) should be able to reach the insurance policy, its cash value, or eventual death benefits, while held

property or liability if someone sues you, so renters' insurance is necessary. If you own a condominium or cooperative apartment, a special policy should be purchased that doesn't duplicate coverage that the homeowners' association or cooperative has but that does cover your personal exposure. Review the bylaws of the homeowners' association or condominium association to determine exactly what they cover and what you must cover.

Renters' Insurance

Simply because you rent an apartment rather than own a home doesn't mean insurance coverage is unnecessary. Renters' insurance, coordinated with personal excess liability coverage, scheduled riders for personal property, and so on, is just as important.

Scheduled Property

Whether you have homeowners', renters', or some other type of insurance, few standard policies provide more than modest coverage for art, jewelry, and other valuables. Therefore, it is important for you to review your asset holdings and determine which should be covered by additional insurance endorsements. These are referred to as *scheduled* or *listed* properties.

Automobile Coverage

Automobile coverage, while important to protect the value of your car in the event of an accident or damage, is secondary to the liability exposure owning a car can create. It can be nearly unlimited. Proper liability coverage is vital.

Caution: Too often, a personal automobile is insured through the business to claim the premiums deductible. In other cases, many people insure business cars as if they are personal because the premiums are lower (although they presumably deduct the depreciation and maintenance costs on the business). Insurance costs and tax deductions pale in comparison to the liability exposure you will have if there is a serious accident and your coverage is jeopardized because it was not handled properly. Think twice about how penny-wise and pound-foolish it is to improperly characterize your car.

Liability Coverage

In addition to homeowners' and automobile coverage, you should have excess personal liability, also called *umbrella,* coverage. This is coverage over and above the liability limits on your homeowners' (and automobile) insurance.

Example: Your homeowners' and automobile insurance have maximum liability coverage of $500,000. Your net worth is $1.5 million. If you are sued for $1 million, the insurance would pay the first $500,000 and you would pay the next $500,000. If you had a personal excess liability policy, it would cover the $500,000 claim above the $500,000 paid by your homeowners' and automobile insurance.

As a rule of thumb, you should have personal excess liability coverage at least equal to your net worth. The cost, compared to the coverage, is usually modest. Be careful, however, to review the actual risks covered by an umbrella policy. It might exclude a home business, profession, and rental property, so you may need to coordinate with those additional coverages to properly protect yourself.

RULES FOR LIFE INSURANCE

Life Insurance as a Protected Asset

Life insurance has some creditor protection and in most states cannot be attached by owners' creditors. Even if the cash value is available for the insured to take, it is protected. The only other asset with this type of protection for a liquid value is a qualified retirement plan. The first step is to determine which state law applies and how much insurance is protected. In some states the amount protected is too small to be helpful to your planning. This will depend on your residence at the time the suit commences. However, if there is a claim, this might be an issue the claimant asserts in an effort to obtain the benefit of a state law more favorable to him or her. There is an important exception to this protection of insurance values. If you purchased the policy or added cash to it after knowing of a claim, the fraudulent conveyance rules would prevent you from taking advantage of the protection. In many situations, a trust, partnership, or other family members own the policy. The

trust itself provides a measure of asset protection, so the issue as to whether the insurance asset itself is protected under state law may not matter. However, the levels and types of protection afforded by the insurance asset and by the trust can differ.

Life Insurance Planning Considerations

Death is a risk your family and others depending on you financially must face. If you make significant transfers of assets as a part of an asset protection strategy, it may be prudent to supplement your life insurance coverage to ensure that your loved ones are protected without the complexity of their having to deal with the asset protection structures. For example, if you establish a foreign situs asset protection trust to hold a significant portion of your assets, it may be easier for the initial period following your death for your family to have access to readily available insurance proceeds. Insurance should consider meeting these liquidity needs in light of the other asset protection steps you take. Decisions must be made as to the type of coverage—term, whole life, universal, variable, or other options. The rule to getting it right is to have the decision made with your team of advisors, which includes your estate attorney and accountant, not just your insurance agent. Remember in making the selection that your asset protection goals may change the approach used. If insurance is a protected asset for you, a permanent policy might make much more sense than a term policy with no cash value. Further, a policy structured so that you can pay the premiums as quickly as possible (without violating the characterization of the policy as "insurance" under the income tax rules) may be the best approach to safeguard assets as quickly as possible.

Planning Tip: Because your goal may be to build a large cash value in the policy for the long term, your analysis differs from other people buying insurance. You may wish to have liberal loan provisions so a beneficiary can access this cash value if needed. For example, if your other assets are lost in a lawsuit, your spouse's borrowing the cash value of an insurance policy may be an important source of cash flow for your family. Also, a long-term, high cash policy means the insurance company is holding a significant asset. You want to be sure the insurance company has strong financial footing. Check the various rating agencies: A.M. Best, Duff & Phelps, Moody's, Weiss, and Standard & Poor's before buying.

---

in trust. Further, you can handpick the trustees or use a combination of cotrustees and other quasi fiduciaries to control the policy and proceeds. The manner in which an insurance trust is structured to avoid estate tax (if an estate tax affects you) is to prohibit you as the insured from being a beneficiary of the trust. Thus, the only way to access the cash value is to set up a trust for your spouse, and the trustee could then borrow the cash value, distribute it from the trust to your spouse, and your spouse could then use it for joint living expenses. This scenario can work and is safer than owning the insurance yourself in many cases. However, are the risks of the *ifs* more than the risks of the creditors? What *if* the trustee doesn't want to borrow against the policy? What *if* the trustee doesn't want to distribute the funds to your spouse? What *if* your spouse divorces you and you won't be able to share in the trust distribution?

- *Your children/heirs:* If you want to access the cash value of the policy if needed in the future (e.g., if a malpractice claim wipes out most of your unprotected assets), how will you do so if the policy is owned by your children? Will that miserable, cheap son-in-law help you out? Do you really want to ask him? What if your daughter divorces the bum? The policy cash value might enter into her divorce proceeding. What if your brilliant daughter, the anesthesiologist, is sued? Your insurance cash value, if owned by her, is an asset available to her creditors. An insurance trust is almost always a better option than children for owning a policy, especially in an asset protection context.

- *Family partnership:* A family partnership can be used to own life insurance. But if the insured is the general or managing partner, will the IRS or claimant argue that you thereby still control the policy?

Example: Father is a 1 percent managing partner of a family general partnership. The partnership owns a $1 million insurance policy on Father. Father gifts 99 percent of the general partnership interests to his children. On Father's death, the children receive 99 percent of the insurance proceeds in proportion to the percentage interests in the partnership previously given to them by gift. The executor for Father's estate would try to argue that only 1 percent of the insurance proceeds are included in Father's estate.

RULES FOR PERSONAL MEDICAL AND OTHER HEALTH INSURANCE

Insuring health and related risks is vital to safeguarding your assets from being dissipated in paying for such care. This planning is vital to safeguard your assets because a major illness affecting you or a loved one or a lengthy nursing home stay in your later years could decimate your savings. With nursing home fees of $75,000 per year and more, even a substantial estate can be materially and adversely affected. Planning for medical and health-related costs is a broad and complex topic. It requires analysis of coverages you or your family may have from employment, personal coverage you have or may wish to obtain, and even governmental programs. If you own your own business so that you can control the "employment" medical benefits, the options grow further. Traditional health insurance, medical savings accounts, cafeteria plans, disability insurance, long-term care insurance, and more should all be considered. While the details of these types of coverage are beyond the scope of this book, some key points are noted briefly to ensure that they don't escape your planning.

Health Insurance

The costs of a major illness can be almost unlimited, so insurance coverage is essential. You might obtain your own coverage by purchasing it from a commercial insurance company or a nonprofit association such as Blue Cross. Alternatively, you may consider a health maintenance organization or physician hospital organization program. You may choose to self-insure for some portion of your health care costs (you personally bear the costs). There are a host of different types of plans. Traditional insurance plans reimburse you for medical expenses incurred after you pay a deductible. Managed care plans attempt to control medical costs by eliminating unnecessary procedures, monitoring treatment, encouraging compensation, and so forth (or at least the theory says they do). You might join an HMO and then use its doctors and facilities for your care. Preferred provider organizations (PPO) are often set up as networks of physician and hospitals. These generally allow you to choose between a PPO facility or pay a higher price and choose a nonmember physician or hospital.

Medicare is a federal health insurance program intended to help individuals age 65 or older. Part A is hospital insurance and Part B is medical insurance. This latter part is optional, and a monthly premium is required. These do not always cover all health care costs; a major illness could result in your incurring substantial medical bills after Medicare pays its share. Therefore, many people supplement their Medicare coverage with additional coverage to fill in any gaps; this is called a Medigap policy.

Long-Term Care Insurance

If you are over age 50, some consideration should be given to long-term care coverage to fund the costly risk of a long-term nursing home stay. *Long-term care* refers to the need for assistance with day-to-day living needs due to illness and/or advanced age, such as bathing, dressing, and eating. This type of care can be administered at your home, in a facility, or in a nursing home. Medical insurance coverages exclude this type of care, so additional provisions have to be made to safeguard your assets. Even if your net worth and income are sufficient to cover these costs, it is still worth the analysis to consider coverage in many cases. The coverage can still be used to safeguard assets for other uses. If long-term care coverage makes sense for you, carefully evaluate the various policies available. Obtain sample policies and coverage statements and review what is actually provided. Analyze the insurance companies you are considering to gain comfort that they are sufficiently strong financially to be in place to pay the coverage you are purchasing.

Disability Insurance

Planning for disability is critical to asset protection planning because steps you take will make it more difficult to reach assets. If the feared malpractice or other lawsuit occurs, your remaining savings may be depleted, and if you're disabled on top of it, your current earnings would also not be available to meet expenses.

Don't rely on Social Security. Even if you qualify, the maximum payments are very limited.

Disability planning should be coordinated with group term disability plans available from trade or other organizations, benefits provided by a corporate employer, lines of credit (which may enable you to borrow to fund a short-term disability), available cash resources (often severely depleted by the a large lawsuit, malpractice claim, or divorce), and any requirements under the divorce decree (because divorce is a significant asset protection risk you must address). A comprehensive overview of disability planning to address the current circumstances is essential for almost everyone, although again, this topic is beyond the scope of this book.

Example: Dr. Smith undertakes a comprehensive asset protection plan. She places a significant portion of her liquid assets into a family limited partnership (FLP) and gifts 40 percent of her partnership interests to a domestic asset protection trust formed in Delaware and 5 percent to each of her children. If Dr. Smith is then sued, her remaining available liquid assets may be lost in defending the suit and meeting the judgment. If she becomes ill and cannot work, she will have more limited sources of funding living expenses. Not only is disability insurance essential to preserve her lifestyle, but it will also support the reasonableness of the assets she transfers because it serves as a backstop to her income on which she is relying.

It may be feasible as part of your asset protection planning, or postdivorce, to negotiate a revision to a closely held business shareholders' agreement to provide for some greater length of compensation continuation in the event of disability. Coordination with business-related documents needs special attention if you undertake a comprehensive asset protection program because such planning almost always involves forming new entities and restructuring existing entities. Disability coverage should also be coordinated with business interruption insurance purchased for your business or professional practice and salary or other compensation continuation provisions in a shareholders' agreement for a closely held business.

In assessing disability insurance coverage, consideration should be given to accepting the longer waiting (elimination) periods and fewer "bells and whistles" to minimize the cost of the coverage and focus on the more significant risks as part of your asset protection plan. Increasing the waiting period from 30 days to one year may provide a tremendous savings in premium costs. On the other hand, as more of your assets are restricted because of asset protection planning steps, you may actually prefer to shorten a waiting period from one year to, for example, 90 days. A barebones policy is far better protection and far more prudent than no coverage at all in many cases. Other policy variables you should consider include whether the policy is guaranteed renewable. Your preference is to obtain a policy that cannot be cancelled and that you can renew at least until your expected retirement. The definition of *disability* is also important. If the definition is too restrictive, you may never collect if you can perform any employable task, whereas if it is broader (such as your not being able to perform in your own occupation), the cost may be prohibitive. Partial disability may afford you protection by paying monthly benefits.

Note: The timing of your application for disability insurance may be affected by asset protection planning. If you report substantial passive income (dividends, interest, etc.) on your personal income tax return, you may not qualify for coverage. However, following implementation of your asset protection planning, that income may be reported on tax returns for family partnerships and trusts, and you may be viewed differently by the insurance company.

A group policy, even if not tailored for your unique needs, may be a less costly option than individual coverage. Often, professional associations offer disability coverage at modest cost. It is often worthwhile to investigate the benefits of joining various new professional associations to identify their benefits.

Lines of credit and increased credit limits on credit cards (perhaps the worst of all options but, again, better than nothing) can be used as temporary emergency stopgaps, pending the ability to obtain additional coverage and time to rebuild savings.

RULES FOR BUSINESS INSURANCE

The first rule in planning to protect your business interests is to identify your business insurance risks. These include obvious risks such as damage to business property and liability loss in the event of a suit, such as a malpractice claim if you are a professional, or a product liability suit if you are a manufacturer. Other risks include covering overhead expenses if property is damaged, suits by employees for harassment, director liability, death of a key employee, and many more. The following discussion can provide only a cursory review of a few of these points. The key is to review each risk with your insurance consultant and other advisors and develop an affirmative plan to minimize those risks, to insure remaining risks that are cost effective to insure, and to then recognize that risks that remain are to be self-insured (your business, which often means you, bears the loss in the event of a claim or damage).

Directors' and Officers' Liability Insurance

In the post-Enron and post-WorldCom world, directors and officers' (D&O) coverage is likely to become more costly, harder to obtain, and more narrow in its coverage. D&O insurance is intended to protect directors and officers from suits by disgruntled shareholders and others. The costs are high and large deductibles may be the only affordable technique. For these reasons, the many other lawsuit protection techniques discussed in this book should be addressed to protect your personal assets from D&O claims that aren't covered by insurance.

In addition, many states permit a business to indemnify officers and directors. This may require an amendment to the legal documents used to form the corporation as a legal entity (certificate of incorporation) or amendment of the corporation's bylaws. Be certain to have corporate counsel address these issues. Indemnification is not, however, foolproof and should not be looked on as a substitute for insurance and other asset protection steps.

Malpractice Insurance

Every professional is concerned about malpractice risks. Jury verdicts have grown. Coverage is costly and sometimes hard to obtain. Even when coverage is obtained, there are always a host of exclusions. Even the best policy should never be relied on as your only protective step. A key aspect of every policy is not only the coverage it provides for malpractice claims, but the payment of the costs to defend those claims. Professional liability coverage comes in a wide array to cover malpractice for doctors, attorneys, and accountants. Medical malpractice policies cover the risks of professional liability for bodily injury. Errors and omissions policies cover architects, accountants, lawyers, and engineers who face risks involving intangible and tangible property. Directors' liability coverage is for members of boards of directors. Malpractice coverage provides coverage for the failure to use the degree of skill and care that a similar professional in your area should have used.

Malpractice coverage is complex; therefore, this discussion can highlight only a few points to consider. The key rule for lawsuit protection is give your malpractice coverage the attention due because it is a key part of your planning. Review coverages and options with your current agent and periodically obtain a second or even third opinion. Stay current with your professional literature to minimize risk and to identify problem areas and malpractice coverage issues.

Be sure to coordinate your commercial package policy for general coverage and your malpractice policy. Most commercial package policies exclude bodily injury and damage resulting from professional errors. If so, be sure that each time excluded by your commercial package is covered by your malpractice policy. A gap can prove financially ruinous.

Consider the differences between an occurrence or claims made coverage. Be careful that there are no gaps in coverage.

An *occurrence policy* covers malpractice acts during the period the policy is in force. It doesn't matter when the claim occurs. With this type of policy if you stop your coverage or if the claim filed occurred in a year when you had coverage, that claim is covered (assuming the insurance company is still in business), even in a later year when you have no coverage.

A *claims made policy* covers any claim made during the period the policy is in force regardless of when the claim occurred. With this latter type of policy, once the policy lapses, you have no coverage. If you have a claims made policy and retire or switch insurance companies and want to be sure that there are no gaps, you can purchase a *tail* policy. This provides coverage for a claim made for the period for which you had coverage, but which was brought after the coverage ended.

Example: Dr. Jones practiced for 12 years with a claims made malpractice policy. She decided to retire in 2004. At that point, she doesn't want to continue paying malpractice premiums (they are, in fact, the primary reason for her retirement), so she instead purchases a *tail* policy covering her from 2004 and later years for claims that occur as a result of actions occurring during the 12 years before retirement. If Dr. Jones cannot obtain affordable tail coverage, she may opt to continue practicing to be able to afford her continued malpractice coverage on a claims made basis.

Business and Buy-Out Insurance

Often, insurance is structured for use in a business buy-out or business key-person coverage (to provide funds for the business to hire a replacement). These needs should all be reviewed and the pros, cons, and cost-effectiveness of insurance to address them should be considered. If a partner dies or is permanently disabled, and you don't have formal buy-out procedures in place and a mechanism to fund that purchase, litigation with the partner's heirs is likely. This litigation often focuses on determining final payments to the deceased or disabled partner, the value of his or her interest, and how it should be paid. Don't risk these types of challenges. Have a binding legal agreement drafted and implemented while both of you are alive (not considering the immediate need for a buy-out) and are both insurable.

Commercial Property and Casualty Insurance

Just as with homeowners' insurance for your home, you need to insure business properties against loss. This coverage should protect business property from loss due to fire, theft, water damage, glass breakage, and so on. Often this coverage is part of a broader business insurance policy known as a *commercial package policy*. Smaller businesses may benefit from a package of insurance coverage referred to as *business owners' policy*. Computer equipment may warrant a special policy or endorsement to address unique risks facing such assets, such as electronic damage. When insuring business property, bear in mind that your business may own assets that have value but have already been deducted for income tax purposes. Be certain that they are covered. Also, address with your insurance consultant the value to be insured. In some instances, you want replacement cost coverage so you can, for example, rebuild a building destroyed by fire. In other cases, a lesser coverage may be all that is available or all that is affordable.

Caution: Be careful of coinsurance provisions. If you insure a property for less than its full value, the insurance company may pay only the same proportion of any loss. Assume your policy has a 90 percent coinsurance clause and your business owns a building worth $2 million. You insure it for only $1.6 million. You suffer a $500,000 loss. The insurance company will have to pay only about $440,000.

Commercial automobile coverage is another related type of business insurance. It should cover your business vehicles in the event of bodily injury, property damage, collision, personal injury, uninsured motorists, and so forth. A host of circumstances can affect the availability and cost of your coverage, including the use of the vehicles (delivery, service, retail, etc.), the distances driven, claims experience, and more. You may have opportunities to reduce your risk or increase your insurance coverage at a lower cost by controlling some of these factors.

Planning Tip: Depending on the circumstances, it may be advisable to create an independent legal entity (a separate corporation or limited liability company) to operate your vehicles to insulate the value of your main company for vehicle-related claims.

Business Interruption Insurance

Business interruption insurance can insure your business against loss of profits and continuing overhead costs. If your business must close temporarily while repairs are made because of a fire, you may still need to pay operating expenses, employees, property taxes, and many other costs (overhead). A business interruption insurance policy is intended to address this risk. Your should consult with your real estate attorney to determine how your obligations under a lease affect this. You may be obligated to continue paying rent even if you cannot use the premises while it is being repaired. To safeguard your business from these losses and to increase the likelihood of maximum coverage if a loss does occur, develop a disaster or emergency plan that ensures the quickest return to operations.

SUMMARY

Insurance coverage is a cornerstone of every lawsuit protection plan. Develop a team approach of involving all your advisors, and review the myriad options available. Try to eliminate unnecessary coverage and low deductibles in favor of broader coverage with higher limits to obtain the protection you really need on the "big risks." Be certain that your insurance coverage is coordinated and updated with the changes you make as you implement additional asset protection steps. Remember, insurance is critical but can never be relied on as your only protection. Gaps exist; coverage can be denied (e.g., you didn't notify the carrier quick enough); and jury awards (even if the government legislates caps on some awards) do exceed policy limits.

8 FRAUDULENT CONVEYANCE RULES CAN UNDERMINE YOUR LAWSUIT PROTECTION

The objective of your lawsuit protection planning is to make it difficult for claimants and creditors to get your assets. The key rule for protecting assets is to transfer them in a manner that will better protect them. However, if your transfer of assets violates the rules of *fraudulent conveyances,* your malpractice claimants and other creditors will be able to reach them regardless of how you transferred them. In short, if you don't respect the fraudulent conveyance rules, you are undermining your asset protection planning steps. When your claimants win a suit and find that most of your assets are protected, you can almost always assume that they will challenge you for violating the fraudulent conveyance rules. So whatever your actual circumstances, you cannot plan without an understanding of these rules. This chapter explains these rules and ways you can plan to avoid their impact.

A *fraudulent conveyance* can be defined simply as a transfer (conveyance) made (or presumed to be made) with the intent to delay or defraud your creditors. The simplicity, however, ends here. Defining each of these terms and phrases and understanding the many nuances created by court cases over the years is extraordinarily complex.

Fraudulent transfers can be transfers made with the intent to de-fraud. This could include, for example, a transfer immediately after a judgment. You just lost the lawsuit; you know the creditor wants to be paid. This type of transfer is obvious. Transfers completed in a manner that constructively appears that they were fraudulent are also considered to be fraudulent conveyances. Now you're getting into the hard to define gray areas. These transfers could include, for example, a transfer that so depletes your assets as to render your net worth so small as to be suspect. How much by way of value of assets must you retain? There are no clear-cut answers.

Transfers for which you receive a fair value are not considered fraudulent because the assets you transferred are replaced by assets of equivalent value.

Example: Assume you sell IBM stock worth $50,000 and receive $50,000 in cash; your transfer of IBM stock is not a fraudulent con-veyance. However, if you sell a closely held business for $50,000 and re-ceive back $50,000 in cash, is this similarly excluded because of your receiving a fair purchase price (consideration)? It depends. How do you determine the value of a closely held business? It's not simple or clear cut. If the sale was to an unrelated person and you retired, perhaps it is a fair price. What if the sale was to a trust you set up, your son, or a long-time employee? It becomes less clear.

The fraudulent conveyance rules are complex. Your advisors may have to consider the Bankruptcy Code, the Uniform Fraudulent Conveyances Act (UFCA), the Uniform Fraudulent Transfers Act (UFTA), and common law (state law) principles. This chapter can-not address this level of detail, so professional advice is essential.

HOW A POTENTIAL FRAUDULENT CONVEYANCE CHALLENGE MUST BE ANALYZED

To analyze the risks that a transfer you want to make to protect your assets might be caught by a fraudulent conveyance claim, you must review the following steps. Only with the following analysis can you and your advisors properly assess the outcome of any asset transfer.

What Law Applies to Determine if You've Made a Fraudulent Conveyance?

Have your attorney determine what laws apply to the analysis. Different laws may create different results. This may require an analysis of rules to determine which state laws apply (conflict of laws).

Did You Actually Intend to Defraud Your Creditors?

Under the laws that apply, analyze the contemplated asset transfers to see if they would constitute fraud based on your actual intent to defraud the potential claimant. Actual intent can be tough to prove, but if the creditor does, they need prove nothing more to get the assets. The bankruptcy laws permit the courts to void transfers you made within certain time periods before filing for bankruptcy protection. But it can be worse than just having your transfer voided. If you convey assets with the actual intent of defrauding, hindering, or delaying present or future creditors, you can also be penalized. You may make your situation worse by making transfers that are fraudulent than by doing nothing at all.

These rules can be tough, and the law may continue to evolve in a manner that is not favorable to those seeking to protect assets. What type of creditor or claim should you be responsible to foresee? How far will the courts go?

Example: A physician created a foreign trust for asset protection purposes and was sued by a plaintiff for malpractice, which occurred approximately one year after the transfer. The trial court drew a distinction between "probable" and "possible future creditors" and classified the plaintiff as the latter. The appellate court discarded the trial court's "probable" versus "possible" creditor argument and remanded the case to determine whether the defendant doctor harbored actual fraudulent intent at the time the assets were transferred. In this instance, it would be extremely difficult to prove that the doctor intended to defraud the plaintiff and actually intended to commit malpractice. However, it would seem easier to prove fraudulent intent where assets were transferred to a foreign trust and an environmental or health hazard existed at the time of the transfer. The key distinction is that the hazard existed before the foreign trust was created; therefore, the argument is stronger that the assets were transferred with actual intent to hinder, delay, or defraud. Although this hurdle may be overcome, it must be considered a potential risk from the outset. Might future courts hold such a doctor responsible for defrauding future malpractice claimants because of the statistical likelihood of such claims being filed? Because of the particular physician's specialty? Because malpractice claims are part of the cost and routine of conducting a medical practice?

Fraudulent conveyance claims can, depending on applicable law, be brought until four years after you made the transfer or one year after the claimant discovers (or should reasonably have discovered) the transfer, whichever is later.

Did You "Constructively" Defraud Your Creditors?

Under the laws that apply, analyze the contemplated asset transfers to see if they would constitute fraud based on your constructively defrauding the potential claimant. To prove such a claim and reach your assets, your claimant must prove that you made a transfer of property within the time periods provided for under law without receiving reasonably equivalent value in the exchange (fair consideration), and you were either insolvent or left insolvent, left with an unreasonably small amount of capital, or intentionally left unable to pay debts as they matured.

A constructive intent to defraud creditors is the more common claim; it is subtle and complex. If the creditor can prove that there were circumstances indicating that you might have had an intent to defraud a creditor, that alone may suffice to make the creditor's case. These circumstances are referred to as *badges of fraud*.

The Transfer Made You Insolvent.   If your transfer of assets renders you insolvent (insufficient assets to meet your needs or debts in excess of your assets), the transfers will be deemed fraudulent. It doesn't matter what your intent was.

The Transfer Leaves You with Inadequate Capital.   If you engage in a transfer or business transaction that leaves you with inadequate assets (capital), it is a sign that the transfers are questionable. While this badge of fraud may sound similar to the preceding one, there is an important difference. Your creditor doesn't have to prove you insolvent—just that you have unreasonably small assets remaining.

Your Relationship with the Recipient of Your Assets.   If you sell assets to a competitor, the odds are this transaction will be respected because there can't be an ulterior motive. If you sell or give assets to a family member or long-time friend, the transfers will "smell fishy" from the outset. Often, you transfer assets to family limited partnerships, trusts, or other entities over which you may have some control. The more control you can exercise, the more unreasonable the transfer will appear.

Transfers When You Incurred a Substantial Debt.   If you make a transfer shortly before or after incurring a large debt, such as a home mortgage or business loan, the transfers will appear to be fraudulent.

Transferring Substantially All Your Assets.   A transfer of substantially all of your assets will appear fraudulent. This is why the "nest egg" approach to protecting some, but not all, assets is advocated in Chapter 2. Additional planning tips are discussed later in this chapter.

Less Than Fair Payment.   If you transfer assets and receive back anything less than a fair purchase price (when you make a gift of assets, for example, to your child or a trust you set up, you get nothing back), the transfer will have a badge of fraud. This means that you must be even more diligent in avoiding any of the other badges of fraud.

As illustrated in the previous example, if you intend to complete a sale, get independent corroboration that the price you receive, especially if there are nonmarketable assets involved, is fair.

If you engage in business transactions with inadequate investments (capital), called *thin capitalization* in tax jargon, it is a sign that the transactions are questionable. For example, if you sold valuable assets to a corporation, especially a controlled one, for a note (i.e., on credit) and the corporation has little capital, the transaction may be set aside even if the price paid is fair.

Hidden Transfers.   If you had to hide a transfer, the presumption is that you were doing something wrong. Asset protection, as explained in Chapter 1, is not about hiding assets. It's about protecting them. Most asset protection transfers are reported in full on U.S. income tax returns—nothing hidden.

Unusual Business Practices.   If your legal and other documents effecting a transfer of assets appear different from what other nonrelated persons would do in the ordinary course of business, the transactions will appear suspect. Be as ordinary and typical as possible.

Timing.   If you transfer assets when you know, or should have known, that there was a suit or claim against you, the transfer will appear to be fraudulent. The lesson of this rule is simple: Implement your asset protection planning sooner, rather than later. The early bird certainly catches the asset protection worm. In addition, as discussed later, when you plan transfers, take steps to demonstrate that you had no known claims at the time the transfers occurred.

Retained Rights.   If, after you transfer assets, you retain rights to use or benefit from those assets, especially rights that are inconsistent with the apparent purposes of the transfers, the transfer will appear more questionable. For example, if you transfer your home to a family limited partnership (usually not a wise move) or an irrevocable trust, you should have no right to live in the house unless you rent it. Renting it means a written lease and fair rent. If you transfer most of your marketable securities to a family limited partnership but continue to distribute all of the income to yourself, this is a badge of fraud that may undermine the transfer. Instead, what you should do is make distributions to all partners in proportion to their partnership interests (see Chapter 10).

The more badges of fraud a transfer has, the more likely that the courts will find in favor of your creditor or claimant and overturn the transfer. The goal of your lawsuit protection planning is to structure any asset transfers so that they are not fraudulent conveyances and so that they have the least appearance of being a fraudulent conveyance (to fend off later claims that they are).

Are There Legal Defenses to the Fraudulent Conveyance?

If there is a risk that a valid fraudulent conveyance claim might exist on either of the previous theories (actual or constructive), have your lawyer analyze whether there are any legal arguments (defenses) you can assert to prevent those claims from succeeding. If you received *fair consideration* for an asset transfer, your claimant cannot win a fraudulent conveyance argument on that transfer.

If You Did Engage in a Fraudulent Conveyance, What Might the Court Do?

If there is a risk that a fraudulent conveyance claim might succeed in spite of any legal arguments your attorney will advance, analyze what steps (remedies) the court is likely to take and how they will impact you. For example, the court may nullify the transfer and order the transferee (e.g., a trust or child you gave assets to) to transfer the assets back to you so that your claimant can get them. The court may recover the actual property transferred or the value of the property transferred. To protect this right, the court may order that the property be attached to prevent its dissipation. The court could appoint an independent person (receiver) to take charge of the property in question.

RULES FOR PROTECTING YOUR LAWSUIT PROTECTION TRANSFERS FROM FRAUDULENT CONVEYANCE CLAIMS

While there is no guarantee that any successful malpractice claimant or creditor won't argue that you've violated the fraudulent conveyance rules, there are a number of rules that, if followed carefully, will help prevent such an attack from succeeding.

Nonasset Protection Motives Support Establishing Trust

There should be predominant nonasset protection motives for the transfer. For example, transferring assets to an irrevocable life insurance trust can be primarily to provide management of assets following death and to avoid federal estate taxes by removing the insurance from your estate. Transferring assets to a foreign trust could be primarily for the purpose of diversifying a large investment portfolio to include assets not available in the United States because of U.S. securities regulations and other restrictions. However, you should have the investment sophistication to understand these asset classes, and the trust should actually invest in them. Setting up a family limited partnership to consolidate disparate family accounts for unified management, minimize asset management fees (which are lower for larger investment accounts), minimize record keeping, and so on are all valid nonasset protection motives. Not only should nonasset protection motives exist, but also they should be documented.

Retain Sufficient Assets and Don't Become Insolvent by Transfers

The transfers you make to trusts or otherwise must not render you insolvent. Have your accountant prepare detailed personal financial statements to demonstrate that the transfer did not render you insolvent and a budget or cash flow analysis to demonstrate that you have adequate resources to meet anticipated expenses.

Caution: This analysis is far from simple. What if in your line of business, lawsuits are common? Must the likely lawsuit awards you could anticipate paying be included in the analysis of what are reasonable assets for you to keep? If not, might the transfers you make be characterized as fraudulent conveyance?

Retain sufficient assets following the transfer to meet expected expenses. For example, a thorough lien and judgment search can be done to ensure that you retain assets to meet any known claims.

Use *Standard* and *Arm's-Length* Documentation to Transfer Assets to Trust

When personal property is transferred, a properly prepared bill of sale should be used. When real estate is transferred, a deed should be used; and all ancillary steps that would be taken in an arm's-length real estate transaction should be taken. These include obtaining casualty and fire insurance in the name of the trust, limited liability company, or other entity; obtaining title insurance; and so forth. If you sell assets to a related party, be sure that the legal documentation and protection are the same that an unrelated party would insist on. If you are selling and receiving a note, there should be adequate security, guarantee, or other arrangements in place. Any related party transfer will be suspect.

Transfers Should Not Be Completed Secretively

If your asset transfers are consummated "in the closet," they will appear much more suspect when discovered. On the other hand, a transfer consummated openly will appear less suspect. Discuss with your attorney whether a memorandum of trust should be recorded in the public record if you are transferring assets to a trust.

Adequate Consideration Should Be Paid for Assets Transferred to a Trust

Where adequate consideration is received on transferring an asset, the transfer should not be subject to fraudulent conveyance or other similar attacks. The problem with transferring an asset for adequate consideration is that in many instances, trusts and other techniques are formed for the primary purpose of removing assets from your estate for federal estate tax purposes, as well as asset protection. For example, if you transfer a noncontrolling, for example, 35 percent interest in a family partnership or business, for tax purposes this interest will be valued at a substantial discount from the actual value of the entities assets because no independent buyer would pay full price knowing they are in a noncontrolling position and subject to the decisions that the family majority owners would make. The determination of these discounts is not a science, and they might be looked at adversely by a court as constituting a transfer for less than fair consideration for fraudulent conveyance purposes.

Example: Joe Smith owns a rental property worth $1 million. He transfers it to a family limited liability company (LLC) to minimize the risks of his home and other personal assets being subjected to claims relating to the property. Joe is also a surgeon and wishes to protect all assets. As part of his overall asset protection plan, Joe forms a domestic asset protection trust in Alaska. Joe then sells 40 percent of the real estate LLC to the trust. Because the 40 percent interest in the LLC is less than a controlling interest, Joe hires an appraiser, who determines that the value is 30 percent less than the underlying asset value. An unrelated buyer would discount the building value by 30 percent to reflect the lack of control they would have as a mere 30 percent owner. Thus, the sale is consummated at $280,000 [(1 − 30 percent) × 40 percent × $1 million] instead of $400,000 [40 percent × $1 million]. Will the court view this as fair consideration?

SUMMARY

Asset protection planning cannot be done without carefully planning any transfers you make to avoid the implications of the fraudulent conveyance rules. This chapter provided an overview and some rules to follow to help your planning succeed. The complexity of these rules and their tremendous importance makes it essential that you seek professional guidance for any planning.

9 MISCELLANEOUS ASSET PROTECTION RULES

Asset protection is a complex process that involves many different issues, laws, and concepts. This chapter provides an overview of a number of important ancillary topics that might affect your planning that were not addressed in preceding chapters. A key concept this chapter addresses is that certain types of assets are safer than others. These special assets are sometimes referred to as *exempt* assets, because your claimants can't reach them. These rules can be used as another component to your lawsuit protection planning.

PICK THE RIGHT ASSETS—HOMES

Your home may be partially or, in a few states, entirely, exempt from the reach of creditors. These laws, called *homestead exemptions,* are based on the concept that creditors should not be able to deprive you of your home. When the homestead exemption applies, it applies to your home, the land, and permanent improvements. The rules, however, differ substantially from state to state. For the majority of states, the exemption is capped at less than $100,000, making it of only limited use. Only nine states permit homestead exemptions of $100,000 or more: Arizona, Florida, Iowa, Kansas, Massachusetts, Minnesota, Nevada, South Dakota, and Texas. Only a few states have unlimited homestead exemptions: South Dakota, Iowa, Texas, and Florida. Thus, for most people, this exemption cannot be a significant portion of their planning.

To qualify for the exemption, the property must be used as your primary residence and you must intend it as your homestead.

Can You Move to a State with Inclusive Laws and Buy a Big House?

You can, but that won't guarantee you a better homestead exemption. The planning idea is simple. Move to a state with a large or unlimited homestead exemption, and put all of your money into the purchase of a home. To protect against nonresidents' abusing this, you must have lived in the state for about two years to obtain a $125,000 homestead exemption. If you lived in Texas 1,015 days, for example, you can qualify for an unlimited homestead exemption. If you lived less time in the state, your exemption is what it was in the state you moved from.

See the discussion of *tenancy by the entirety* in Chapter 3. State law may provide another method of protecting your home even if your state's homestead exemption is small.

The federal homestead exemption is limited. For debtors in bankruptcy, the amount is under $20,000.

PICK THE RIGHT ASSETS—PENSIONS

Pension and retirement plans are generally exempt from the reach of claimants if qualified under federal laws governing pension plans (ERISA). Some uncertainties and gaps remain. IRAs, for example, are not exempt under federal law, but may be protected by state law. Under a new bankruptcy bill, which is pending, it will be clearer that pension plans will be exempt if they are qualified under ERISA and the tax code. IRAs may also be protected as exempt assets up to a $1 million limit. Be careful in evaluating whether a Roth IRA is exempt under your state's laws. Some state exemption laws refer to plans under Section 408 of the Internal Revenue Code, the section governing traditional IRAs. Roth IRAs were enacted under a new Code Section 408A. Depending on your state's laws, traditional IRAs may be protected while Roth IRAs may not be. Deferred compensation plans, incentive stock option plans, and other employee benefits are generally not covered.

PICK THE RIGHT ASSETS—LIFE INSURANCE
AND ANNUITIES

Many states provide that life insurance and annuities are partially or wholly exempt from the reach of your claimants. However, if you've transferred funds into insurance or annuities in a manner that runs afoul of the fraudulent conveyance rules in Chapter 8, these protections won't apply. For a life insurance policy that hasn't matured (you're still alive), some states protect the cash value of the policy but limits can be small. Once you've died and the insurance policy is paid, many states continue to protect the proceeds from your creditors if the proceeds are paid to your dependents. The beneficiaries are not protected. It is recommended that insurance be held in a trust because of these gaps.

Some states exempt annuity payments from the reach of claimants. However, these exemptions are limited, some as small as $200 to $500 per month. The exemption may also be influenced by when you purchased them. In some states, annuities must be specifically tied into life insurance coverage to obtain protection.

RULES FOR USING A LIFE ESTATE TO
PROTECT PROPERTY

Life estates can provide a means of having more than one person own an interest in property, such as your house, although those interests are not effective at the same time. The life estate arrangement is often used when the testator wishes to give a designated person the right to use property for life (such as a second spouse) but wishes to control the distribution of that property following the death (or some other event) of the life tenant (e.g., to ensure that your children inherit it). The life estate is perhaps considered a method of achieving these goals without the cost and expense of a trust. The prices to pay, however, include the inclusion of the value of the asset in the life tenant's estate where the life tenant had an interest in the property for life, potentially complex gift tax calculations, less security and certainty than the use of a trust, and so on.

Another example of a life estate is giving your house to your children, while preserving (retaining) your right to use property for the duration of your life. Or, your spouse owns your home (because of your malpractice concerns). Your spouse's will bequeaths a life estate to you, and on your death, your children will own the entire house (remainder interest). Both of these examples illustrate how a life estate can be used to protect your assets from a claimant. The only right you have is the right to live in your home. You cannot sell or mortgage it because you don't own it. While this type of restriction limits the value of the home to you, it also severely limits the value of your home to a malpractice or other claimant seeking your assets. If your goal is to live in the home, you may find the restrictions on you are less worrisome than the reach of potential creditors.

Another common use of a life estate is to protect a senior's right to live in a home without risking the home being taken to pay for medical and nursing home bills. This is a form of asset protection planning (see Chapter 7). Although it could be argued that the life estate has value, Medicaid seems at present to accept this as having no value for eligibility purposes.

RULES FOR MORTGAGING PROPERTY TO PROTECT ASSETS

Mortgaging an asset doesn't sound like much of a way to protect your interests; it puts cash in your pocket. However, if you own an asset that is tough to protect, for example, your home (assuming that the other techniques noted in this book don't appeal to you), you could mortgage your home and then invest the proceeds in a manner that is protected. Thus, the value of the unprotected asset, your home, is diminished by the mortgage, and the cash proceeds are given to an irrevocable trust or family limited partnership to protect them. Your home becomes a less attractive asset to a claimant because it has less value and is encumbered by a large mortgage. The cash is unappealing to a claimant because you have tied it up in a partnership or trust.

RULES FOR USING DISCLAIMERS TO PROTECT PROPERTY

Asset protection planning does not mean protecting only assets you own. It might mean avoiding the receipt of assets, which would expose them to the reach of your claimants. For example, your wealthy aunt dies and bequeaths $300,000 to you. Unfortunately, you are in the midst of a large malpractice suit. Receiving the inheritance may not only jeopardize the money, but also encourage your claimant onward. You could refuse to accept the assets involved by filing the appropriate court documents (disclaimer or renunciation). The assets would then pass on to whoever would receive them under your aunt's will if you had died before your aunt. This might be your own children. If not, perhaps it is a family member that you would rather enrich than your creditor.

For a disclaimer to be effective, it must comply with the requirements of the federal tax laws under Section 2518 of the Internal Revenue Code:

- It must be irrevocable (you can't change your mind later).
- It must be in writing.
- It must be unqualified. You can't place any conditions on the disclaimer.
- You can't have accepted the property to be disclaimed or obtained any benefit from it.
- Once disclaimed, the property must pass to the next beneficiary without any directions from you and without any benefit to you. The only exception to this latter requirement is made for a surviving spouse. Thus, a surviving spouse could disclaim a bequest and the disclaimer would qualify even if the result would be for the disclaimed assets to be transferred to a trust of which the disclaiming spouse is a beneficiary.
- The disclaimer must be completed within nine months of the decedent's death.

BANKRUPTCY RULES CAN HELP PROTECT YOUR ASSETS

How Bankruptcy Rules Affect Your Lawsuit Protection Planning

If all else fails, bankruptcy filing may be your last chance to resolve the demands of your malpractice claimants and creditors. Federal bankruptcy rules provide that certain limited assets are exempt from the reach of your claimants (qualified pension plan assets, a modest amount of real property used as your residence and some personal property in your home, a modest amount of life insurance, etc.). It will also enable you to settle your debts that are dischargeable in bankruptcy for amounts you can pay and pursuant to a plan. This gives you the ability to preserve some assets and get a fresh start—not exactly the hoped-for solution you had in mind when you started the planning process. Some debts, such as those due the IRS or relating to divorce, cannot be discharged.

BANKRUPTCY AND DIVORCE

Bankruptcy Could Be Used by Your Ex-Spouse to Increase Alimony and Child Support

A state court may occasionally consider the bankruptcy to be a cause for a change in circumstances and modify the divorce decree. But before you view this as a positive development, it can have a negative impact if, as a result of your bankruptcy, you have no debt while your ex-spouse still has substantial debt. If you're released in bankruptcy from your debts, the court may modify your divorce agreement and require you to pay greater child support and alimony if the original divorce settlement was based on your paying debts. Now, as a result of your bankruptcy, your ex-spouse may have to pay joint debts, so you may lose out in any event. Other courts won't do this because of the "supremacy clause" of the U.S. Constitution, which provides that state courts must defer to federal bankruptcy court. If your ex-spouse tries to go back to court to argue for an increase in alimony and child support as a result of your discharge of debts in your bankruptcy, discuss with your lawyer an argument being made against this on the basis that a modification would undo what the bankruptcy was to accomplish. A modification would undermine the fresh start you are supposed to get from the bankruptcy process.

How Your Bankruptcy Can Help You

Support obligations such as alimony, maintenance, and child support cannot be discharged in bankruptcy. But a property settlement can be. Support is nondischargeable only if it is in the nature of support. Therefore, if you declare bankruptcy, you would prefer that your divorce agreement had been couched in terms of a property transfer, not a maintenance payment. Keeping a roof over your spouse and children is support. Distributions from your company if your ex-spouse is no longer an owner may be considered property by the bankruptcy court. Different courts have different standards; just make sure the agreement is clear as to whether a particular obligation you have is a property transfer or a support payment. The bankruptcy court can characterize a distribution of assets differently than the matrimonial documents did. For tax reasons, you may try to treat a payment as maintenance so it's deductible. Thus, you may say in the divorce agreement that $500 per month for five years is maintenance in a divorce agreement. The court may look at this agreement and decide that it's not maintenance, but rather, it's a property distribution. And as a property distribution, your obligation can be wiped out in bankruptcy forever.

Support arrears are not discharged in bankruptcy and must be paid. If you file bankruptcy under Chapter 13 and the plan provides that you are to pay off your creditors over three to five years, you will also continue to pay your ex-spouse any property settlement remaining through the bankruptcy plan over the same time period based on your pro rata share. If creditors all get 30 percent, your ex-spouse gets his or her 30 percent at the same time. In a Chapter 7 bankruptcy, this is an instant discharge; therefore, your ex-spouse can go after your wages the day after you file.

How Your Ex-Spouse's Bankruptcy Can Hurt You

If your ex-spouse files bankruptcy, it is very important for you to pay attention. Have your attorney review the schedules your spouse files with the bankruptcy court to make sure all assets are listed and find out how it impacts you. The best place for trustees to get data on fraud by a debtor in bankruptcy is from an ex-spouse. It's amazing how many people forget their boat in storage, the antique jewelry in the attic, and so on. If the trustee finds out that there is money to pay, they will pursue it. You want to make sure that all of your ex-spouse's assets are reported so you don't get saddled with his or her debt later.

SUMMARY

This chapter reviewed a grab bag of miscellaneous, although often important, lawsuit and divorce protection techniques. It also demonstrated how broad and complex the process can be and how you can use planning that, at first look, doesn't appear to be asset protection planning to protect you.

PART FOUR

RULES FOR USING BUSINESS ENTITIES TO PROTECT AGAINST LAWSUITS

10 FAMILY LIMITED PARTNERSHIPS (FLPs) AND LAWSUIT PROTECTION PLANNING

WHAT IS A FAMILY LIMITED PARTNERSHIP?

A family limited partnership (FLP) is a limited partnership where a majority, or all, of the interests are controlled by members of the same family. FLPs are formed under your state's partnership laws. However, it is often advantageous to form a partnership in a state that has more favorable partnership laws (i.e., has greater limits on a claimant's rights to break a partnership). To do so, however, you must have some legitimate connection with that state.

FLPs are an important planning technique in lawsuit protection and family estate planning generally. This is because the limited partnership structure can permit you as a parent, for example, to serve as general partner, and thus control the entire partnership within certain reasonable parameters. Although the parent may control the entire partnership through control over the general partner, the parent's estate, for purposes of estate taxes and for the reach of creditors, should include only that percentage interest in the entire partnership actually owned by the parent. Further, the limited partnership interests are often valued at a substantial discount from their pro rata share of the fair market value of the underlying partnership assets. This discount, attributable to the lack of marketability or the nature of a minority interest (i.e., lack of control), facilitates the parent's gift planning because it makes it easier to remove the partnership from the parent's estate. These same factors lower the value of the partnership interest in the hands of a malpractice claimant or other creditor and, therefore, simultaneously serve as an inhibition to potential claimants.

Limited partnerships have two types of partners—general and limited. The general partners have unlimited liability (they can be held personally responsible for all partnership liabilities) and the right to manage partnership affairs. The limited partners have limited liability (they cannot be held personally responsible for partnership liabilities) but cannot participate in management. Every limited partnership must have at least one general partner.

LAWSUIT PROTECTION

Family limited partnerships are a favored asset protection tool. This chapter defines FLPs, describes how to use them to protect yourself from lawsuits, and discusses some of the limitations on their benefits. The focus is on FLPs because lawsuit protection planning is generally focused on protecting family assets. Limited partnerships can be used for nonfamily transactions with similar benefits.

Merely transferring assets to an FLP will not ensure that those assets can never be reached by creditors or other claimants. Fraudulent conveyance challenges could be asserted if you transferred assets to an FLP or gave away the FLP interests to defraud or hinder creditors (see Chapter 8). FLP interests can be subject to claims filed in U.S. federal or state courts that have jurisdiction and are thus subject to the vagaries of the legal system. The result is that many attorneys combine, where possible, the use of an FLP with a domestic or foreign situs trust (see Chapters 17 and 18).

LIMITED PARTNERS HAVE LIMITED LIABILITY

Asset protection considerations are often important in the decision to structure a transaction as an FLP. A fundamental principle of an FLP is that the limited partners have a limitation on their personal liability for partnership acts. Their liability is generally limited to their investment in the partnership. The general partner, however, has unlimited liability for partnership liabilities and recourse debts. This aspect of FLPs is important to protect the partners from lawsuits or claims resulting from partnership assets and activities. Sometimes referred to as *inside-out* protection, it protects the partners' personal assets from claims arising inside the FLP.

Example: Joe Attorney and Sue Dentist are married and own a rental property in which they have their professional offices. They also rent space to several other tenants. If a tenant is injured and sues, all of their personal assets, home, and investments could be reached to satisfy the tenant's claim. Joe and Sue transfer the building to an FLP owned by them and their children. They form an S corporation to serve as general partner (see later discussion in this chapter and Chapter 12). If a tenant now sues, all of Joe and Sue's personal assets are protected. The tenant can reach only the value of assets held by the FLP.

GENERAL PARTNERS CAN ALSO LIMIT LIABILITY

The most common method of addressing this risk to the general partner is to have an entity (e.g., S corporation or limited liability company [LLC]) serve as general partner instead of an individual. Thus, if the entity has unlimited liability for FLP debts, the entity's assets are limited and personal assets remain protected (shareholders of the S corporation and members of LLCs have limited liability).

The corporate or LLC general partner should also have substance and not be a mere paper entity. Minutes of the board of directors of the corporate general partner authorizing their investment in, and serving as general partner for, the partnership should be prepared. Employment agreements for the employees of the general partners and consulting agreements for certain consultants and contractors retained by the general partners should be executed to demonstrate that the general partner corporation has personnel sufficient to carry out reasonable operating functions associated with actual management of the limited partnership's operations.

PROTECTING ASSETS FROM NONPARTNERSHIP CLAIMS (SUCH AS MALPRACTICE)

FLPs offer two types of lawsuit protection. As explained previously, an FLP can protect your personal assets from a lawsuit from claims arising from FLP assets or business—inside-out protection. While this is a great reason to use FLPs to protect personal assets, it is not the primary reason FLPs are such a great lawsuit protection tool. FLPs also offer what is called *outside-in* protection for FLP assets from claims originating *outside* the partnership and challenging assets *in* the FLP.

Example: Joe Attorney and Sue Dentist own a rental property in an FLP owned by them and their children. One of Sue's patients sues her for malpractice. The claim exceeds Sue's malpractice coverage and the patient tries to collect the value of Sue's interest in the building to satisfy it. The value of the building, because it is owned by an FLP, is protected from the patient's claims. While the patient might get Sue's FLP interests, collecting real economic value for it won't be so easy. These difficulties will enable Sue to negotiate a better settlement, thus protecting the value of her investment in the building from a claim.

HOW FLPs PROTECT FLP ASSETS

If a malpractice claimant or other creditor gets a court award to take your assets to satisfy a judgment and if one of your assets is an ownership interest in an FLP, the creditor can get a limited right to receive your share of FLP income (called a *charging order*). This does not give the creditor the right to take a proportionate share of partnership assets or even to force the sale of those assets. This is why FLP interests you own are not a creditor-friendly asset. These restrictions are explained later.

State law and language in the limited partnership agreement can prevent a creditor from becoming a partner (a *substituted limited partner*) without consent of the general partner or unless specified requirements are met. If your creditor cannot become a partner, he or she will obtain only a limited right to a partnership interest, which is referred to as an *assignee* of a partnership interest.

As an assignee of a limited partnership interest under a charging order, the creditor cannot have any control over the operations or distributions made by the limited partnership. Because a partnership interest is personal property, no partner has any direct interest in the underlying assets of the partnership. Thus, your claimants have no right to obtain such interest either. A creditor will not generally have the right to force a sale of an FLP interest.

A creditor of yours, as an assignee of your FLP interest, is generally entitled to receive only the profit (or loss) allocated by the partnership to the assigned partnership interest. The assignor would have been entitled to this same interest. The general partner could thus limit distributions substantially or, in some instances, entirely. If the general partner limited distributions to an amount less than the income tax due on the partnership income earned, the result could be that the limited partner could receive phantom income reportable for tax purposes but without any commensurate cash distribution to pay the taxes.

Example: Dr. Jones is married to Mr. Smith, an attorney. Both fear malpractice claims. They establish the Jones and Smith Holdings, Limited Partnership, and each contributes substantial portions of their real estate and stock investments to the FLP. They each give 20 percent of their FLP holdings to an irrevocable trust formed in Alaska, leaving them each with only 30 percent limited partnership interests. A corporation owned by various family members serves as general partner. Dr. Jones is sued and her malpractice claimant tries to attach her only significant asset, her 30 percent limited partnership interest in the Jones and Smith Holdings, Limited Partnership. The FLP earns $100,000, but the general partner decides to distribute nothing, retaining all earnings to purchase a new real estate property. Dr. Jones's creditor, as owner of 30 percent of the FLP, reports $30,000 (30 percent × $100,000) of partnership income on his personal income tax return, resulting in a $15,000 state and federal income tax. However, with no distribution, the claimant is out of pocket for the "benefit" of owning the FLP interest. This type of result encourages the claimant to make a more favorable settlement.

As an assignee, rather than a substituted limited partner, a creditor should not have any right to examine partnership books and records.

A typical state statute limits an assignee's rights as follows:

Except as provided in the partnership agreement, a partnership interest is assignable in whole or in part. An assignment of a partnership interest does not dissolve a limited partnership or entitle the assignee to become or to exercise any rights of a partner. An assignment entitles the assignee to receive, to the extent assigned, only the distribution to which the assignor would be entitled. Except as provided in the partnership agreement, a partner ceases to be a partner upon assignment of all his partnership interest. Notwithstanding the foregoing, a general partner who assigns all of his general partnership interest shall cease to be a general partner only upon filing of a certificate reflecting that fact in accordance with this chapter.

The court may charge the partnership interest of the partner with payment of the unsatisfied amount of the judgment with interest. To the extent so charged, the judgment creditor has only the rights of an assignee of the partnership interest.

Don't assume that this type of FLP protection is guaranteed. A claimant may challenge your transfer of asset to the FLP as a fraudulent conveyance. Your FLP may have been so lax in observing the requisite legal formalities that a court may disregard the FLP entirely. In addition, as more FLPs are used in asset protection planning, courts may find more ways to treat claimants fairly by piercing FLPs. This is why many approaches and layers to your asset protection plan are recommended.

FAMILY LIMITED PARTNERSHIPS AND DIVORCE PLANNING

FLPs can also help protect family assets from the ravages of a child's (or other heir's) divorce. If you make gifts of stock to your son, if he is not careful to avoid commingling those assets with marital assets, they can be converted from separate gift (or inherited) assets, which his wife cannot reach in a divorce, into marital assets that she may claim an interest in. If the interests you give your son are limited partnership interests, because a limited partner is not permitted to participate in the management of the FLP (and make sure the partnership agreement says so), this can prevent any argument that your son's interests were converted from separate property (not subject to distribution in a divorce) into marital property by virtue of his active management of those assets during marriage.

FAMILY LIMITED PARTNERSHIPS MUST BE HANDLED CAREFULLY

Limited partnerships, whether with family members or unrelated third parties, can be effective tools in thwarting creditors and achieving other valid personal and estate planning goals. When evaluating the use of the limited partnerships, the analysis should not be limited solely to those situations where limited partnerships can be structured with only family members. The objective of the *family* limited partnership, as contrasted to limited partnerships in general, is to obtain the protection of limited liability and avoid creditor claims, while preserving an asset within the family group.

When asset protection planning is an important objective, having nonrelated persons, as well as family members, involved in the limited partnership can add credibility to the transaction.

When an FLP is used with solely related parties (family members), a greater amount of care must be exercised to properly and fully document any transactions. As one court noted: "Although there is no presumption that transactions between close relatives are per se fraudulent . . . , when such a confidential relationship is shown to exist, the parties are held to a fuller and stricter proof of the consideration and the fairness of the transaction."

COMPARING FLPs TO OTHER ENTITIES

The decision to use an FLP or another entity, as well as a better understanding of what an FLP is, can best be made by comparing FLPs to other common entities. Many of these other entities are explained in greater detail in the chapters that follow.

FLP versus Corporation

A partnership form of entity gives the partners more flexibility than a corporation can give to its shareholders. For example, the partners in a partnership may want the personal use of tax benefits of the partnership, such as tax losses. This is possible in a partnership but not in a C corporation. In an S corporation, flexibility is significantly curtailed. Moreover, in a partnership, it is far easier from a tax perspective to distribute money or property from the partnership than from a corporation. In the event of death, under the current estate tax rules, the income tax basis (used to determine gains and losses) in the assets held by a partnership can qualify to be increased, whereas those of a corporation, even an S corporation, cannot. This can mean significant income tax savings.

FLP versus Limited Liability Company

A limited liability company can offer many of the same advantages as an FLP. An LLC can offer control by designating who the manager is (analogous to the general partner in an FLP for control purposes), the interests of the other members (analogous to the limited partners in an FLP) can be severely restricted, and limited liability can be achieved. This can be done without the costs of forming yet a second entity (e.g., the S corporation typically used as general partner of the FLP) and, hence, without the tax risks that the partnership will be characterized as an association taxable as a corporation. An LLC deserves consideration in the appropriate circumstances. The real decision depends on a comparison of the specific state FLP and LLC laws in the states in which you can reasonably form the entity. See a more detailed analysis of LLCs later.

Converting a General Partnership into a Limited Partnership

A general partnership is a simple form of business with each partner having equal and complete control over partnership matters. No partner has limited liability. Both of these characteristics can have substantial drawbacks to an asset protection plan. If a building, business, investment, or other asset is owned in a general partnership format, many of the benefits of an FLP can be obtained by converting the general partnership into an FLP. This raises a number of issues. A potential tax problem that can arise on conversion of a general partnership interest into a limited partnership interest occurs if the conversion reduces a partner's share of partnership liabilities. If the reduction exceeds the partner's basis in his or her partnership interest, tax can result. Similar problems can arise if there are changes in any partner's interest in the partnership capital or if profits change. Thus, any conversions should be reviewed by your tax accountant before proceeding.

GENERAL CONCEPTS

Retention of Control

Although the transfer of assets to an FLP can serve as a vehicle to facilitate divesture and can effectively encumber the value of the asset (e.g., for estate and gift tax purposes and in the eyes of a potential judgment creditor), you as the transferor can still exert some measure of control over the assets through control over the provisions of the partnership agreement when the FLP is created and through continued input or even control over the general partner. You can retain some or all control (although less than controlling is best) of the general partnership interests and, hence, control over the management and investment control over the FLP's assets. The general partner can be given rather broad discretion to determine the amount and timing of distributions to the partners. The partnership agreement can limit (or perhaps prohibit) the right of a partner to demand a distribution or a return of his or her capital account.

Example: Dr. Transferor contributes property to an FLP. In exchange, Dr. Transferor receives from the partnership both general and limited partnership interests. Thereafter, the transferor makes yearly gifts of the limited partnership interests to his family members (or a trust for their benefit) in an amount equivalent to the annual exclusion, $11,000 per year per donee (or $22,000 if the doctor and his wife elect to make split gifts). Dr. Transferor retains the general partnership interest in the partnership, and, as the general partner, Dr. Transferor retains control over the partnership assets. Thus, Dr. Transferor has divested himself of the ownership of the asset for estate tax purposes and for purposes of creditor claims (assuming no fraudulent conveyance, etc.), while effectively retaining control of the asset by having a general partnership interest in the partnership.

Divestment or Encumbrance of Asset Value

You can transfer assets you own, such as rental real estate (e.g., the office your accounting practice uses), securities, and other assets to your FLP; and you can use the FLP as a means of transferring ownership through gifts to family members, trusts, and so on. Even when the limited partnership interests are not transferred, the conversion of economic interests (e.g., control over investment assets) into limited partnership interests in a partnership that owns the asset can effectively change the value of the asset because of the restrictions that the nature of a limited partnership interest creates on the ownership of the underlying asset.

Tax Consequences

Through the use of the FLP as an estate planning vehicle, a family may be able to shift wealth to a younger generation without the imposition of estate or gift tax. This can be accomplished because the partnership structure can facilitate gift programs (making an indivisible asset, such as a shopping center, easily divisible into $11,000, $22,000, or other values) and by bolstering the ability to claim minority and lack of marketability discounts. To qualify for the annual gift tax exclusion, the gift must be a gift of a present interest. The limited partnership agreement (and perhaps the conduct of the general partner) could possibly taint the gifts of limited partnership interests as not qualifying as gifts of a present interest. The amount of control retained by the general partner over the potential distributions to the limited partner must be considered. The purpose of these rules is to prevent the general partner from arbitrarily incurring unreasonable expenses such that the profits, which should have been available for distribution to the limited partners, are siphoned off to the general partner.

Your direct power to affect the distributable income of the other partners is not necessarily a power that would cause the transferred partnership interests (e.g., the limited partnership interests given to the other partners such as your children) to be included in your taxable estate.

An FLP is also a tool for saving income taxes if the children and others you give partnership interests to are in a lower income tax bracket than you.

Your use of an FLP can be combined with other planning techniques, such as the trusts discussed in Chapter 16. For example, you could use a grantor retained annuity trust (GRAT) by donor/transferor partner, which can permit the transfer of an even greater percentage interest in the FLP to a younger generation (or other designated beneficiary) through the discounting of the future value of the gift of the partnership interest.

Ancillary Probate Administration Consequences

The FLP can provide a mechanism to avoid ancillary probate—a legal proceeding following your death to administer your assets in a state other than where you lived. If you live in New Jersey but own real estate in Florida, your estate would have to institute a legal proceeding in Florida to transfer the real estate. An FLP may afford a simpler option. If, instead, your real estate is held by a partnership, the asset you then own, a partnership interest, is personal property—not real property. Therefore, the administration of your estate would be required in only the jurisdiction of your domicile (your permanent home) and not in the second (or multiple additional) jurisdictions where real property owned by the FLP was located. The avoidance of probate is consistent with the goal of asset protection under the general principle that the less costs and legal proceedings, the better. The same technique enables you to transfer real estate to an asset protection trust in another state.

Requirements for the IRS to Respect the FLP Transaction

While the IRS's respecting your FLP is not essential to having a court respect it when challenged by a claimant, many of the factors that the IRS looks at to respect the integrity of your FLP are similar to the factors courts will consider. Furthermore, handling your FLP in conformity with applicable tax laws also supports the proposition of your respecting the independent formalities of your FLP, which will encourage, in turn, a court to respect it as well.

Family Limited Partnership Rules Must Be Followed for Partners to Recognize Income. For gifts of limited partnership interests to be respected, the FLP will be tested under the income tax provisions of the family partnership rules under Section 704(e) of the Internal Revenue Code. For the allocation of income to children and other donees as partners to be respected by the IRS, the partnership agreement and operations must pass muster under these rules. A failure to meet these tests could result in a portion or all of the FLP income being taxed solely to you as the transferor partner, rather than to your children (or other heirs) as the donees of the FLP limited partnership interests.

Capital must be a material income-producing factor in the partnership. This requirement is perhaps most easily met for transactions involving the transfer of real estate properties to an FLP because capital is usually the primary, if not only, material income-producing factor in a real estate investment. Other transactions can be far less certain.

The donee partners (e.g., your children or other heirs) must be the real owners of the capital interests given to them. The donee partners must have genuine interests in the FLP. They must be entitled to receive a portion of the assets on withdrawal from the partnership, and they must be able to transfer their interests in the FLP without financial detriment. These requirements can be interpreted as implying that the donees are the real economic owners of their capital interests in the FLP. The donees must have dominion and control over their FLP interests.

Donee Partner Must Have Minimum Rights for Gifts to Be Respected. The donee partner should possess certain powers, controls, and rights to avoid tainting the validity of the transaction. If the donee partner, even as a limited partner, for example, cannot realize the economic value of his or her partnership interests, the transfers may not be complete and respected. The buy-out provisions of the FLP partnership agreement must be carefully analyzed. For example, your FLP's partnership agreement could give all partners the right to sell their partnership interests to anyone, as long as the FLP itself has the option to buy the FLP interests at the same price (right of first refusal). If the donee doesn't really own the partnership interest your creditors will still be able to reach it.

MINORITY DISCOUNTS

Properly valuing an interest in an FLP is important. As explained in Chapter 8, if you sell interests in any asset, such as an FLP, if it is not valued properly so that you do not receive back fair consideration, the sale could be characterized as a fraudulent conveyance. When valuing the interest for purposes of a sale, for estate planning for gifts or a bequest under a will, or evaluating the collateral for a loan or other financing transaction, general valuation concepts should be applied. These include comparative market analysis, replacement costs, and capitalization methods. An especially important concept is a determination of the appropriate discounts to be applied if the interest being valued is a noncontrolling (less than 50 percent) interest. One court described the discount concept in the context of a corporation, which is analogous to FLPs and LLCs, as follows:

> Courts have long recognized that the shares of stock of a corporation which represent a minority interest are usually worth less than a proportionate share of the value of the assets of the corporation. . . . The minority discount is recognized because the holder of a minority interest lacks control over corporate policy, cannot direct the payment of dividend, and cannot compel a liquidation of corporate assets. . . . Although these cases deal with minority interests in closely held corporations, we see no reason for a different rule for valuing partnership interests in this case. . . . The critical factor is lack of control, be it as a minority partner or as a minority shareholder.

The concept of a minority discount is that the sum of the parts is worth less than the whole. An undivided minority interest is worth less than the allocable share of the entire value because of the restrictions and limitations that affect such minority interest. The nature of such a discount and the appropriate magnitude of the discount are supported by an extensive body of case law.

REQUIRED FLP DOCUMENTS

Certificate of Limited Partnership

A certificate of limited partnership must be filed in accordance with applicable state law to form your FLP.

Limited Partnership Agreement

Most importantly from the perspective of asset protection considerations, your FLP should have a governing document, which determines the rights and obligations of the partners, how the partnership is managed, and so forth. This agreement, the limited partnership agreement, should also contain as severe restrictions as possible with respect to the transfer or assignment of partnership interests. These restrictions must be tempered against the possibly contradictory requirements of complying with applicable tax laws to meet estate and income tax planning objectives.

A written agreement is essential to demonstrating the validity of the FLP. This agreement could be amended periodically to reflect the varying partnership interests as they change over time, due to the gifts, sales, and so forth. Periodic and methodical updating of the agreement demonstrates the validity of the FLP arrangement.

Note: See www.laweasy.com for sample forms and additional planning ideas.

Assignments of Partnership Interests

Assignment of partnership interest forms are used to effect any transfers of limited partnership interests by gift or otherwise.

Appraisal

A formal appraisal of any assets transferred to the partnership should be made. Where sales or gifts of the limited partnership interests will be made, an appraisal of the limited partnership interests is also necessary to value the interests for gift or estate tax purposes and to demonstrate that any sales are not fraudulent conveyances.

SUMMARY

This chapter provided an overview of the use of family limited partnerships as an asset protection planning tool. FLPs are complex, and the rules differ from state to state. There are also numerous income tax issues, which need to be addressed. Therefore, in spite of the common use of FLPs, always obtain professional advice.

FOR YOUR NOTEBOOK

SAMPLE CLAUSE FOR LIMITED PARTNERSHIP AGREEMENT RESTRICTING TRANSFERS

General Requirements of Transfer: No transfer of any nature shall be made of any interest in this Partnership, unless the provisions of this Article are complied with. No Partner, or estate of a deceased Partner, or guardian or custodian for a disabled Partner shall, without the prior written consent of the General Partner, which may be withheld for any reason in the absolute discretion of the general partner, mortgage, pledge, sell, assign, hypothecate, or otherwise encumber, transfer, or permit to be transferred in any manner or by any means whatever, whether voluntarily or by operation of law, all or any part of their interests in the Partnership, except as provided for in the buy out provisions of this Article.

Transfer of Limited Partners' Interest: Subject to the provisions of Section X hereof, a Limited Partner may not, without the consent of the General Partner sell, transfer, assign or otherwise dispose of all or any portion of his Partnership Interest nor may a Limited Partner permit a Transfer (as hereinafter defined) of any interest of such Limited Partner. Any such purported sale, transfer, assignment or other disposition of a Partnership Interest (hereinafter referred to collectively as a "Transfer") without such consent shall be void and shall not bind the Partnership. However, if (i) the General Partner in its sole discretion shall have consented to such Transfer, (ii) the provisions of Section X hereof do not otherwise prohibit such Transfer, (iii) a duly executed and acknowledged counterpart of the instrument effecting such Transfer in form and substance satisfactory to the General Partner shall have been delivered to the General Partner, (iv) the assignee shall have expressly agreed to be bound by the provisions of this Agreement and to assume all of the obligations imposed upon a Limited Partner hereunder, (v) the assignor and the assignee shall have executed or delivered such other instruments as the General Partner may deem necessary or desirable to effectuate such admission, including but not limited to, an opinion of counsel that the Transfer complies with the registration provisions of the Securities Act of 1933, as amended (the "Act") and any applicable securities or

"Blue Sky" law of any state or other jurisdiction and (vi) the assignor or assignee shall have paid all reasonable expenses and legal fees incurred by the Partnership relating to his admission as a Limited Partner, including, but not limited to, the cost of any required counsel's opinion and of preparing, filing and publishing any amendment to the Partnership's Certificate of Limited Partnership necessary to effect such admission, then the Transfer may be made. Any valid Transfer shall be recognized not later than the last day of the calendar month following receipt of notice of the Transfer and required documentation and payment of the fees and expenses set forth above.

Limitations on Transfers of Limited Partners' Interests: No transfer may be permitted if the Transfer would result in the termination of the Partnership under the Code, and, if so attempted, the transfer shall be void and shall not be effective upon the Partnership. In making the determination whether a transfer will result in such a termination, the General Partner, in its absolute discretion, may require the assignee to furnish an opinion of counsel passing on this issue. Such opinion shall be at the assignee's expense. In no event may a transfer be made to (and no successor Limited Partner shall be admitted to the Partnership who is) a person below the age of majority in the State, or a person who has been adjudged to be insane or incompetent, and any purported Transfer to any such person shall be void and shall not be effective upon the Partnership. No Transferee shall be admitted as a Substitute Limited Partner without the consent of the General Partner which consent may be withheld for any reason or for no reason, whether or not such withholding of consent is reasonable. As a condition of recognizing a transfer, the General Partner may require such proof of the age and competency of the assignee as the General Partner may deem necessary.

11 LIMITED LIABILITY COMPANIES (LLCs) AND LAWSUIT PROTECTION PLANNING

INTRODUCTION TO LIMITED LIABILITY COMPANIES

Limited liability companies (LLCs) are a relatively new type of entity becoming popular in only the past 10 years. They offer a great tool in your lawsuit protection arsenal.

Perhaps the best way to understand what an LLC is and the advantages it can offer you is to compare it with the two most common traditional forms of organizing a business—an S corporation and a partnership. Following this basic overview, some of the jargon, documents, and procedures you should become familiar with are discussed.

Note: For more detailed information on LLCs, see Shenkman, Weiner, and Taback, *Starting Your Own Limited Liability Company* (2nd ed.), John Wiley & Sons, Inc., 2003. For additional sample forms, see www.laweasy.com.

COMPARING LLCs TO FLPs

Many of the concepts and issues concerning the use of LLCs for lawsuit protection are identical to those issues discussed for family limited partnerships (FLPs) in Chapter 10. LLCs are almost always treated as partnerships for income tax purposes (although there are some exceptions for state income taxation). Thus, all of the tax concepts discussed in Chapter 10 apply almost identically to LLCs. The key asset protection aspects of LLCs, *inside-out* and *outside-in* protection, are very similar to those of FLPs as well. The key rule to note is that both FLPs and LLCs are created under state law; therefore, your attorney should carefully review the FLP and LLC laws in the states you are considering before making a decision as to which type of entity to use.

A partnership and an LLC are similar for tax purposes.

LLCs DIFFER IN KEY WAYS FROM FLPs

There are a couple of important differences between FLPs and LLCs, which you should review with your attorney and accountant before making a decision as to which one to use:

- An LLC can have one owner (member) whereas an FLP must have at least two. A one-member LLC is ignored for tax purposes. This can make the LLC the ideal choice for some transactions; for example, to own real estate (to provide inside-out protection if there is a suit for the property) yet permit certain tax-advantageous transactions, such as a swap for other real estate without triggering tax (tax-deferred like-kind exchange).

- All members of an LLC have limited liability. This makes it easier to have complete asset protection for inside-out liabilities if the LLC owns assets, such as a business or real estate, which have their own lawsuit risks. To accomplish this in an FLP is more complex. Every general partner is fully and personally liable for all partnership debts and claims. This is a substantial disadvantage when compared to either an S corporation or an LLC. A limited partnership can offer this benefit of limited liability. However, to accomplish this goal requires a more complex, expensive, and cumbersome organizational structure. The limited partnership requires at least one general partner, so at least one principal must agree to remain personally liable. Rarely is this acceptable. Thus, in most instances, a limited partnership is structured with an S corporation as general partner. This requires two entities and the legal documentation and fees for each. Thus, the LLC can offer the advantages of a limited partnership structure for less cost, in a more simple manner, and with less tax risk.

- Limited partners in an FLP are generally prohibited from participating in management. This can have an appeal to you to ensure that your children or others to whom you give FLP interests cannot get involved in management matters. In an LLC, you have to contractually set up these limitations. In the event of a divorce, if your daughter owns only limited partnership interests, it will be much harder for her ex-husband to argue that she converted separate nonmarital assets into marital assets by her participation in management. She cannot. This argument may take a different course in the LLC because every member can participate in the management of the LLC unless the legal documentation establishes a different arrangement.

HOW DOES AN LLC COMPARE TO AN S CORPORATION?

The traditional form of structuring most closely held businesses had been the S corporation. The advantage of the S corporation is that it provides the limited liability protection of a corporation while income can generally flow through to the principals with no corporate-level tax. However, this form of ownership has many shortcomings, many of which are addressed by the LLC. Unlike an S corporation, an LLC has no restrictions on the number of owners. This contrasts favorably with an S corporation, which can have no more than 75 owners. In addition, there are far fewer restrictions on the nature and character of those who can be owners of an LLC. S corporations have substantial restrictions, which can wreak havoc with the best of plans. For example, only specific types of trusts are permitted to be owners of stock in an S corporation, nonresident aliens are not permitted to be shareholders, and an estate can hold stock for only a limited time period. The limitation on which trusts can own S corporation stock is a major advantage for lawsuit protection planning because the entity interests you establish (whether FLP, LLC, etc.) are often owned by various trusts to provide a second line of defense.

An LLC can provide for almost any type of allocations structure of its cash flow, income, expense, and gains between the owners.

An S corporation is inflexible because it must have the same distributions per share for each owner. The LLC can provide tremendous and important flexibility in this regard.

If the business will be financed, the tax basis of the investors for purposes of determining deductible losses can differ substantially between an LLC and an S corporation. Assume each of the two S corporation shareholders contributed $10,000 in cash to the corporation, and the corporation borrowed $200,000. The S corporation shareholder's basis is limited to the $10,000 invested. LLC owners, however, have a basis of $110,000 because they can include their pro rata share of entity level debt.

An LLC, similar to a partnership, can provide a step-up in tax basis to a new owner purchasing an interest in the LLC. Thus, if an owner purchases an interest in an LLC that owns appreciated property, the owner can obtain depreciation deductions based on the purchase price paid for this interest. A shareholder in an S corporation is limited to his or her pro rata share of the S corporation's depreciation deduction.

TAX CONSEQUENCES OF LLCs

An LLC is almost always characterized as a partnership for federal tax purposes. This means that all income, deductions, gains, and losses flow through to, and are reported on, the tax returns of the owners. The LLC itself pays no tax.

HOW TO SET UP AN LLC

To form an LLC, a simple legal document (certificate of formation or articles of organization) must be filed with the secretary of state and a modest filing fee must be paid. The certificate provides the name of the LLC, the address for the registered office and registered agent for the service of process, and perhaps a few other key items required under your state's laws or recommended by your attorney to include. For example, the certificate may state that the LLC may carry on any lawful business or purposes permitted under state law. It may be advantageous in some situations to provide a more restrictive definition of the activities of the LLC. The filing of the certificate creates and forms the LLC. The certificate must be amended only when the information contained in the certificate on file has changed.

Once the LLC is formed, a legal contract or agreement (operating agreement) should be prepared. This agreement provides for the allocation of profits and losses and other aspects of the business transaction between the members of the LLC. It should address the transfer of membership interests between other members and third parties. This step is extremely important in asset protection planning. Severe restrictions on transfer should be imposed, analogous to those discussed in Chapter 10, for the transfer of a limited partnership interest. Relative classes, rights, powers, and duties of each class or group of members and voting rights of members should be addressed. You may provide that certain actions may require certain percentage votes, and other actions may be taken without a vote. Whether management of the LLC operations will be vested in the manager or in the members as a unit can be addressed. In asset protection planning, naming a manager with complete control to diminish the value of the interests of the nonmanager members may be preferable. On the other hand, if family members constitute all of the members, perhaps a vote may be appropriate so that no partner as manager has additional powers. If no manager is designated, the majority vote would rule unless provision is made to the contrary. For asset protection benefits, you may wish to require a higher threshold, such as two-thirds or even unanimous consent, for some actions. If a manager is named to operate the LLC, details as to the rights and obligations of the manager should be provided for. It may be practical to include penalties or other provisions addressing what should happen in the event that the manager or a member fails to comply with the revisions of the agreement.

ADVANTAGEOUS USES FOR THE LLC

Real Estate Investments

An LLC can be an effective structure for owning real estate investments. Too many investors have structured real estate ownership in their individual names or in general partnership format. While these approaches have the benefit of simplicity from both a tax and legal perspective, there is no limitation on liability for claims stemming from the property (inside-out liability). While many lenders may require personal guarantees of the principals in any event, the use of an entity that provides limited liability for other potential claims, such as environmental and personal injury claims, should always be considered.

Professional Practices

For professionals, the most common form of ownership of a professional practice has been the partnership. The problem this creates is vicarious liability of one partner for the acts of another partner. The partner in a partnership is liable for the debts of the business in addition to being potentially liable for the negligent or wrongful acts of colleagues. An LLC member should not be liable for these risks, depending on the applicable law. Advantages of a professional LLC as compared to a professional corporation (PC), such as flexibility in allocations, will undoubtedly encourage professionals to use LLCs.

High Technology Enterprises, Venture Capital

Limited liability is attractive if significant risks are involved because highly risky investments often use special allocations to compensate the various persons involved for the different types of risks they may each take. Further, the limitation on liability is essential. Finally, investors in many small, high-risk, start-up ventures wish to have more control and input than a mere limited partner. Thus, the combination of limited liability, participation in management, and flexible allocations makes an LLC an ideal structure. In the context of venture capital situations, for the reasons noted, an LLC may provide an alternative to forming a captive subsidiary to undertake a new project.

Foreign Investors

LLCs resemble entities long in use in other countries. This should make them familiar to some foreign investors who are less familiar with entities such as limited partnerships. For non-U.S. persons, the LLC becomes an ideal vehicle to structure investment and business transactions because the restrictions that an S corporation has on excluding non-U.S. persons do not apply to LLCs and their liability (inside-out) can be limited.

Estate Planning

You can give gifts of LLC membership interests while still retaining control. The LLC operating agreement can restrict the sale of interests to strangers and determine the rights of the members to distributions. However, care must be taken to ensure that your powers as manager are not so broad as to prevent the IRS from respecting the gift as having been made or the income as being earned by the donee (e.g., your child).

Trusts may invest in LLCs. This provides far greater flexibility than the use of qualified S corporation trusts in lawsuit protection and estate planning. This permits two layers of protection.

An interest in an LLC is deemed to be personal property. This can be important to avoid having a second legal process (an ancillary probate proceeding) in a state where you own real estate. If, instead, you transfer the real estate owned outside the state in which you live to an LLC, the only probate your heirs must deal with are in the state in which you had your primary residence.

PROBLEMS, RISKS, AND ISSUES TO ADDRESS

Piercing the LLC "Veil"

If an LLC fails to observe the formalities of the LLC form of operation, your claimant may succeed in having the courts disregard, or pierce, the LLC entity (veil) to reach the LLC assets personally to satisfy a judgment. Care must always be taken to be certain that all documents and contracts are signed in the name of the LLC by the manager if so required under the operating agreement and that all necessary tax filings are made. LLC funds should never be commingled with personal funds. The LLC should have adequate funds (capital) to conduct its business. If additional certificates (Certificate of

Amendment, Certificate of Assumed Name, etc.) are required, these, too, should be properly filed. Leases, licenses, and other ancillary agreements should all be completed in the proper name of the LLC. The provisions of the LLC operating agreement should be followed.

Fiduciary Obligation of Manager

If you serve as the manager of your LLC, you owe a fiduciary duty to other LLC members. This means that you are in a position of trust and must treat them accordingly. You cannot gift or sell LLC membership interests to trusts or other family members and then ignore the reality of their ownership interests. As a manager, you should operate with respect to their LLCs as if they had the same fiduciary responsibility to the members as a general partner does to a limited partner in a limited partnership. When in doubt, proceed with caution and as if the other members were not related to you.

Note: See www.laweasy.com for sample forms.

SUMMARY

This chapter highlighted the differences between partnerships and LLCs and explained some of the unique aspects of LLCs. However, you should refer to Chapter 10 for tax and asset protection (e.g., charging orders) aspects of LLCs because, in most instances, they are the same for LLCs and limited partnerships. The LLC is a newer, and often the best, form of owning assets as part of your overall asset protection plan. The LLC offers distinct advantages, in many cases, over other techniques you can use. However, the decision is complex, and, in some instances, your personal circumstances or your state's laws may favor using a family limited partnership or other approach.

FOR YOUR NOTEBOOK

GIFT ASSIGNMENT OF AN
LLC MEMBERSHIP INTEREST

The undersigned hereby assigns by devise to RichKid Jones, (the "Assignee"), a percentage interest in Jones Family LLC, a Limited Liability Company (LLC) formed under the state laws of Somestate. The percentage interest hereby assigned is Two (2) percent of the total interests in the LLC.

The value of this LLC Membership interest is $22,000.

ASSIGNOR/DONOR:

_____ Date: December 31, 2005
Daddy Jones

ACKNOWLEDGED AND APPROVED:
Jones Family, LLC

By: _____
       Mommy Jones, Manager

State of Somestate   )
                                          ss:
County of Anycounty   )

On this December 31, 2005, before me personally came, Daddy Jones, a member of Jones Family LLC, known to me to be the individual described in and who executed the forgoing instrument, and he or she duly acknowledged to me that he or she understood the meaning of the instrument and that he or she executed the same for the purposes therein stated.

_____

Notary Public State of Somestate
Commission Expires: _____

FOR YOUR NOTEBOOK

DECLARATION OF GIFT OF LLC
MEMBERSHIP INTEREST

We, Mommy Jones and Daddy Jones, hereby state and declare that:

1. We are residents of the State of Somestate, residing at 123 Main Street, Big City, Somestate.

2. I, Daddy Jones, have this day executed an Assignment of Membership Interests concerning limited liability company Membership interests to transfer Two and 00/100s Percent (2.00 percent) Membership Interests in Jones Family, LLC to my son RichKid Jones, who resides at 123 Beachway, Surfcity, Somestate, valued at $22,000, by way of gift and without any consideration.

3. I, Mommy Jones, hereby join in making such gift.

4. We declare under the penalties of perjury that the foregoing is true and correct and further declare that this Declaration of Gift is being executed this December 31, 2005.

_____ _____

Daddy Jones   Mommy Jones

12 RULES ON USING CORPORATIONS TO PROTECT ASSETS

Corporations are not discussed in asset protection planning nearly as much as limited partnerships (FLPs) and limited liability companies (LLCs) because FLPs and LLCs offer a better combination of flexibility, asset protection, and tax benefits. So why are corporations so important to the process? Because the vast majority of closely held businesses and professional practices were organized as corporations before FLPs and LLCs became as popular as they are today. Even if the FLP or LLC form is better for you than a corporation, income tax laws often make it so costly to change from a corporation to an FLP or LLC that you will have to continue using your corporation. From a lawsuit protection perspective, this is not a significant negative because corporations afford important asset protection benefits if used properly. This chapter provides you with an overview of some of the procedures you should follow so that your corporation will be respected and some of the tax and other consequences you need to be aware of.

Most importantly, the vast majority of closely held corporations are organized as S corporations (explained later) to achieve certain important income tax benefits. These corporations present unique problems if their ownership interests (stock) is transferred to trusts. Because the transfer of entity ownership interests (FLPs, LLCs, S corporation stock, etc.) to trusts is an essential component of most asset protection plans (to achieve two levels of protection, fractionalize control, etc.), the issues of how various trusts can own S corporation stock is of vital importance to every closely held corporate business owner's lawsuit protection planning.

DIFFERENT TYPES OF CORPORATIONS

There are several different types of corporations. A C corporation is a corporation that is taxed as a separate entity. An S corporation is a corporation that generally passes all of its income and deductions to its shareholders, who then report their shares on their personal income tax returns. C versus S is solely an income tax concept and is discussed later.

The third type of corporation is formed by professionals who use professional corporations (PCs) or professional associations (PAs) for their practices. These can be C corporations or S corporations. The unique aspect of PCs and PAs is that the shareholder/professional remains liable for his or her own malpractice, but not for the malpractice of other shareholder/professionals. Using a PC or PA also enables you to limit your liability for nonprofessional lawsuits (e.g., a patient trips on the floor and sues).

Whatever type of corporation you have—C, S, or professional—you should adhere to the appropriate corporate formalities to minimize risk that a claimant will successfully pierce your corporation and reach the underlying assets held by the corporation, or worse, that a claimant of the corporation will convince a court that the corporation should be disregarded and your personal assets should be made available to pay the claim (piercing the corporate veil). These legal formalities, common to each of these corporations, are reviewed after the initial tax discussion.

C CORPORATION

C corporations pay income tax on the profits they earn. Profits are computed based on the various tax elections (such as depreciation method, etc.) and tax year determined at the corporate level (i.e., independent of the tax elections and tax year of its owners). When these net-of-tax profits are ultimately distributed to the corporation's shareholders as dividends, the shareholders have historically paid tax on the amounts received, although at this time, written proposals are pending to eliminate the taxation of dividends. If the proposals are not enacted or if dividends aren't made wholly tax free, this scenario results in two layers of taxation—double taxation. This can be rather unfavorable when compared to the result obtained with a limited liability company, a partnership, or an S corporation (see later discussion). These latter entities generally do not pay a tax at the entity level. Rather, their earnings are distributed to their owners who pay any tax due.

Another result follows from this corporate tax scheme. If the corporation is subject to its own tax system and if the corporation realizes losses, the shareholders cannot benefit from these losses. Again, this can compare rather unfavorably with the result available with a partnership, LLC, or S corporation. These latter entities can pass any tax losses they realize through to their owners. However, if a C corporation incurs losses, these losses can be carried back to the three preceding tax years or carried forward to the next 15 successive tax years. The result is that losses of a C corporation may not be wasted because they will offset future income.

Shareholder Compensation

For many closely held corporations, the shareholders are likely to be active principles in the business. Where this occurs, much of the income of the corporation will be distributed as salaries and bonuses. These are deductible by the corporation and taxable to the individual as income. Paying all income as a salary avoids the double taxation on dividends (although this will become less relevant or irrelevant if pending proposals to make dividends nontaxable are enacted). This type of planning can minimize an important advantage often cited for flow-through entities, partnerships, LLCs, and S corporations. The IRS, however, can challenge these salaries under the doctrines of unreasonable compensation or assignment of income. Thus, even a regular corporation can avoid any corporate-level tax. For asset protection, paying all income out of the corporation eliminates any protection of those funds.

C Corporations Are Subject to the Alternative Minimum Tax

Corporations can also be subject to a second tax system to ensure that they pay minimum levels of income tax (the *alternative minimum tax* [AMT]). The corporate minimum tax requires corporations to increase their taxable income by various items (tax preferences), make certain other adjustments, and multiply the result by a specified tax rate.

Double Taxation on Sale of C Corporation Assets

The risk of double taxation on the sale of corporate assets can have a tremendous impact on the net economic earnings a shareholder can realize. Both the corporation and its shareholders can be subject to a tax if the corporation distributes its assets or liquidates. With limited exception, gain and loss must be recognized if the corporation distributes assets to its shareholders, as if the assets had been sold to those shareholders at their fair market value. Corporations also recognize gain on nonliquidating distributions of appreciated property.

Shareholders face two types of taxes with respect to their ownership of stock in a C corporation: taxation on dividend distributions and the tax on the sale of the shares. In most instances, any sale will be controlled by the buy-out provisions contained in the shareholders' agreement. The sale of stock should qualify as a capital gain. Similarly, capital gain may be realized when the corporation redeems the shareholders' stock.

These rules are far less favorable than the tax rules that apply to partnerships and LLCs.

S CORPORATIONS

S corporations for many years were the entity of choice for most closely held businesses. While the LLC may have advantages in many instances, S corporations will continue to predominate for years to come if for no reason other than the large number of businesses previously organized in this format. The result is that the characteristics of S corporations must be carefully addressed in asset protection planning for the closely held business.

S corporations are generally not taxed; rather, they act as a conduit, and income and loss flows through to the individual shareholders and is taxed to them. A shareholder in an S corporation, like any corporate shareholder, can benefit from limited liability.

Only the amount invested is at risk. This is always touted as an important factor favoring an S corporation over a general partnership or a sole proprietorship. However, for a start-up business, limited liability is rarely absolute because personal guarantees are often required for bank loans, leases, and other transactions.

What Happens When a C Corporation Becomes an S Corporation

Because of the advantages of an S corporation over a C corporation, if you own a regular or C corporation, review with your accountant having it elect to be taxed as an S corporation. Two special tax traps must be considered. In the first, the built-in gains tax will be imposed on the S corporation on any gain that arose before the corporation was converted from a regular corporation to an S corporation. This special tax applies during the 10-year period following the election to be taxed as an S corporation. The tax is assessed at the highest corporate tax rate. The maximum gain subject to this special tax is limited to the net unrealized built-in gain that existed at the date the corporation became an S corporation.

Note: If a corporation owned a building with a depreciated book value of $1 million and a worth of $2 million at the date the corporation was converted to an S corporation, the built-in gain would be $1 million. If the S corporation was sold or liquidated within 10 years, a corporate tax would have to be paid.

As a result of this built-in gains tax, it is best to have the assets of any regular corporation valued in a written and independent appraisal as of the date an election is made for it to become an S corporation.

A second problem in converting a regular C corporation to an S corporation is a limitation on passive income. If the regular corporation has earnings and profits when it elects to be an S corporation, the S corporation could face a corporate-level tax and possible loss of its S corporation status if excessive passive income is earned. If more than 25 percent of the taxable income for an S corporation subject to these rules is passive, a tax will be charged on excess net passive income. If this 25 percent threshold is exceeded for three consecutive years, the S corporation status will be terminated.

S Corporations and Tax Losses

An S corporation shareholder can deduct only losses passed through up to the amount of his or her tax basis. Only the basis in the shareholder's stock, such as the price paid and amounts directly due to the shareholder from the corporation, are included in the tax basis under IRC Section 1366(d). The S corporation shareholder cannot include a pro rata share of entity level debts (a nonrecourse mortgage on the property) in the basis as a partner can. This dichotomy greatly favors the partnership form when real estate assets are owned.

How Distributions from S Corporations Are Taxed

If an S corporation has earnings and profits (analogous to financial statement retained earnings) from a tax year before it became an S corporation (i.e., when it was a C corporation), distributions are taxed based on the following priority of rules:

- A nontaxable return of investment up to the amount of the S corporation's accumulated adjustment account (AAA). The AAA is generally the sum of all income reduced by the following: nontaxable distributions, losses and deductions, and certain non-tax deductible amounts.
- Dividends to the extent of accumulated earnings and profits.
- Nontaxable return of investment up to the amount of the shareholder's basis in the stock.
- Gain from the sale of stock.

Trusts as Shareholders of S Corporations

For asset protection purposes, this is the key planning consideration. Only three specified types of trusts can qualify to own S corporation stock: electing small business trusts (ESBTs), qualified

Subchapter S trusts (QSSTs), and grantor trusts. Many common types of trusts cannot be S corporation shareholders. If you transfer S corporation stock to the wrong type of trust, you could destroy the S corporation income tax advantages (i.e., the corporation would be taxed as a C corporation). This adverse tax result applies to not only the stock you incorrectly transferred, but also all shareholders. It is vital in planning that these requirements be carefully addressed.

ESBTs: Electing Small Business Trusts.   Electing small business trusts can be shareholders of S corporations. The ESBT is an exception to the general S corporation rule that an individual must pay the tax on S corporation earnings; instead, the trust pays tax. For a trust to qualify, all of its beneficiaries must be individuals or estates (i.e., partnerships, corporations, and so on cannot be beneficiaries of the trust). An ESBT can have a special needs trust as a beneficiary. Certain charities can be contingent remainderman (i.e, the beneficiaries who receive trust income or assets if all prior beneficiaries die or cease to qualify as beneficiaries). Most commonly, an ESBT is a trust created to benefit several beneficiaries (e.g., your spouse and children; called a *spray, sprinkle,* or *discretionary* trust). ESBTs can provide greater flexibility then the QSSTs, described later, in that they can have many current income beneficiaries. This means several different people can receive income each year from the trust. QSSTs require a separate trust for each beneficiary.

If your trustee files the appropriate statement (election) with the IRS for the trust to be taxed as an ESBT, the trust is taxed on all its share of S corporation income. This is a costly result because the tax is a flat tax at the highest rate, with no offsets or deductions and without the benefit of any lower marginal rates. ESBT gets almost no deductions other than state and local taxes and administrative expenses. There is no charitable deduction for an ESBT. All distributions to beneficiaries are tax free (as they should be because the trust paid the tax for them at the highest possible rate).

When counting the general 75 shareholder limit for S corporations when an ESBT is a shareholder, you must look through ESBT to identify and count the individual ESBT beneficiaries. Anyone who is a potential distributee from an ESBT spray trust should be counted when adding the number of shareholders for compliance with the 75 shareholder test. For example, if the ESBT trustee can distribute income among all of your descendants, all of your descendants are included. If a beneficiary can receive ESBT distributions only following the exercise of a power of appointment, that beneficiary is not counted as an S corporation shareholder until the power of appointment is exercised.

QSSTs Can Qualify to Own S Corporation Stock.   Trusts that meet the requirements of a QSST can own stock in an S corporation. A QSST can be a very useful income tax, estate tax, and creditor protection planning technique.

Example: Father owns 55 percent of a mortgage servicing corporation, which is organized as an S corporation. He decides that it is time to start transferring stock to his children to reduce his potential federal estate taxes. He wants to protect the stock in the event a child divorces or is sued. He sets up a qualified S corporation trust for each of his minor children. He joins with his spouse to jointly gift $22,000 in value (based on an appraisal of the corporation) of stock to each child's trust. This approach enables him to control the use of the assets for the benefit of each child; the stock could be insulated from both his creditors and the children's creditors. He also reduces himself to a noncontrol position (under 50 percent) which makes his remaining stock less valuable to a claimant.

Many of the trusts that are created to qualify for the marital deduction for federal gift and estate tax purposes can also meet the requirements of a QSST. For example, the qualified terminable interest property (QTIP) trust discussed in Chapter 14 can be a QSST. Many of the typical trusts established for the benefit of minor children do not qualify for QSST treatment without modification because they give the trustee the authority to accumulate income rather than pay it currently to the minor child. The minor child's trusts are discussed in Chapter 14.

To qualify for QSST treatment, the following requirements must be met:

- *Election:* The income beneficiary (such as your child) must file a statement with the IRS choosing to be taxed as the owner of the S corporation stock for income tax purposes. The election must be made within 2½ months of the trust's becoming a shareholder or within 2½ months of the beginning of the first tax year of the S corporation.

- *Tax reporting:* The single beneficiary of the QSST trust will be treated as if he or she owns the portion of the trust that consists of stock in the S corporation. The effect of the election is to treat the beneficiary as the deemed owner of the S corporation stock. This means that the S corporation's income allocable to the shares of stock owned by the QSST flow directly to the beneficiary as if he or she were the shareholder.

- *Required income distributions:* During the life of the current income beneficiary (a child in the previous example), the trust's income must be required by the terms of the trust agreement to be distributed to one beneficiary.

Example: Father sets up a trust for the benefit of his minor child, Junior. Father makes gifts of two assets to the trust: (1) 10 shares of stock in XYZ Company, Inc., an S corporation, and (2) a certificate of deposit. The S corporation pays a dividend of $245 per share. The certificate of deposit pays $530 interest. The trust agreement should require the distribution of the $2,450 S corporation dividend. However, the trust agreement could provide for a different treatment of the $530 interest. This distinction is important for asset protection.

If an S corporation doesn't distribute all of its income, the trust is not required to distribute income that it did not receive.

Example: XYZ Company, Inc., earned $450 per share. It distributed, however, only $245 per share. The Joe Junior Qualified S Corporation Trust, which owns 10 shares, must report $4,500 in income. However, it will not be required to distribute to the beneficiary more than $2,450. The trust's share of the $2,050 of undistributed XYZ Company, Inc., S corporation income ($4,500 − $2,450) need not be distributed.

- *Beneficiaries:* There can be only one beneficiary. Any distributions of trust assets (corpus) during the life of the current income beneficiary can be made to only that one beneficiary.

- *End of required distributions:* The current income beneficiary's income interest in the trust must end at the earlier of his or her death or the termination of the trust. The trust can, however, end at an earlier date (e.g., when your child, who is the beneficiary, reaches age 30). However, for divorce and creditor protection benefits, the trust should continue for the beneficiary's life.

- *Distribution on termination of QSST:* If the trust ends during the current income beneficiary's life, the trust assets must be distributed to the current income beneficiary.

Grantor Trusts Owning S Corporation Stock. Trusts that have a certain status for income tax purposes can own S corporation stock. These trusts, called *grantor trusts,* and all of the trust income of these trusts is taxable fully to you as if the trust did not exist. An example is the commonly used revocable living trust (which provides no asset protection). Not all grantor trusts qualify to hold S corporation stock. Some provide asset protection, some do not. Therefore, have your estate planner carefully review any trust agreement before transferring S corporation stock to that trust.

BUYOUT AGREEMENTS AND LAWSUIT PROTECTION

Many closely held corporations have buyout agreements governing who will buy the stock if one shareholder dies. These agreements often use insurance to pay for the stock. From an asset protection perspective, many are not handled properly. Any cash accumulations on insurance policies owned by the corporation are subject to the general creditors of the corporation. If the perceived risks are material, a cross-purchase arrangement, where each shareholder owns insurance on the life of the others, may be preferable.

Example: Four doctors join forces in a new fertility practice. Their attorney recommends that they organize as a professional corporation to minimize liability exposure. When drafting their shareholders' agreement, a buy-sell provision is included. Although it is cumbersome and more costly to use a cross-purchase arrangement with so many shareholders involved, the doctors unanimously choose this approach because they don't want to risk placing the permanent insurance (which will eventually have substantial value) at the risk of potential malpractice claimants. Individually, they review the use of irrevocable life insurance trusts to further protect the insurance policies from personal creditors and malpractice claimants.

RULES TO ENSURE THAT YOUR CORPORATION CAN WITHSTAND A LAWSUIT

One of the major problems with most closely held businesses is that the formalities of a business entity separate and distinct from its owners are too often ignored. Further, many closely held business owners are reluctant to incur the costs necessary to properly document even common or important transactions. This informality is often not problematic. However, in the event of an IRS audit, a lawsuit or claim by a third party, or disagreement among the owner group, such informality can exacerbate the problems or, at worst, lead to the disregard of the corporate form, recharacterization of transactions for tax purposes, and even failure of the business. Make sure your professionals have helped you address these items:

- The necessary legal document must have been filed with the appropriate state authority to form the corporation (certificate of incorporation), and it should reflect current and correct information. Often, the person (agent) on which the state can serve notice of a lawsuit (process) has long ago moved or is dead. Have your attorney review and update the certificate. In addition, your state may permit the certificate to include an indemnification of directors, which was not permitted when the corporation was first formed. This is an amendment worth considering.

- For a corporation to remain valid, once properly formed, it must file periodic reports with the state and pay periodic fees. If you're not certain that your corporation is valid, your attorney can usually obtain a certification from the state that it is valid (a *good standing certificate*).

- The corporation should have a formal set of legal records (corporate kit). This should include a copy of the certificate of incorporation and all amendments. The incorporator should have resigned and a board of directors should have been appointed, officers appointed, the form of stock certificate that evidences ownership in the corporation should have been acknowledged by the shareholders, and stock should have been issued. If any of these formalities was not completed when the corporation was formed, your corporate attorney can address them now. The "For Your Notebook" section following this chapter includes a sample set of minutes to accomplish this.

- Be certain that the names of the officers and stock ownership conform with what your accountant reports on the corporation's income tax return. Too often, changes are made over the years, and the legal and tax filings become inconsistent. These are great differences for a claimant to exploit in trying to pierce the corporation and reach your personal assets.

- Be sure the stock certificates were actually delivered to each shareholder (issued). They should not be left in the corporate kit.

- Hold an annual meeting and prepare minutes to be signed by all shareholders and directors. These should appoint directors and officers and confirm major legal transactions.

- The corporation should have its own tax identification number.

- No corporate funds should ever be commingled with personal funds.

- Every significant legal transaction, especially if it is with family or other controlled entities, should be documented in a separate, formal, written contract prepared with the same care and formality as it would be for a transaction with a nonfamily member. For example, if your business corporation leases real estate from a family limited partnership, have a written lease (see Chapter 13).

- Always sign corporate documents in the name of the corporation, not in your personal name. If a signature line on a bill of lading or other document has only your name, correct it. The only format you should use to sign is as follows:

Corporate Name

By: _____
    Your Name, Your Title

CORPORATE LIABILITY PROTECTION IS NEVER COMPLETE

No corporation is a foolproof safeguard against lawsuits. If you transfer assets into the corporation or transfer stock in the corporation, which is a fraudulent conveyance, a claimant can set it aside. If your corporation has not paid payroll taxes it has withheld from employees' wages or sales taxes received from customers, you can be held personally liable if you are a "responsible" person.

INTEGRATING YOUR CORPORATION INTO YOUR OVERALL LAWSUIT PROTECTION PLAN

Your asset protection plan should be a comprehensive plan consisting of many "baskets" of different entities and agreements, as well as different "layers" or lines of defense. Your corporation should be integrated into this overall plan. The following are some of the common methods:

- Shares of stock in your corporation are divided among various family members and trusts. This prevents you from having total control.

- By having trusts own shares of stock in your family corporation (other than a professional corporation), a claimant will have to succeed against both the corporation and the second tier of the trust owners.

- Use separate entities for different assets. The most common example is to have different retail stores or real estate and an operating company owned in separate entities. For older businesses, these entities are commonly corporations. This creates separate baskets, which makes it more difficult for someone injured by one store to sue and get a judgment against all of your stores. A physician can have expensive equipment owned by an LLC and leased to the practice. It is vital for this type of planning to work that all intercompany transactions be handled as they would between unrelated parties.

DIVORCE PROTECTION FOR THE FAMILY CORPORATION

Many families have the important goal of keeping the family business within the family (see Chapter 5). Here are some of the steps you should consider:

- Insist that every child sign a prenuptial agreement before marriage, which expressly excludes the new spouse from making any claim on the family business corporation.

- If the spouse-to-be won't sign a prenuptial agreement, try to have the new spouse sign a limited agreement not to take stock in the family business.

- Some attorneys include provisions in the shareholders' agreement for a closely held corporation prohibiting transfers incident to divorce and have the spouses sign the agreement acknowledging that provision and agreeing to be bound by it.

- Carefully review with your attorney and accountant how distributions, perquisites, and compensation will be paid out of your corporation. In the event of divorce, if your soon-to-be ex-in-law is on the books as an employee with a car, it won't make the settlement easier or cheaper.

Note: For additional planning ideas and sample forms see www.laweasy.com.

SUMMARY

Planning for the closely held business corporation is a key part of many lawsuit protection plans. This chapter explained some of the different types of corporations and presented suggestions for how they can be integrated into your overall asset protection planning.

FOR YOUR NOTEBOOK

SAMPLE CORPORATE MINUTES

CORPNAME
Unanimous Consent of All Shareholders and Directors
of CORPNAME In Lieu of Meeting
To Adopt By-Laws, Stock Certificate, Seal, S-Election, etc.

The undersigned, being all of the directors and shareholders of the Corporation, hereby take the following actions:

RESOLVED, a certified copy of the Certificate of Incorporation, the original of which has been filed in the State of Statename on June 12, 1995, was ordered kept in the minute book.

RESOLVED, that the By-laws now submitted to the meeting are hereby adopted as the By-laws of the Corporation, and that a copy be kept permanently in the minute book, attached to this Unanimous Consent.

RESOLVED, that the seal of this Corporation is circular in form, and has the name of the Corporation around the circumference, and the words and figures, "Corporate Seal, New Jersey, 1995," in the center. This Seal is impressed on this page, below, and is adopted as the Seal of the Corporation:

RESOLVED, that the form of stock certificate attached to this Unanimous Consent is adopted as the stock certificate of the Corporation.

RESOLVED, that the Board of Directors is authorized and requested to issue the capital stock of the corporation for cash or property to such persons and in such manner as they from time to time may determine.

RESOLVED, the following persons are elected to serve as directors of the Corporation until their successors are elected and qualified:

Dad Smith
Jane Smith
Daughter Smith

RESOLVED, the following persons are elected to serve as officers of the Corporation until their successors are elected and qualified:

President	—Dad Smith
Vice President	—Jane Smith
Secretary	—Jane Smith
Assistant Secretary	—Dad Smith
Treasurer	—Junior Smith
Assistant Treasurer	—Daughter Smith

RESOLVED, That the following officers be paid the compensation set forth herein for the fiscal year next ending following the date of this unanimous consent:

President	—$100,000
Vice President	—$20,000
Secretary	—$5,000
Assistant Secretary	—$2,000
Treasurer	—$5,000
Assistant Treasurer	—$2,000

RESOLVED, the corporation hereby adopts any and all acts heretofore done or undertaken by the Incorporator. The Corporation hereby agrees to indemnify and hold harmless the Incorporator for any acts done or undertaken on behalf of the Corporation. The Incorporator hereby tenders his or her resignation and the Corporation hereby accepts the resignation of the Incorporator.

RESOLVED, That Susan Accountant shall be retained by the Corporation to compile financial statements for the corporation for the fiscal year next ending.

RESOLVED, That the Corporation elect to be taxed as a Subchapter S Corporation for income tax purposes, and that the necessary tax filings and elections be made to obtain this status.

RESOLVED, that the officers are directed and authorized to undertake any acts necessary to carry out the above resolutions.

Dated: June 4, 2004   CORPORATE SEAL:

_____

Dad Smith, Shareholder

_____

Junior Smith, Shareholder

_____

Daughter Smith, Shareholder

_____

Dad Smith, Director

_____

Jane Smith, Director

_____

Daughter Smith, Director

13 OTHER BUSINESS ASSET PROTECTION TECHNIQUES

INTRODUCTION—IT'S NOT ONLY ABOUT USING ENTITIES TO ACHIEVE ASSET PROTECTION PLANNING

LLCs, FLPs, foreign trusts, and other entities are typically the first techniques thought of when asset protection concerns are addressed. However, using entities alone is not sufficient in most cases to achieve your goals and to thwart creditors' claims. You should, with your attorney and accountant, carefully analyze a broad range of entities and contractual arrangements that can be beneficial. In the best of plans, different types and layers of entities and contractual relationships are used to build a structure for ownership and operation that is even more impervious to attack. Any of the techniques described in the following sections could be appropriate.

LEASE

Real estate or valuable tangible property (e.g., construction equipment, medical equipment) can be given by way of gift or part gift/part sale to family members, children, or trusts for children (trusts being the preferred approach from an asset protection perspective). Ideally, the property would first be transferred into a family limited partnership (FLP) or a limited liability company (LLC) and then the interests in the entity transferred to the trusts for your children. These assets can then be leased back to ensure the business the use of the assets. Lease arrangements can be structured as gift-leaseback arrangements, or by the children, trusts, or others purchasing the assets directly. From an asset protection perspective, if you or your business is then sued, you or your business does not own the asset. If the initial transfer cannot be set aside as a fraudulent conveyance (or under some other theory), the valuable real estate or other tangible property can be protected.

To be respected, however, the lease terms should be reasonable. The lease agreement should be typical of that used in regular non-family business transactions. Too many people get sloppy about these formalities and could thus jeopardize the independence of the entity owning the property, the lease, and the entity leasing the property. The terms of the lease should be respected. If, for example, your business needs to make a repair to the property and if the lease requires the lessor's approval, get a letter in writing from the FLP or LLC owning the equipment or building authorizing the improvement.

LICENSE

Concepts similar to the lease arrangement in the preceding paragraph can be used to carve out the rights to important intangible assets, vest ownership in a person or entity less at risk to creditor or malpractice claims, and then pay a license fee to obtain the use of these assets. This planning is consistent with the general asset protection concept of creating separate baskets for different assets. If your main business is sued, the intangible rights it is merely licensing, and which it no longer owns, may be protected.

Example: The name and logo for a restaurant or other business could be owned by a family trust or partnership. The restaurant can then license the right to use the name and logo. In the event of a suit or challenge to the restaurant business, these assets could have some measure of protection. This same technique can facilitate the transfer of income to lower tax bracket family members, remove assets from the estate of an older generation family member, and so forth. In the event that the concept for the restaurant takes off, the children, through the FLP or other entity, would own the license to the name, logo, and related intangibles. These could be licensed to future restaurant locations. Thus, a future appreciation would be outside your estate.

For this type of planning to be effective, and especially if there is a sale and you wish to avoid implications of the fraudulent conveyance rule, obtain a written and independent appraisal of the value of these assets and the fair license fee to pay.

CONSULTING/EMPLOYMENT AGREEMENTS

If you or another family member is providing services to a family business corporation, FLP, or LLC, consider having your lawyer prepare a separate consulting or employment agreement documenting the relationship, the compensation, the specific services you are providing, and other key terms. Family transactions are subject to very close scrutiny in the event of a suit or claim. Having as much independent documentation as possible to demonstrate the fairness of prices and terms (arm's length) will help fend off a challenge. It will also help support the positions your accountant will take with the IRS.

LOAN TRANSACTIONS

You cannot use your closely held business corporation, FLP, or LLC for the payment of personal expenses. You cannot transfer funds back and forth from the corporation, FLP, or LLC to your personal account as you run short of money. The only ways you can take money out of your entity are as salary (or other compensation), dividend distribution, or loan. If the funds are not a salary or dividend/distribution (which must be in proportion to share ownership), it must be a loan. Every loan must have a signed loan agreement and should be repaid with interest. This is one of the most obvious ways claimants and the IRS attack the legitimacy of a closely held corporation, FLP, or LLC. The "For Your Notebook" section following this chapter includes a sample note.

OTHER TECHNIQUES

The techniques that should be used are those with the most non-asset protection benefits and appearances, that can be implemented with the most certainty, and that can most effectively meet all of the objectives of the parties involved. This broad approach suggests that the answer differs in each situation and the professional advisor should become adept at addressing the various situations.

SUMMARY

For your various corporate, partnership, and LLC entities to be respected, all of their operations and transactions need to be handled in a manner similar to operations and transactions in a real, competitive business environment with independent, unrelated persons. An important step in demonstrating this and in helping you recognize the formalities is to use common business documents for each transaction. A key purpose of these documents is to ensure that you and your advisors focus on setting all prices and fees charged between your related entities in a reasonable manner.

FOR YOUR NOTEBOOK

SAMPLE LOAN DOCUMENTATION

CORPNAME
Action Taken by Unanimous Written Consent
of the
Board of Directors and Shareholders
To Authorize Loans by the Corporation

The undersigned, being all of the directors and shareholders of the Corporation, hereby take the following actions:

RESOLVED, The Corporation shall loan Dad Smith, a shareholder, officer and director of the Corporation on the terms and conditions set forth in the Promissory Note attached.

RESOLVED, The Corporation enter into a loan, and disburse the necessary funds, substantially in accordance with the form attached.

RESOLVED, The officers of the Corporation are hereby authorized to take any and all actions to effect the above.

Dated: June 4, 2004   CORPORATE SEAL:

_____

Dad Smith, Shareholder

_____

Junior Smith, Shareholder

_____

Daughter Smith, Shareholder

_____

Dad Smith, Director

_____

Jane Smith, Director

_____

Daughter Smith, Director

PROMISSORY NOTE

$25,000.00
Big City, Somestate
Date: June 4, 2004

FOR VALUE RECEIVED, the Undersigned promises to pay to the order of CORPNAME, or the holder hereof ("the Payee") at 456 Business Way, Big City, Somestate, or at such other place as the Payee may designate in writing to the Undersigned, the principal sum of Twenty Thousand Dollars ($20,000.00) in lawful money of the United States of America.

This Note shall be repaid in full upon the maturity hereof, on June 3, 2005. Repayment shall include all then unpaid principal and any accrued but unpaid interest on this Note.

Interest shall accrue on this Note at the rate of Six percent (6.00 percent) per annum. Interest shall be due and payable within Thirty (30) days of each anniversary date of this Note.

The Undersigned shall, at any time, have the right to prepay, without penalty or premium, all or any portion of the loan evidenced by this Note.

The Payee shall not exercise any right or remedy provided for in this Note because of any default of the Undersigned to pay the sums due hereunder, until after the expiration of a Five (5) day grace period from the Undersigned's receipt of any demand for payment.

If the Payee shall institute any action to enforce collection of this Note, there shall become due and payable from the Undersigned, in addition to the unpaid principal and interest, all costs and expenses of such action (including reasonable attorneys' fees) and the Payee shall be entitled to judgment for all such additional amounts.

The Undersigned irrevocably consents to the sole and exclusive jurisdiction of the courts of the State of Somestate and of any federal court located in Somestate in connection with any action or proceeding arising out of, or related to, this Note. In any such proceeding, the undersigned waives personal service of any summons, complaint or other process and agrees that service thereof shall be deemed made when mailed by registered or certified mail, return receipt requested, to the undersigned. Within Twenty (20) days after such service, the undersigned shall appear or answer the summons, complaint or other process. If the undersigned shall fail to appear or answer within that Twenty (20) day period, the Undersigned shall be deemed in default and judgment may be entered by the Payee against the Undersigned for the amount demanded in the summons, complaint or other process.

No delay or failure on the part of the Payee on this Note to exercise any power or right given hereunder shall operate as a waiver thereof, and no right or remedy of the Payee shall be deemed abridged or modified by any course of conduct.

The Undersigned waives presentment, demand for payment, notice of dishonor and all other notices or demands in connection with the delivery, acceptance, performance, default or endorsement of this Note.

This Note shall be governed by and construed in accordance with the State of Somestate applicable to agreements made and to be performed in Somestate.

This Note cannot be changed orally.

UNDERSIGNED:

By: _____
    Dad Smith

Address for Communication:
123 Main Street
Big City, Somestate

PART FIVE

RULES FOR USING TRUSTS TO PROTECT AGAINST LAWSUITS AND DIVORCE

14 WHAT ARE TRUSTS AND HOW CAN THEY HELP YOU PROTECT ASSETS?

Trusts are contractual arrangements in which you create a contract naming a person to manage the assets for the benefit of specified people. Trusts, as compared to outright ownership of the assets, can provide important measures of protection against creditors and other claimants. If you give or sell assets to a trust that cannot be changed (irrevocable) and there is no fraudulent conveyance involved (see Chapter 8), the trust serves as a barrier, making it more difficult for your claimants to reach the assets held by the trust. Further, the assets held in the trust are protected for the benefit of your children or other beneficiaries. Trusts can protect against divorce as well (see Chapter 5). Explanations of specific trusts appear in Chapters 16 and 17. A discussion of how these trust concepts can be used to protect your assets and your heirs from divorce appears in Chapter 15.

Note: See Shenkman, *The Complete Book of Trusts* (3rd ed.), John Wiley & Sons, Inc., 2002 for a detailed analysis of trusts. For additional sample trust forms and commentary, see www.laweasy.com.

A trust can be structured to accomplish almost any legal act desired. It can provide for the management of assets in the event of sickness and disability. Trusts can provide for significant tax benefits. Trusts can protect assets from creditors and other claimants, to some extent. In accomplishing all of these important goals, the trust can often remain confidential. Again, confidentiality is not a basic tenant of asset protection planning—what is unknown (or at least more difficult to identify) is likely to appear more suspect.

To address the use of trusts in asset protection planning and to clarify the powers and benefits that trusts can offer, we first discuss the basic characteristics of a trust.

WHAT IS A TRUST?

A trust, like a corporation, is a creation of the law. A trust exists because you set it up in accordance with the procedures required by the laws of the state where the trust is domiciled.

A trust is formed by having a legal document prepared and signed. This trust document is a contract between the grantor, the person who sets up the trust, and the trustee, who administers the trust. The provisions of this document are essential to the success of the trust as an asset protection tool. (The sample clauses and drafting suggestions throughout this book highlight some of the considerations to address in drafting an asset protection trust.) Next, assets are transferred to the trust. The timing and structure of the transfers are critical to avoiding a fraudulent conveyance, which could nullify your planning efforts. This completes the establishment of the trust. Next, the trust is administered for its duration. Finally, when the trust has fulfilled its purposes, the money and assets it holds are distributed, and the trust is terminated. At this final stage, any asset protection benefits of the trust are terminated.

Trusts Separate Legal and Beneficial Ownership of Assets

A trust arrangement can be used to separate the legal ownership of an asset from the benefit of that asset. The person holding the legal title, the trustee, has a fiduciary duty to the persons entitled to the benefits of the trust property. A fiduciary duty is a responsibility of care. The trustee is charged with exercising certain specified care in carrying out the requirements and intent of the trust document governing the relationship of the trustee to the property and to the beneficiary. This duty of care can be imposed on the trustee by the provisions of the trust document. State law can also create certain obligations and duties of the trustee.

The benefits of a trust arrangement come from this separation of ownership and benefit. Where the IRS is willing to recognize the separation, certain important tax benefits may be available. Where the persons to benefit cannot, or should not, be in control of the assets, a trust provides an ideal vehicle to provide for management of those assets. Trusts, for example, can permit a bank or financially astute family member to manage money for the benefit of children or incapacitated family members who cannot manage the funds for their own benefit. Where the separation of the ownership and benefit is recognized, assets can be used for the benefit of the beneficiaries but may escape the clutches of creditors of the beneficiaries. This is the key characteristic for any trust that is to also function as an asset protection trust.

Key Elements of Every Trust

In a trust, a *grantor* transfers *trust property* to a *trustee* to hold for the benefit of the *beneficiary* in accordance with the purpose or *intent* of the trust. Every trust requires the five elements italicized in the previous sentence. The grantor is the person who transfers the trust property to the trust. This intent of the grantor to form a trust must be manifested. This is generally in the form of a written and signed trust agreement. In general, the less interest the grantor retains in the trust, the less likely the grantor's creditors can reach the trust corpus. If the grantor is a primary beneficiary of the trust, restrictions on the use of a self-settled trust to protect a person's own assets from his or her own creditors could come into play. Courts generally do not permit grantors to self-fund trusts with their own assets and seek to use the trust to protect those assets from the grantor's claimants (see Chapters 17 and 18).

Trust assets are the principal subject matter of the trust. The property must be properly transferred to the trust for any protection to be realized. In most trusts, a formal legal description of the trust property is attached to the end of the trust as a schedule. This, however, may be insufficient; formal steps should be taken to formally transfer ownership of assets to the trust:

- *Bill of sale*—transfer personal property.
- *Deed*—transfer real estate.
- *Stock power; stock certificate*—transfer stock in a corporation.
- *Partnership assignment*—transfer partnership interest.

If the assets are not properly transferred to the trust with the requisite legal formalities, any asset protection benefits the trust may have will likely prove illusory.

The *trustee* is the person responsible for managing and administering your trust. The trustee should make a declaration, often by signing the trust agreement, that he or she accepts the trust property. The trustee may be the grantor (generally not the preferable approach if asset protection goals are important), a trusted friend, a family member, a bank trust department, or any combination of these and other persons. The main legal requirement to serve as trustee is that the trustee have the legal capacity to accept title (ownership) of the trust property. The trustee generally has specific duties and responsibilities for the trust property or has certain powers concerning the disposition of the trust property. Title to the trust property is held by the beneficiaries of the trust.

The *beneficiaries* are the persons who are to receive the benefits and advantages of the property transferred to the trust. If asset protection motives are important, consideration should be given to naming a class of potential beneficiaries instead of having the person who wishes to protect assets be the sole beneficiary. The asset protection benefits can be further enhanced if an independent trustee is given discretionary authority to allocate distributions among members of the class of beneficiaries. From an asset protection perspective, the rights of the beneficiary to control the trust and to reach trust corpus should be restricted. For example, if the power of the beneficiary to remove a trustee is excessively broad, the IRS or other claimants may argue that the powers of the trustee should be attributable to the beneficiary and the trust corpus reachable.

Every trust has a purpose, or *intent,* which motivates the grantor to set up the trust in the first place. Apart from the obvious requirement that the intent must be legal, there are few restrictions on the grantor's intent. The intent can relate to benefiting a particular beneficiary (self, spouse, child), providing for the management of certain assets (real estate, stock in a closely held corporation), achieving certain tax benefits (charitable remainder trust, marital trust), or a combination of all three. The intent of the trust should be detailed in the trust document, with as much external evidence as reasonable, and should clearly support that the purpose for the trust was something other than mere asset protection. This is important with respect to asset protection planning to combat a claim of fraudulent intent.

STEPS THAT CAN GENERALLY ENHANCE A TRUST'S ABILITY TO PROTECT ASSETS

Affirmative steps can be taken in forming any trust to increase the likelihood of the trust's being respected as a defense against claimants, including the steps we discuss next.

You Should Not Be the Only Trustee

If you are seeking protection through the use of the trust, you should at most be a cotrustee so that you cannot independently act to distribute assets to creditors. It would be preferable that the person seeking protection not be a trustee at all. Further, whatever decision is made as to your serving as a trustee, the provisions of the trust agreement should be carefully reviewed to be certain that the powers granted either trustee alone are not so expansive as to taint the potential asset protection benefits.

Example: Your parents understand your concern for asset protection planning and revise their wills, bequeathing your inheritance into a trust to last for your lifetime. You could serve as a cotrustee with another person or independent institution (i.e., not your spouse).

If you are setting up the trust to benefit yourself, you should preferably not serve as a trustee (see Chapters 17 and 18).

Ascertainable Standard

Limiting the standards under which the person seeking creditor protection can receive distributions is advisable. This is sometimes referred to as a *support trust* because trust assets may be used only to pay for support items for the beneficiary. These include health, maintenance, and support. This is a rather restrictive standard, which may enable the trustee to fend off claimants' efforts to force a distribution not covered by such a restrictive standard. Caution: A claimant may try to enforce distributions at that level from the trust and then attach them. Where independent trustees are used (e.g., a bank), the trust agreement can give broad discretion to the trustee to make, or withhold, distributions, which can be beneficial because the creditor should not be able to achieve more power than the beneficiary. For this to be effective, the trustee should have absolute and uncontrolled discretion to pay and apply trust income and principal. The power must be so absolute that the trustee can exclude the beneficiary seeking asset protection planning from distributions. This type of power is often combined with the spendthrift provision discussed later.

Sample Clause: The independent trustee of any trust created under this trust agreement is authorized, at any time, with respect to any beneficiary of any trust formed under this trust agreement then eligible to receive the net income from such trust, to pay to, or apply for, the benefit of such persons all, some, or none of such sums out of the principal of such trust as the trustee considers advisable.

Independent Trustee with Discretionary Distribution Powers

If you or your spouse will serve as a cotrustee, the trust agreement can expressly exclude you or your spouse from making distributions by restricting distribution decisions to only an independent trustee.

Sample Clause: Only the independent trustee shall: Participate in any decision to exercise, or not to exercise, any discretionary power over payments, distributions, applications, appointments, or accumulations of income or principal; Exercise discretion to allocate receipts or expenses between principal and income; Exercise any discretionary power with respect to any insurance policy held under this trust insurant the life of such individual or such individual's spouse; Hold property as a custodian for a minor or as donee of a power during minority, or selecting any such custodian or donee; Determine tax elections; Amend or otherwise affect any beneficiaries' withdrawal rights over additions to the trust estate of any trust; or Determine the selection of property to be allocated to a marital deduction trust, if any, created under a preceding section of this trust.

For these purposes, an independent trustee is defined as a trustee who has no legal obligation to support the beneficiaries affected by any decision in the preceding paragraph, and who cannot appoint trust income or principal to himself or herself, his or her creditors, his or her estate, creditors of his or her estate, or to or for the benefit of any child or other person to whom he or she owes a legal obligation of support and for which such appointment of income or principal would constitute a discharge of such legal obligation of support.

Sprinkle Power

Have the trust document name multiple beneficiaries in addition to the person seeking creditor protection. Combine this with a broad discretionary power over distributions vested in an independent trustee so that no determinable amount can be identified for attachment.

Sample Clause: The trustee shall hold the trust estate, in trust, to pay or apply to or for the benefit of any one or more of the following persons: grantor's spouse, as such person shall exist from time to time, and grantor's children Jane Doe, James Doe, and Jerold Doe ("children"), and grantor's friend Bob Buddy, as shall be living during grantor's life (collectively, grantor's spouse, and the children are called the "recipients"). The net income of the trust shall be applied in amounts, whether equal or unequal, as the trustee, in the exercise of absolute discretion, may consider desirable for the maintenance and support of any one of the recipients.

Limiting the Protected Person's Interest

Trigger mechanisms can be included in a trust that exclude a particular person as a beneficiary if certain types of claims are made against the trust or that particular beneficiary (trigger events). A trigger could be used as a prerequisite to distributions to the beneficiary seeking asset protection. For example, no distributions could be permitted unless and until the person in question is solvent or attains a specified age. The problems with this approach are considerable. The triggers are obviously included for creditor protection purposes and thus give the trust an appearance of being formed primarily or solely for asset protection purposes. If the person seeking creditor protection is removed as a beneficiary, he or she may not wish to establish the trust in the first place.

Indirect Benefits

Every trust intended to provide asset protection should afford the trustee the right to distribute money "for the benefit of the beneficiary," not only "to the beneficiary." If the beneficiary is being sued, a distribution of cash to the beneficiary may only serve to make that cash available to the beneficiary's creditor or malpractice claimant. Instead, if the trustee can pay medical, clothing, and other bills directly for the beneficiary to unrelated persons (i.e., make payments "for the benefit of" the beneficiary), the beneficiary's claimants should not be able to access those funds.

Trustee Can Purchase Assets and Make Their Use Available to the Beneficiary

Instead of making a distribution to the beneficiary to buy a personal use asset (e.g., boat, airplane, art, or a house), the trustee should be authorized to purchase the house in the trust. The trust can then own the house, boat, or other asset and let the beneficiary use that asset. The trust document should give the trustee the authority to pay all reasonable expenses associated with this personal use asset, permit the beneficiary to use it rent free, and absolve the trustee of any responsibility in the event that the personal use asset doesn't prove to be a good investment.

Limit or Exclude Powers of Appointment in Beneficiaries

A *power of appointment* is a legal right given to a beneficiary to designate, for example, to whom and how trust assets should be distributed on the beneficiary's death.

Example: Jane Smith set up a trust for her physician son, Marcus. Marcus is concerned about malpractice risks. If he is sued, he wants his entire inheritance held in trust for his life. Jane obliged, seeking to protect her son. However, not knowing how his family situation will develop, Jane asked her lawyer to give Marcus the unlimited power to designate in his will where the trust assets will be distributed on his death. This right is called a *general power of appointment*.

A general power of appointment is illustrated by the sample trust provision wording in the following example.

Sample Trust Provision: Upon the death of such beneficiary, the trustee shall transfer the principal of the trust to such persons other than child, but including his estate, his creditors, and the creditors of his estate, to such extent, in such amounts or proportions, and in such lawful interests or estates, whether absolute or in trust, as such child may by his last will and testament appoint by a specific reference to this power.

The effect of a general power of appointment is to make the assets in the trust reachable by the beneficiary's creditors. The best approach is not to include any power of appointment. If one is included, a limited power of appointment, which expressly precludes beneficiaries from giving trust assets to themselves, their creditors, their estates, or creditors of their estates, is recommended.

Spendthrift Provision

Include a spendthrift provision in the trust agreement. This prevents any beneficiary from assigning the trust assets to creditors. This protection, as explained in the following discussion, is not absolute.

Sample Clause: Except as may be otherwise provided in this trust agreement, no transfer disposition, charge, or encumbrance on the income or principal of any trust created under this trust agreement, by any beneficiary by way of anticipation shall be valid or in any way binding upon the trustee. The right of any beneficiary to any payment of income or principal is subject to any charge or deduction which the trustee makes against it under the authority granted to them by any statute, law, or by any provision of this trust agreement. No beneficiary shall have the right to transfer, dispose of, assign, or encumber such income or principal until the assets shall be paid to that beneficiary by the trustee. No income or principal shall be liable to any claim of any creditor of any such beneficiary.

Spendthrift laws differ from state to state. This is a factor you should discuss with your attorney in deciding which state laws should govern your trust. Whatever law applies, once the assets are distributed to the beneficiary, the spendthrift protection is lost. Therefore, the longer the term of the trust and the more discretion the trustee is given on making distributions, the safer trust assets will be.

Application of Favorable Law

Review with your attorney which states or countries (Chapters 17 and 18) have the laws most supportive of your objectives.

LIMITATIONS ON ANY TRUST PROTECTION ASSETS

There are a number of limitations on the ability of almost any trust to provide protection from claimants. These limitations include, but are not limited to, the following.

The Provision of Necessities

Where necessities are provided to a beneficiary, it may be possible for the provider to obtain reimbursement from a trust for the benefit of that beneficiary.

Example: A minor child is the sole beneficiary of a spendthrift trust, which has an independent trustee with sole discretion over distributions. The minor contracts with a third party for the provision of necessary medical services. The services are provided in good faith. The minor has no means of paying for the services. The trust can probably be pierced and the trustee required to pay for the medical services.

Internal Revenue Service Claims

If monies are due the Internal Revenue Service (IRS), expect any trust to be challenged for payment. The IRS is more likely than other creditors to be able to pierce the trust for outstanding balances.

Fraudulent Conveyance

If the initial transfer of assets to the trust was a fraudulent conveyance or is deemed to be constructively fraudulent, the transfer could be set aside and any purported benefits lost.

Alimony

Depending on the facts and circumstances and the jurisdiction involved, claims for alimony and child support may be successful in piercing a trust, which general creditors may be unable to.

Using Irrevocable Trusts to Insulate Assets

The transfer of nonrisk property or assets to an irrevocable trust may insulate those assets from the reach of your creditors. If you remain the primary beneficiary of such trusts, it is unlikely that sufficient insulation of the trust assets from creditors can be achieved. Most courts tend to look askance at self-funded trusts where grantors seek to protect their own assets from their claimants by transferring them to a trust to benefit themselves. The exceptions to this are the domestic and foreign asset protection trusts (see Chapters 17 and 18). Alternatively, to the extent that assets are transferred to a trust to benefit persons other than you, such as your spouse or children or perhaps other family members, the risks of a self-funded trust should not be an issue. While this is not a guarantee against a challenge or attack on trust assets, it appears that this approach will afford a greater measure of protection, especially when the assets are transferred to the trust as part of an overall estate plan (i.e., for reasons other than protection from creditors) and prior to the cause of action. For example, funds could be transferred to an irrevocable trust for the benefit of your spouse and the funds used to purchase a permanent insurance policy on your life. The investments of all trust assets in insurance may afford an additional barrier to a creditor's challenge. In later years, assuming the stability of your marriage, your trustee could borrow funds from the insurance policy and make distributions to your spouse as a beneficiary, and your spouse could in turn use them to meet living expenses.

Where the trust is revocable, such as the typical inter vivos or living revocable trust, or if you retain excessive rights or powers over the trust, the asset protection benefits will not be realized.

Note: See Shenkman, Weiner, and Taback, *Starting a Limited Liability Company* (2nd ed.), John Wiley & Sons, Inc. 2003 for more information.

SUMMARY

Trusts are a key component of your lawsuit protection planning. Trusts can be used to own and invest assets for you and other family members while insulating assets from claimants. Trusts can own interests in family partnerships, LLCs, and, in many cases, even S corporations. This can provide a double layer of protection for key assets. The first layer is the entity itself; the second layer is the trust. This chapter reviewed some of the rules for using trusts to achieve these goals.

15 RULES FOR USING TRUSTS TO PROTECT AGAINST DIVORCE

TRUSTS AND DIVORCE PROTECTION

Trusts frequently have important matrimonial implications. With a 50 percent divorce rate and a higher rate for second and later marriages, a careful understanding of the matrimonial implications to trusts is essential for protecting assets for you and your heirs. Protecting against future matrimonial actions, facilitating the conclusion of acrimonious divorces, and planning for remarriage can all be facilitated by proper trust planning. Practical implementation and operation of the trusts before, during, and after a divorce present additional issues. This matrimonial planning must also be coordinated with overall asset protection planning.

Example: Dr. Surgeon is very concerned about malpractice. His colleagues tell him to put everything he has into his wife's name. However, he is not so confident that his marriage will last. He also worries that because of his wife's lack of responsibility, she is a likely candidate for a lawsuit or other problem. Any assets Dr. Surgeon transfers that were earned during the marriage are marital property over which his wife may have equal claim. He must endeavor to protect assets from malpractice claimants while not exacerbating his problems in the event that he divorces.

This chapter provides a survey of the many planning considerations affecting trusts and what can be accomplished by trusts through each phase of you (or your heir's) marital status (premarriage, during marriage, divorce). In addition, it discusses how this planning affects, and can be coordinated with, your lawsuit protection planning.

PREMARRIAGE TRUST PLANNING

You can create trusts to safeguard assets given to, or to be bequeathed to, your child or other heirs from their possible divorce. You can also create trusts for yourself to safeguard separate assets before you marry. A number of issues must be dealt with in this type of planning.

Common Scenarios

Unknown Future Spouse. Many parents simply exclude any "in-law" from the list of potential beneficiaries of an irrevocable trust. This simplistic approach is not always ideal, and a more flexible approach can be used so that a possible future spouse can be benefited if future circumstances warrant. Several approaches can be used.

In lieu of naming a spouse (or even the relationship *spouse* to include a future spouse), a trust can include a broad distribution clause for the primary beneficiary, such as the child (e.g., a comfort and welfare standard), which can provide the ability for that named beneficiary to indirectly provide for a future spouse through distributions he or she receives. This approach of using a broad distribution standard, however, might be used in divorce proceedings by the ex-spouse to argue that the trust assets and/or income are fully available to meet alimony, child support, or equitable distribution claims. This argument might be especially cogent if there has been a history of regular distributions under that broad standard from the trust to your child.

Another approach is to include a *floating spouse clause,* which could provide that any person legally married to a specified beneficiary (e.g., your child) would be a permitted beneficiary until the execution of a legally binding separation agreement or divorce. A more restrictive distribution standard (e.g., to maintain a specified standard of living) might be used in this approach because the spouse is named and can thus be benefited directly. A matrimonial court would likely honor such a clause, especially one created before the marriage by someone other than the child getting divorced. Although this may not make the trust impervious to an ex-spouse to the extent that a court might consider gift/inherited trust assets in structuring a settlement, it might fare better than the approach in the preceding paragraph of using a broad distribution provision.

A third alternative is to name an independent quasi-fiduciary (someone with powers like a trustee, but not quite), such as a distribution committee or trust protector, and vest in such person the authority to add or delete a beneficiary's future spouse as a beneficiary. This approach must be structured in a manner that avoids inadvertent inclusion of the trust assets in your estate or the estate of the beneficiary. This protection is necessary to ensure that other asset protection goals are not violated.

Sign a Prenuptial Agreement or Lose Beneficiary Status.   Some parents endeavoring to ensure that an heir execute a prenuptial agreement before marriage have incorporated a "do it or else" provision into trusts, mandating that if a prenuptial agreement is not signed, the beneficiary will lose the status as a distributee under the trust (no prenuptial, no money) or face a more restrictive standard for receiving distributions (e.g., a limited standard of living rather than a broad comfort standard). This type of clause creates a host of issues, not the least of which is often an angry or resentful heir. From a public policy standpoint, if the heir is not a minor child (whom you have an obligation to support), this type of provision should be enforceable. However, it can be impossible to anticipate the scope of a provision sufficient to accomplish your objectives years in advance of the actual marriage. Must the trust mandate the minimum terms of the prenuptial agreement? If not, merely mandating a prenuptial agreement may be a hollow demand easily met by the heir, with an agreement lacking any significant substance. A matrimonial court should not have issue with such a clause if created in a third-party trust before marriage.

Third-Party Irrevocable Trusts Established before Marriage

It is common for parents and others to establish irrevocable trusts before a beneficiary's marriage. The matrimonial consequences of these trusts should not differ from similar third-party irrevocable trusts established during the marriage if the gifts or bequests are made solely to the grantor/testator's heir and not the heir's spouse.

Common trusts include a child or grandchild's trust established under a will or *inter vivos,* an insurance trust, a family dynasty trust, and so on. Many factors may influence the later matrimonial consequences of these trusts, which planners should consider.

If a trust mandates the payment of income or a total return distribution on an annual or other periodic basis, the history of these regular payments is likely to be viewed as a more certain cash flow in a matrimonial negotiation or contest than would a purely discretionary distribution standard.

A key factor to consider is the time that distributions are made from such a trust. If the trust mandates corpus distribution when the beneficiary attains a certain age, those distributed funds could be distributed to the married heir before divorce. While separate identification of those assets may preserve their separate property status, the risk of commingling and destroying that favored status is magnified. Further, if the property leaves the protected trust envelope, the spouse might become an active participant in the investment, management, or operation of those assets, thus transmuting them (depending on state law) into marital property. Finally, even if the separate property status is maintained, the distribution limitations of the trust vehicle are gone, and a matrimonial court would naturally view them as more available than it would view trust assets subject to restrictions.

If the heir is a sole beneficiary of a trust, this is another negative factor from a matrimonial protective perspective in contrast to a trust with several beneficiaries and a sprinkle power afforded to the trustee. Finally, even if the beneficiary can be the sole beneficiary and a trustee under state law (limited to an ascertainable standard of distribution), this situation would not be viewed favorably by a matrimonial court as contrasted with a similar trust with an independent trustee or one with an independent cotrustee and a restriction on the ability of the named beneficiary/trustee/divorcing heir to prevent making distributions for himself or herself or to discharge the legal obligation of support. These planning recommendations all serve to make the same trust assets more difficult to reach for the beneficiary's claimants.

Self-Settled Trusts

Before marriage, you might self-fund a trust, such as a revocable living trust or a domestic asset protection trust. The only difference in matrimonial consequences to such a trust funded before marriage, as compared to one funded during the marriage, is that there would be no issue of the possible use of marital assets in the funding. Thus, this approach is an affirmative planning opportunity if you are contemplating marriage. Segregate and safeguard the separate asset nature of premarital property.

When drafting such a trust instrument, language should be added clarifying that the trust has been funded solely with gift, inheritance, or premarital assets; this fact should ideally be acknowledged in a prenuptial agreement by specific reference to the trust. Exercise caution in avoiding later gifts to such a trust if they are not clearly identifiable as gift, inheritance, or separate assets.

TRUSTS ESTABLISHED DURING THE MARRIAGE

When trusts are established for an intact family, a number of issues might arise that can have later consequences if the marriage falters. If the trust is funded with marital assets, the use of a trust won't change this characterization, although the legal impediments created by the trust may create more complexity and difficulty in how the matrimonial court will deal with this. This and other issues need to be addressed when the trust is planned and formed and later should be interpreted and addressed if divorce occurs. A survey of some of those issues follows.

General Issues

Ex-Spousal Removal Clauses.   Some trusts are drafted with a provision stating that if there is a divorce, the spouse who is a cotrustee and/or beneficiary loses that status. These clauses, if included in a trust established by a third party, should be respected by a matrimonial court. If such a clause were included in a trust established by the married couple, the spouse to be removed might challenge the clause. However, it is unclear whether a matrimonial court could have any control over the enforceability of such a clause.

Use Modification Provisions in Existing Trust to Meet Divorce Requirements.   When drafting trusts, it is becoming increasingly common to incorporate provisions to provide drafting flexibility to address the uncertainty about the future of the estate tax, the increasing fractionalization of family units, and other risks. The impact of these provisions needs to be addressed when drafting trusts that might be affected by a future divorce and in negotiating property settlements in a future divorce.

If the trust provides for discretion in the trustee (or a quasi-fiduciary such as a trust protector) to modify provisions of a trust, these may be used to modify the trust to be more suitable for the postdivorce family needs, to meet provisions of a divorce agreement, and to minimize postdivorce friction. For example, if the succession of trustees provides for family members from each ex-spouse's family to serve jointly, followed by an institutional trustee, perhaps the individual family members could resign, leaving as a neutral trustee the independent institution. If there is merely one trustee who is objectionable to the spousal beneficiary, that trustee might be requested to resign in exchange for forgoing other property settlement provisions in the negotiations. It may be feasible under the applicable state's principal and income act to convert an income-only trust into a total return trust, which makes an annuity payment based on a specified percentage of principal. This approach might provide greater certainty to the ex-spouse payee and eliminate discretion that the trustees might have over investments that could be used to reduce distributions to the ex-spouse payee/beneficiary.

From an asset protection standpoint, any powers to modify or otherwise affect the trust, which is held by the beneficiary seeking to keep assets protected, are a potential detriment. The more power held by a beneficiary, the more likely a claimant is to reach the assets. Therefore, for both matrimonial and lawsuit protection purposes, effort should be made to have amendment powers held by independent persons.

Terminate Irrevocable Trust.   You might want the flexibility of including clauses that provide some options for terminating what is otherwise an irrevocable trust. This might be accomplished by providing a trust protector the authority to terminate a trust without restriction or only in specified circumstances (such as a divorce nullifying the intent of the trust). A trustee might be given the power to make unlimited principal distributions, thus effectively terminating a trust, or perhaps an express power to terminate in the event that the trust is uneconomical to operate, and so on. In the event of a later divorce, the opposing spouse may seize on these provisions to encourage a matrimonial court to order the termination of the trust or to treat trust assets as fully reachable by the beneficiary/payor ex-spouse.

Trusts Established during the Marriage by the Married Couple

A host of trusts may be established by a married couple for a myriad of reasons. The following sections present an overview of a number of the trusts and some common situations these trusts can present in a later matrimonial case. Many of these trusts are discussed in Chapter 16.

Insurance Trusts.   Insurance trusts are commonly established by married couples. These sometimes take the form of a trust established by the wife, holding insurance on her life, for the benefit of the husband, and vice versa. A survivorship insurance trust holding survivorship or second-to-die insurance on both spouses' lives is also common. Because divorce agreements commonly include insurance requirements, existing trusts and coverage should be reviewed to determine if they are feasible to use or adapt for these purposes. Doing so often has considerable economic benefits through cheaper premiums when the insurance has been in force for many years (when the insured was younger and perhaps healthier). In such instances, provisions of the trust should be reviewed and perhaps modified through available trust instrument flexibility, as described previously. If the existing insurance is cancelled, the cash value, if any, may be distributed to the current income beneficiaries under the terms of the trust agreement, or it may be held for the benefit of children beneficiaries under the existing trust agreement. This distribution could defeat any asset protection benefits the trust may have afforded.

Qualified Personal Residence Trusts

THRESHOLD QPRT ISSUES.   Qualified personal residence trusts (QPRTs) are often used by wealthy, intact families to leverage a gift of a valuable primary residence or vacation home to the children of the marriage and to provide a measure of protection for their residence from creditors. Divorce is rarely considered in these trusts. In the event of divorce, several issues arise. The threshold issues are whether, economically, the divorced family can or should retain the home and to determine how the QPRT was structured. The most common method is for the husband and wife to each transfer a tenant-in-common interest in the residence into their own respective QPRT. In other instances, because of malpractice or similar concerns, the source of funds to purchase the home (e.g., one family), or a significant difference in the age of the spouses, the house may be transferred from one spouse alone into a single QPRT. Because of different ages or health conditions, the husband and wife often have QPRTs for different terms.

EACH SPOUSE'S QPRT PURCHASES NEW HOME.   If two QPRTs exist, one for each ex-spouse, they could sell the home pursuant to terms set forth in the divorce agreement, exclude gain to the extent feasible, and then use the proceeds in their respective QPRTs toward the purchase of new separate residences. This can be an effective method of continuing the estate tax and asset protection benefits of the QPRT as initially planned, but facilitating each ex-spouse in securing his or her independent residence.

PROCEEDS OF HOME SALE LESS THAN COST OF NEW HOME PURCHASED.   What if the net proceeds to each QPRT are insufficient to purchase the new home? Each spouse could own part of his or her respective new residence as a tenant-in-common with his or her QPRT. Another alternative would be for that ex-spouse to contribute additional funds to his or her QPRT, making a new gift tax calculation for the additional transfer. The QPRT would then use the combination of these new funds and the proceeds from the sale of the interest in the former marital residence to purchase a new home for that ex-spouse.

PROCEEDS OF HOME SALE EXCEED COST OF NEW HOME PURCHASED.   Another scenario is for the proceeds of the sale of the former marital residence (or the one-half tenants-in-common interest in it) to exceed the amount reinvested due to the detrimental financial impact that the divorce proceedings have on the respective ex-spouse. In fact, the ex-spouse may determine that it is not advisable to repurchase a new residence, instead renting to conserve cash. In such an instance, the unreinvested sales proceeds would be retained in the QPRT. These funds would be invested and a periodic annuity paid to the ex-spouse beneficiary for the remainder of the QPRT term under the qualified annuity trust (QAT) provisions of the QPRT document. When both ex-spouses are equal beneficiaries of the respective trusts, each having previously owned a one-half interest in the marital residence, each ex-spouse would have an annuity payment for the remaining term of the trust, which should be factored into the calculations of alimony and support.

Child's Trust.   Intact families commonly establish trusts to benefit children and grandchildren. These trusts typically are intended (whether expressly stated or not) to provide for educational benefits for the children. In the event of a later divorce, these trusts can be used to meet education and perhaps other financial needs of the children (depending on the trust agreement, the terms of the divorce agreement, and the financial needs of the postdivorce family). When negotiating the terms of such arrangements, the provisions of the trust must be analyzed: Are distributions mandatory? discretionary? by whom and to what extent? Who are the beneficiaries—solely the children of the marriage or a "pot" trust including other beneficiaries? These terms may be argued by either ex-spouse as supporting or detracting from the right to count these funds in the settlement or to mandate their use.

Inter Vivos *QTIP*.   If you have substantially greater assets or liability exposure than your spouse, you can transfer assets to him or her to safeguard them. However, as previous discussions have made clear, this is not a prudent step. Your spouse might be sued, you could get divorced, or other problems could arise. The better answer is to set up a trust for your spouse. To avoid any gift tax consequence, this trust is set up to qualify for the marital deduction trust, an *inter vivos* QTIP trust. In the event of a later divorce, a number of options may be considered. If feasible under the QTIP trust instrument, some or all of the corpus may be distributed to the spouse/beneficiary as part of a property settlement negotiation. More likely, however, the QTIP trust will be continued and treated as a cash flow to the ex-spouse/beneficiary and factored into the determination of alimony and perhaps even the property settlement. In such instances, the ex-spouse/beneficiary may seek permitted modifications of the trust instrument (resignation of an unfavorable trustee, conversion into a total return trust, etc.) to provide comfort in exchange for other negotiated provisions in the divorce agreement. If your ex-spouse, who is the beneficiary of the QTIP, has lawsuit worries, this plan remains ideal because the assets remain protected.

The matrimonial courts will likely consider the anticipated mandatory income distributions from a QTIP as income available to the spouse/beneficiary for purposes of meeting living expenses and alimony. The investment flexibility, asset composition, and other provisions of the QTIP trust agreement and its historic as well as possible future operation should be carefully evaluated by counsel for the ex-spouse beneficiary to identify discretion that could be used to adversely impact distributions. For example, if historically, income has been distributed monthly but the QTIP trust agreement permits annual or more frequent distributions, can the trustee's discretion be controlled to prevent the trustee from delaying distributions to once per annum postdivorce as a punitive measure?

Self-Funded Trusts Established during the Marriage by One Spouse

It is not uncommon for one spouse to establish a trust for himself or herself during the marriage. This might be done for a host of reasons by one or even both spouses.

Revocable Living Trusts.   Revocable living trusts are frequently established by both spouses (in some jurisdictions, as a single trust) to facilitate avoidance of probate, management of assets in the event of disability, and other objectives. Because you have the unfettered right to revoke or modify such a trust, there should be no particular impact of such a trust on your future divorce. There are, however, several points to consider. If you have inherited assets or received gifts of assets that are separate property, a common technique is to sequester these assets in a revocable living trust for identification purposes to preserve the separate property character. While the trust itself has no effect on the initial characterization of the assets under state law as immune separate assets, it can be an effective vehicle to avoid commingling and to avoid purported management participation by your ex-spouse. This use can be effective for this limited purpose and would impact any subsequent divorce accordingly.

Self-Funded Domestic Asset Protection Trust.   The use of domestic asset protection trusts is becoming increasingly common among those with more moderate wealth, especially when the transferors are concerned about asset protection. In such instances, if the transfer is made of marital assets to a domestic asset protection trust, consideration of how a matrimonial court would view these transfers during a later divorce is critical. If both spouses are beneficiaries, the issues discussed previously as to how the trust can be modified or operated in the future must be addressed. If the domestic asset protection trust is structured with an institutional trustee or distribution committee provision, perhaps the divorce agreement can include an instruction letter to the trustee or distribution committee concerning future distributions. While unlikely to be legally binding on an independent trustee governed by a previously established irrevocable trust agreement, such a trustee is likely to give considerable weight to such a directive (especially as the divorce agreement will be approved by the court when the divorce is finalized) in making any future distribution decisions. If only one spouse is a beneficiary, perhaps such a distribution instruction could be given addressing distributions to children of the marriage. However, an irrevocable transfer to a domestic asset protection trust, occurring before any divorce proceeding, may be beyond the reach or influence of a matrimonial court, especially one located in another jurisdiction from that in which the trust is established. In such situations, however, the nonbeneficiary ex-spouse may prevail on the court to deem the beneficiary ex-spouse to receive certain distributions from the trust in determining any litigated property settlement.

Trusts Established by Third Parties during the Marriage

The considerations affecting trusts established by third parties (e.g., a parent of a divorcing party) during the marriage should not differ in any material manner from those established before the marriage by third parties. The only difference may be that the donors may have had actual experience with the intended donee's spouse and might thus be more precise in how that spouse should (or often, should not) be treated in the trust.

Specific Types of Trusts Used to Facilitate the Divorce

Practically any type of trust can be used in the context of structuring a matrimonial settlement. If you or your ex-spouse is concerned about asset protection, the use of trusts to secure as many aspects of the postdivorced family wealth is important for everyone. If you lose your remaining assets to a malpractice claimant, it won't give your ex-spouse any comfort that he or she will receive the agreed-on alimony and child support payments. The following discussion highlights a few of the more common trusts and their application.

Alimony Trusts. A trust can be used to fund alimony payments to minimize the interaction of the ex-spouses and to provide the payee/ex-spouse greater certainty regarding receipt of alimony payments. Assets held in such a trust may be afforded some level of protection from claimants, thus benefiting both the payor and the payee spouse. From an economic perspective, an alimony trust can be structured with distributions to be made to the ex-spouse for life (or whatever other termination provisions are included in the divorce agreement and hence the trust), and on death the trust assets are distributed to the children. The trust eliminates the payee/ex-spouse's worry over receiving alimony payments when due.

Insurance Trusts. Insurance is a key financial component of most divorce settlements. Insurance coverage may be mandated for a particular time period (e.g., as long as alimony is paid). How the divorce agreement insurance mandates are funded is a critical planning issue. The decisions have important tax and asset protection issues as well. What type of insurance should be used? Who should own the coverage? What can be done in the future if the obligations change?

Depending on state law, the occurrence of a divorce may not affect the beneficiary designation on an insurance policy; therefore, beneficiary designations should be updated. If the policy is in a qualified retirement plan, federal law would preempt state law and the former spouse's designation may be revoked.

The payment of a life insurance premium can be deducted as alimony by the payor ex-spouse if the beneficiary/ex-spouse owns the policy. Ownership by a trust does not meet this requirement.

The type of insurance policy is often ignored in the divorce agreement and is of considerable importance to protecting the economic results, and it also has important significance to the asset protection and trust planning ultimately used. If lifetime alimony is awarded, the insured/payor spouse may determine that a whole life or variable policy may be preferable to a term policy to fund the obligation. Term insurance is not available in some states beyond a specified age. If the life insurance must be maintained indefinitely unless alimony ceases per the divorce agreement, a permanent insurance policy is, therefore, necessary to meet the obligations.

Making the ex-spouse/beneficiary the owner of a valuable permanent policy (in contrast to a term policy) is generally unacceptable to the insured/payor spouse because of the control that ownership may afford. The better approach is to structure an irrevocable life insurance trust (ILIT) to own the policy. Using an ILIT in such a context generally requires drafting three sequences of distribution provisions: (1) tracking the divorce agreement requirements and termination dates, (2) addressing insurance coverage above the divorce agreement requirements, and (3) distribution provisions following the reduction/termination of the divorce agreement requirements.

The insurance trust can provide that the death benefit required in the divorce agreement be paid to the ex-spouse, but any coverage above such amount can be allocated as the insured/grantor desires (e.g., to the children, a new spouse). Thus, the insurance proceeds can be excluded from the insured's estate but still directed to the desired beneficiary in the event that a contingency in the divorce agreement occurs.

The use of an ILIT can benefit the beneficiary ex-spouse if appropriate measures are taken. For example, the trustee could be obligated to notify the beneficiary ex-spouse (or the attorney for the ex-spouse) if a premium is not paid or a policy lapse notice is received. The use of an independent trustee can also make a person other than a vindictive ex-spouse responsible for any elections under the policy.

Voting Trust for Business Stock.   A voting trust is a legal arrangement in the form of a trust through which shareholders have their stock in a closely held company voted by a designated person who is the trustee of the voting trust. A voting trust agreement provides the trustee an irrevocable right to vote stock in the particular corporation for a designated period of time. The trust does not grant the trustee the right to sell the stock or receive the dividends paid on the stock. Depending on state law, it may even be illegal for the trust to provide for these rights.

A voting trust can be an effective tool for structuring a divorce settlement if a significant marital asset is stock in a closely held business. The spouse who is active in the business and other shareholders will generally insist that the uninvolved ex-spouse not be involved in business matters and, in particular, not have any right to vote. Voting trusts are an excellent method to permit the ex-spouse who is active in a business to continue to control the business, while the other ex-spouse can protect his or her interest in the divorce agreement by actually owning the stock in the business.

Example: Ex-wife owns 70 percent of a real estate brokerage business. Ex-husband is awarded 25 percent of the value of the business as part of the equitable distribution divorce settlement negotiations. If ex-wife transferred 25 percent of the total shares to the ex-husband, she would lose control over the corporation, dropping to a 45 percent interest. Worse yet, an angry ex-husband might vote his shares to the detriment of the ex-wife. One solution is to give the ex-husband the 25 percent of the stock but require that his shares be transferred to a voting trust controlled by the ex-wife. The ex-wife would retain voting control, while the ex-husband would receive the economic interests necessary to resolve the divorce. To fully protect the ex-husband's interests, however, he should also negotiate an agreement that has reasonable restrictions on how much the ex-wife and other shareholders can withdraw as salary or benefits.

In one case, a court refused to permit an ex-spouse to revoke a voting trust agreement. The court reasoned that because the use of the voting trust arrangement for a closely held business was bargained for at arm's length and was an integral part of the divorce settlement agreement, the ex-spouse should not be able to change it.

The responsibilities, duties, powers, and rights of the trustee must be specified in the trust agreement. These obviously must consider the terms of the divorce agreement and the restrictions on the nonactive shareholder. If the trustee is to be compensated, the exact arrangements should be spelled out in the agreement. This depends in significant part on whether a neutral person who is not involved with the business will be serving as trustee. The agreement should clarify the rights of the nonactive spouse receiving stock held in the voting trust.

Using Children's Trusts in Divorce.   Providing for college and other education for the children after a divorce is a common problem. Either or both of the ex-spouses may, depending on their respective financial situations, contribute to the future college costs. The problem this approach creates is that the agreement is merely a promise to pay at some future date—an issue of enforcing a reticent ex-spouse to contribute his or her share years after the divorce was finalized. The better approach, when feasible, is the use of a funded education trust formed pursuant to the terms embodied in the divorce agreement. This avoids later fights to secure the promised payments. If structured with sufficient specificity and care, it can minimize or even avoid the many other arguments, such as how and when payments should be made, which educational expenses should be covered, and so on. If such a trust is set up, matrimonial counsel should strive to include provisions in the divorce agreement to address the key terms of such a trust. Use of trusts protects the assets from claimants and the children's own divorces.

Provisions to Consider.   What terms should be included in the divorce agreement and/or actual trust? The type of education should be specified. The generic specification of "college" or "post-high school" is common. However, what if the child does not pursue a college degree and instead seeks training in a technical school or in the arts? If this is not addressed, distributions from the trust may be prohibited.

Should the contributions by each of the ex-spouses to the trust be mandated as to form; for example, in cash, securities, or other property? If cash or property other than marketable securities is used to fund the trust, complications of valuation may arise. It is generally preferable to mandate contributions of solely marketable securities or cash. Tax basis issues may be relevant. If each ex-spouse commits to contribute $100,000 and one ex-spouse contributes cash and the other zero-basis stock, the income tax costs of the latter spouse are being passed off on the trust and the beneficiaries.

How should the costs of drafting, operating, and investing trust assets be handled? Equal sharing of the fees is often appropriate to encourage both ex-spouses to cooperate and be involved. However, what if one ex-spouse creates substantial difficulties with knowledge that the other ex-spouse must bear half the cost? Perhaps each spouse should bear half of the cost of drafting the document while paying for any other costs individually.

It is essential to provide how funds remaining after the completion of college should be distributed. These provisions should be drafted with sufficient flexibility to ensure that if the child does not attend college, the funds are used appropriately. What if the child attends college only after a delay to work? What about postgraduate studies? Apart from these more obvious issues, it is advisable to specify the intent of the parties as to whether the trustee should endeavor to ensure that funds remain after college. Since the variations of the new uniform Prudent Investor Act have been passed in most states, a statement as to whether funds should remain after college payments, to what extent, and for what purpose is essential to the trustee's determining the time horizon for investments.

Trust Income Taxation; Kiddie Tax May Affect Distributions. Trust income is taxed in a manner similar to individuals but at a compressed rate. Often, trust drafters permit distributions that draw out taxable income to a beneficiary. Once distributed, the child/beneficiary's income tax would be affected. From an income tax perspective, there can be an advantage of having some amount of investment assets taxed directly to the child. Even with the Kiddie Tax (which results in income of a child under age 14 being taxed generally at the highest taxed parent's rate), a portion of income can be taxed at lower rates than had the income been retained in the trust. Many parents attempt to secure this benefit by distributing some funds in a custodial account (Uniform Gift to Minor Act [UGMA] or Uniform Transfer to Minor Act [UTMA]).

In the divorce context, this creates additional concerns because management of the custodial accounts must then be addressed.

If trust income is used to pay college expenses of your children and if your state law makes such payments part of the parent's support obligation, the trust income will be taxed to you as a parent. This income tax cost should be considered in the divorce agreement when drafting terms for a child's trust, whether an existing trust or one drafted solely for purposes of the divorce.

SUMMARY

Trusts are complex and can address a wide range of marital and divorce situations. This planning can and should be coordinated with lawsuit protection planning for both you and your ex-spouse. Careful trust planning can help facilitate the conclusion of the divorce, as well as coordinate with tax, asset protection, and other planning.

16 GENERAL RULES FOR USING DOMESTIC TRUSTS TO PROTECT AGAINST LAWSUITS

WHAT ARE DOMESTIC TRUSTS?

This chapter explains the rules for using many different types of domestic trusts. These trusts are formed under the laws of a particular state, as contrasted with the laws of a foreign country. The only trust excluded is the domestic asset protection or self-settled trust, which is discussed in Chapter 17. For background on trusts and some of the key provisions to consider in working with your advisors in preparing trusts for asset protection, see the discussions in Chapter 14. For divorce protection implications of domestic trusts, see Chapter 15.

DIFFERENT TYPES OF TRUSTS THAT CAN BE USED FOR ASSET PROTECTION PLANNING BENEFITS

Trusts are powerful planning tools for protecting assets and accomplishing a range of other important personal, tax, financial, and estate planning objectives. The use of trusts to protect assets is a legitimate and appropriate endeavor, to be distinguished from many of the fraudulent trusts that have been sold to unsuspecting consumers, usually with a laundry list of too-good-to-be-true tax and other promises. The simplest way to protect yourself is to use well-recommended professionals who are independent of each other: accountant, attorney, financial planner, and so on.

Note: Protect yourself. Before completing any trust transaction, check the IRS Web site. The IRS criminal investigation division Web site highlights abusive trusts.

Many Types of Trusts Can Be Used in Asset Protection Planning

Trusts can be as varied as the people who set them up and the goals and objectives they are established to achieve. The selection of the appropriate trusts must begin with a thorough and objective analysis of personal, lawsuit protection, financial, estate planning, business, and other goals. This type of analysis and documentation of the reasons are essential when asset protection is a goal. A comprehensive example illustrates the selection of the appropriate trusts.

Example: Joe and Dr. Ruth are married. Their net worth is approximately $3.4 million (exclusive of life insurance). Dr. Ruth is a physician, and Joe is an attorney. They are both concerned about limiting exposure to malpractice claims. In addition, their estate planner recommends that they use bypass trusts so that each of their estates can benefit from the once-in-a-lifetime $1 million exclusion (scheduled to increase). Because of their desire to minimize tax and uncertainty over the amount that can be given tax free and because of their need for all inherited assets to be in trust, each will bequeaths all assets to a marital trust (QTIP) for the surviving spouse. Each will specifically directs the executor to decide how much of the trust assets qualify for a marital deduction and how much should be sheltered by the applicable exclusion amount that can be given away estate-tax free. They've tried to give their executor the benefit of hindsight to make an optimal decision. Because most of their nonpension assets are held in a family limited partnership (FLP), the trust in either of their estates will have only a noncontrolling interest in the entity, not actual assets outright. This makes the value or interest of both the estate and the surviving spouse more uncertain. A spendthrift provision is also included in each QTIP. Following the second-to-die spouse's death, the assets from the QTIP trust are distributed to the couple's children in lifetime trusts to afford the children similar protection. Thus, all assets received by the surviving spouse are in trust. Because of similar concerns for their children, as well as concerns over the potential for divorce, all funds to their children are held in trust. With this arrangement, there won't be any federal estate tax due on the first spouse's death. To protect his family,

Joe has a $1 million whole life insurance policy held in an irrevocable trust. If there is an estate tax due, after consideration of the exclusions available to each estate and the discounts created by the family limited partnership, the insurance will address it.

The insurance and the trust also safeguard the cash value. If Joe or Dr. Ruth owns this policy, it will create a tax cost on the death of the latter of Dr. Ruth or Joe. In addition, the proceeds collected on Joe's death could then be subject to the claims of Dr. Ruth's malpractice claimants or other creditors. The solution is to have an irrevocable life insurance trust own the policy. Because Dr. Ruth and Joe's children are minors, they have decided to form presently trusts for their children. These trusts name a succession of close and trusted friends to handle the financial affairs of their children. Neither Joe nor Dr. Ruth has opted to be trustees to minimize any challenges concerning their control over the trusts. Dr. Ruth and Joe have decided to fund trusts for their children now (rather than only under their wills) to protect annual exclusion gifts made to the trusts. A separate trust will be formed for each child. These trusts each receive gifts of family limited partnership interests, which reduce Joe's and Dr. Ruth's ownership to less than 50 percent each, so neither controls the FLP.

Dr. Ruth owns 65 percent of the stock of a corporation, which operates a manufacturing business. The corporation is organized as an S corporation. As their children and estate grow, Dr. Ruth wishes to begin giving gifts of the stock to the children to remove the value from her estate. However, she wishes to retain some protection and control over the children's use of the stock. Dr. Ruth structures each of the children's trusts to qualify as a qualified subchapter S trust (QSST) to hold the stock.

Estate and Gift Tax Laws Affect Many of the Trusts Also Used in Asset Protection Planning

The estate and gift tax laws generally tax any transfer unless a specific exemption applies. The three most common exemptions are:

- The annual $11,000 per donee gift tax exclusion. This is commonly used to fund children's, grandchildren's, life insurance, and other irrevocable trusts for the benefit of persons other than the grantor. This figure is indexed for inflation.

- The once-in-a-lifetime $1 million gift tax exclusion. It is important to note that this figure is not scheduled to be increased even as the amount that can be transferred at death free of estate tax is increased. The amount you can bequeath is scheduled to increase to $1.5 million in 2004 and up to $3.5 million in 2009 before the estate tax is repealed. These amounts may be accelerated or deferred by future legislation.

This limit on gifts is important because, for wealthy families seeking to engage in asset protection planning, this is the cap on the amount you can transfer free of gift tax. For transfers to protect large amounts of wealth, gift tax planning to leverage and discount gifts is essential. There is little point in making large gifts to protect them from creditors if the IRS takes half at the outset. Some of the tax-oriented trusts in the following discussion can help protect assets and leverage gifts.

- The unlimited marital deduction for transfers to your spouse. See later discussion of QTIP trusts.

Note: See Shenkman, *The Complete Book of Trusts* (3rd ed.), John Wiley & Sons, Inc., 2002, for a detailed discussion of each of the trusts discussed. See www.laweasy.com for sample forms for many of the trusts discussed.

Charitable Remainder Trusts (CRT) and Asset Protection Planning

If a CRT is validly established, the ownership of the assets passes immediately to the charity so that the assets should (absent fraudulent conveyance and other challenges) be outside the reach of your creditors. The periodic annuity payments you receive from the charitable trust, however, may be reached.

A charitable remainder trust (CRT) can be used to protect assets. However, because a CRT results in the charity's—not you or your heirs—receiving the residual interest in the property, a CRT alone is not a true asset protection vehicle. However, if the tax savings and income generated by a CRT are used to purchase life insurance in an irrevocable life insurance trust, a significant measure of protection may be achieved with favorable tax consequences.

A CRT transaction would proceed as follows: You donate property (real property, stock, and so forth) to a charity and receive a charitable contribution tax deduction in the year of the donation. The charity receives the full benefit of the property only at some future time (a fixed number of years or the death of you and other named beneficiaries). For example, you can reserve an annuity interest in the charitable remainder trust for your life and the life of your spouse as the income beneficiaries. If this is done, the income generated from the donated property will be paid to you for your life and thereafter to your spouse for his or her life. After the death of the latter of you and your spouse, the charity obtains full use and benefit of the donated property.

The amount of the charitable contribution deduction is equal to the fair market value of the property at the time of the donation to the charitable remainder trust, less the present value of the income interest retained by you and your spouse (or other designated beneficiary).

There are several different types of charitable remainder trusts, including: (1) annuity trusts, in which a fixed annuity is provided to the income beneficiaries, and (2) unitrusts, in which a variable income return is provided to the income beneficiaries based on the fair market value of the property each year. With the exception of gifts of a remainder interest in a personal residence or farm property, you will not qualify for an income, gift, and estate tax deduction for a donation to a remainder trust, unless the donation is in a trust that qualifies as either an annuity trust or a unitrust.

An annuity trust provides a fixed annuity to the people you designate in the trust agreement as the income beneficiaries. The minimum rate of return to the designated beneficiaries cannot be less than 5 percent, and it must be a fixed or determinable amount. Their income is calculated based on the fair market value of the property transferred to the trust. Once the trust is established, no further contributions can be made to it. If the trust income is insufficient to meet the required annual return, principal must generally be invaded.

A unitrust provides a form of variable annuity benefit to its income beneficiaries. The minimum rate of return to the income beneficiaries must be 5 percent. This rate of return is calculated on the fair market value of the property determined on an annual basis. This effectively requires an annual appraisal, which, for any property that is difficult to value (e.g., closely held business interests and real estate), could be a prohibitive cost. For this reason, an annuity trust approach is likely to prove more appropriate when such assets are to be contributed. The trust may provide that if the annual income earned by the trust property is insufficient to meet the required distribution to the income beneficiaries, principal may be invaded. If not required to invade principal, the trust must provide that the deficit will be made up in later years. After a unitrust is established, additional contributions may be made in later years under certain conditions.

The valuation of the remainder interest of the unitrust is determined under methods provided for in the Treasury regulations. The valuation considers the value of the property transferred to the trust, the age of the income beneficiary, and the payout rate.

Life insurance can be combined with a CRT to provide a means of removing a valuable asset that is not liquid from the transferor's estate and the reach of creditors and claimants.

A common method for combining insurance products with a charitable remainder plan is to preserve intact the value of the estate passing to the heirs. The concept is simple: Establish an irrevocable life insurance trust for the benefit of your heirs (e.g., children). The following goals can be achieved:

1. You can meet your desired charitable goals of providing for a favored cause or organization.

2. The income tax savings provide cash flow to make gifts to an irrevocable life insurance trust or to the heir directly.

3. The trustee of the irrevocable life insurance trust (or the heir, where direct gifts are made) purchases life insurance on your life in an amount sufficient to replace the value of the assets that the donor transferred to the charitable remainder trust.

4. On your death, the insurance proceeds are not taxable in your estate. Your heirs receive the insurance proceeds in an amount approximating the value of the assets that you transferred to the charitable remainder trust.

From an asset protection standpoint, your claimant will have a steady cash flow from the CRT to attach. While you may try to include spendthrift protection (Chapter 14), most state laws won't respect this as a self-settled trust. While it may be possible to structure a CRT in a state permitting self-settled trusts, the result is not guaranteed. If you name your spouse and children as beneficiaries or gift the assets to your spouse, who then sets up the CRT, the cash flow may be protected if there is no fraudulent conveyance issue. These alternatives should be reviewed with your attorney before completing the trust.

Trusts That Can Hold S Corporation Stock

One common business and investment asset that requires special attention is the stock in an S corporation. Because so many family and closely held businesses are organized as S corporations, it is important to consider how they affect the planning process. Three types of trusts can hold S corporation stock: a qualified Subchapter S trust (QSST), an electing small business trust (ESBT), and certain grantor trusts. This was discussed at length in Chapter 12. The key planning idea is to make gifts of S corporation stock to trusts that meet these qualifications so that the stock is protected by the irrevocable trust, meeting as many of the requirements discussed in Chapter 15 as possible. These transfers also can reduce your control over the stock to further safeguard your position and reduce the value of your holdings to a noncontrolling position.

Bypass or Applicable Exclusion Trusts

A cornerstone of most basic estate plans is to take advantage of the amount you can bequeath free of estate tax, called the *applicable exclusion*. In most estate plans, it is advantageous for estate tax reasons to use the $1 million exclusion (increasing in later years) in both spouses' estates. The optimal protection of this exclusion in the estate of the first spouse to die will keep those assets estate-tax free in the first estate and ensure that they do not even enter the surviving spouse's taxable estate. The classic zero tax approach using this is to establish a bypass trust (also called *applicable exclusion trust* or *credit shelter trust*) to hold the maximum amount of assets that can pass free of estate tax (although changes in state level taxation may change this). These assets are not only protected from estate taxation, but also this trust, with minor or even no change, can be an excellent asset protection tool.

In many bypass trusts, the surviving spouse and all children are listed as beneficiaries. The trustee, at least one of whom should be an independent trustee, is often given the right to distribute any portion, all, or none of the income and principal to any of the surviving spouse and children or certain other beneficiaries. These trusts frequently have spendthrift provisions. Thus, a typical bypass trust includes, or can easily be modified to include, many of the trust asset protection concepts discussed in Chapter 14. The key planning idea is to focus on asset protection benefits of this common trust when your lawyer is drafting your will, not just the estate tax benefits.

Trusts for Children

Because children (and other minor heirs) have important financial needs for their education and care and the immaturity that requires another to manage their assets, the use of trusts is often ideal for nonasset protection motives. The need to provide for management of assets and to protect children from themselves, from a potential divorce, or creditors makes trusts the ideal approach to provide for your children or other heirs. Funding a child's trust with assets also protects the assets you use if there is no fraudulent conveyance. Assets transferred from the parent to the children's trust may be unreachable by creditors and may still be applied for certain expenses for the child, which the parent, absent the trust, would have paid from his or her own funds.

A child's trust can be funded with annual gifts to take advantage of the annual $11,000 gift tax exclusion. However, if the goal is protection of assets, funding with a larger gift that uses up a portion of your $1 million gift tax exclusion may be more advantageous because it will complete a transfer of significant assets more quickly. To leverage gifts and to provide a second level of protection, gifts of family partnership, closely held business, or other assets valued at discounts should be used. If the gifts made are significant, the next question is whether the gifts will become large enough that a trust should be used. This is primarily a question of costs and assessment of potential risks.

You must decide at what ages your children should be given the assets from the trust. A common approach is one-third at ages 25, 30, and 35. The idea is to accustom the child to receiving money over a period of time so that if the child is irresponsible at the first distribution, there will be two more opportunities to learn responsibility. You must determine whether to have one trust for all of your children or separate trusts for each child. If asset protection concerns are important, two important changes to these approaches should be considered. It is advantageous to lengthen the period of time that the child must wait for unfettered access to the funds for the duration of the child's life and, absent GST consequences, for as long as the rule against perpetuities (a law existing in some states that limits the duration of a trust) permits. In addition, the use of multiple trusts (e.g., one for each child) should probably be preferred over a single trust arrangement.

Income Only Trust: Section 2503(b) Trust.   This trust must require that the income be distributed annually to your child or other beneficiary. This permits you to make a gift of up to $11,000 per year and qualify for the annual gift tax exclusion. The child is then taxed on all of the income earned by the trust. If the child is under 14, the Kiddie Tax described previously applies. The income can be distributed to a Uniform Gift to Minors Act trust without affecting the benefits of the annual exclusion. The assets in the trust must be income producing for the IRS to respect the arrangement (e.g., raw land that is not leased will not work). From the perspective of protecting the child's assets, the mandate that income must be distributed is not an advantage.

Right to Withdraw under Crummey Power.   With the exception of a special trust for minor children discussed later, if a trust can accumulate income, you will not qualify for the annual $11,000 gift tax exclusion on gifts to the trust. However, a gift to a trust qualifies as a gift of a present interest (i.e., qualifies for the annual exclusion) up to the amount the child can withdraw each year from the trust. This is called a *Crummey Power*. This gives the child beneficiary the absolute right to presently enjoy the gift made by the parent. Even if the child does not exercise this right and the money remains in the trust, the existence of this right enables you as the parent to make the gifts to avoid any gift tax or use of your lifetime gift tax exclusion. There are a host of complications to this type of planning, which should be reviewed carefully with the attorney assisting you with estate planning.

Special Trust for Children Under Age 21: Section 2503(c) Trust. The law provides for a special rule that permits you to transfer $11,000 per year to a trust; the trust can accumulate the income, and you can still qualify for the annual gift tax exclusion. To qualify, the trust must be set up to benefit a minor child. The trustee must have the ability to use the income for the benefit of the minor child without restriction. The trust assets must be invested in income-producing assets (stocks, bonds, and CDs—not raw land). When the child reaches age 21, the trust must be distributed to the child. The child can be given the right to require that the assets of the trust be distributed when he or she reaches age 21 but voluntarily choose not to elect to take the money. Giving the child the right to take the money may increase the risk that the child will obtain the assets of the trust earlier than with a trust using a Crummey power, but it is a safer approach to assuring the benefits of the annual exclusion. If the child dies before age 21, the trust assets must be distributed to the child's estate or in a manner that the child appoints. This type of trust is commonly used in planning for minor children. For income tax purposes, the trust pays income tax on income it keeps, and the child pays income tax on income distributed to it. From the perspective of protecting the child's assets, this approach is not advisable. If the child were to be in the midst of a suit or divorce when the distribution has to be made, the assets could be jeopardized. Further, if the child opts not to take the trust assets at that time, the trust could be characterized as a self-settled trust reachable by the child's creditors.

Trusts versus Section 529 College Savings Plans in Asset Protection

Section 529 college savings plans have become popular planning for children's education investments. The pros and cons of these plans in comparison to trusts should be considered when formulating your planning. The 529 plan should be evaluated as an alternative to trusts or in conjunction with trusts (if applicable state law permits a trust to be an account owner for a 529 plan).

A key issue to consider is that if you fund a 529 plan for a child or other heir, you as the account owner can withdraw funds from the 529 plan and pay income taxes and a 10 percent penalty. This type of access is not permissible from a child's trust. The key issue is whether from an asset protection perspective, this withdrawal right will enable your claimants to reach the 529 plan assets. If state law doesn't expressly protect the 529 plan assets, caution must be exercised. If the tax and other characteristics of the 529 plan make it advisable, you should consider structuring it so that someone other than you is the account owner. Even if state law protects a 529 plan you contribute to, be careful; the laws are new and untested.

Qualified Personal Residence Trusts (QPRT)

QPRTs are special trusts designed to hold interests in your primary residence. Their general use was explained in the context of divorce planning in Chapter 15. For general asset protection purposes, the QPRT can provide a measure of protection for your residence. The QPRT is an irrevocable trust with children typically as the remainder beneficiaries. It would appear difficult, absent a fraudulent conveyance issue, for a court to overturn a properly drafted and implemented irrevocable trust and ignore the interests of the remainder beneficiaries. However, the mechanism of the QPRT has a flaw that is important to consider from an asset protection perspective. In most QPRTs, if the house is sold or fails to meet the qualifications of a QPRT, a periodic annuity payment must be paid to you for the life of the trust. Further, most people setting up a QPRT name themselves as cotrustees, which perhaps should be avoided. A court might infer that if you as a cotrustee have authority to sell the house and would then automatically be entitled to a periodic annuity, such a payment should be reachable by your claimants. However, even if this were to occur, the principal value of the trust would remain intact. Thus, a QPRT can provide an important measure of protection.

The decision as to whether a QPRT should be used for your residence should be made by comparing the other asset protection options available for your residence to the pros, cons, and complexities of dealing with a QPRT:

- Mortgage the house and invest the mortgage proceeds in a manner that provides protection. The value of the house, as reduced by the mortgage, should not have as much value or exposure to claimants.
- Ownership of the house as tenancy by the entirety (see Chapter 3).
- Contribution of the house to a QTIP trust.

QTIP or Marital Trusts

Marital trusts can be an excellent lawsuit protection tool, subject to the risks of the stability of your marriage. A qualified terminable interest property (QTIP) trust can be created while you are alive (*inter vivos*) or following death (testamentary).

The inclusion of a testamentary QTIP trust in your will has been discussed in preceding sections. The key concept from an asset protection perspective is that if you face liability risks, any assets your spouse bequeaths to you should be in trust to provide protection. Any assets over the applicable exclusion amount, presently $1 million but increasing in future years, should be bequeathed to a marital trust to avoid triggering estate tax on the first death.

A marital trust can be created during your lifetime as an asset protection plan. For example, if both you and your spouse are concerned about malpractice or other liability claims, you can transfer assets to a marital trust for your spouse instead of directly to her. If your spouse dies before you, assets can be distributed in further trust back for your benefit. This use of a marital trust can provide an alternative to your retaining assets subject to the risk of your claimants or transferring them outright (i.e., without a trust) to your spouse and thus subjecting them to the risk of your spouse's claimants.

Whether the marital trust is set up while you are alive or after your death, the transfer must qualify for the unlimited gift or estate tax marital deduction (assuming your spouse is a U.S. citizen). A number of requirements must be met so that a transfer to, or for the benefit of, your spouse will qualify for the gift or estate tax marital deduction. The property intended to qualify for the marital deduction must pass from you (the decedent for a testamentary transfer) to your surviving spouse. The rights and property transferred to the surviving spouse cannot be a terminable interest. This interest will terminate or fail as the result of the passing of time, the occurrence of an event or contingency, or the failure of an event or contingency to occur. There are a number of exceptions to this terminable interest rule, and these are critical to the use of trusts for transfers to a surviving spouse. Perhaps the most common of the exceptions is for a QTIP trust. Such a trust can then qualify for the unlimited estate tax marital deduction, while including independent trustees, spendthrift provisions, and other clauses with asset protection benefits (see Chapter 14).

On the death of the surviving spouse, the entire value of the QTIP property is included in his or her gross estate. These assets are taxed at the spouse's top marginal tax brackets.

Life Insurance Trusts

Insurance can be one of the most valuable and flexible assets used in an estate, financial, and asset protection plan. The biggest benefit insurance offers, however, can also create some of its most significant problems. Insurance matures on death into a substantial amount of money. This wealth can create substantial tax costs, attract creditors, malpractice claimants, and others who see a potential resource to tap. One of the best solutions to these problems is to use a life insurance trust to own any life insurance policies and to retain and manage the proceeds of those policies after death.

Properly established, an irrevocable life insurance trust can enable both your estate and your spouse's estate to avoid tax on insurance proceeds. An additional measure of protection from creditors and divorce is also obtained because insurance owned outside the trust may independently have a measure of protection, depending on state law. Your surviving spouse can be a discretionary beneficiary of the trust and thus receive some, none, or all of the income and principal from the insurance trust.

Planning Note: Asset protection goals may suggest a somewhat different decision process concerning the use of an insurance trust than would traditional estate planning. Traditional estate planning would almost always favor having insurance held by a trust. However, if insurance owned directly has a significant level of protection under your state's laws, the additional protection afforded by the trust may not be that significant for your claimants. Therefore, if you have used a significant portion of your $1 million lifetime gift tax exclusion and annual $11,000 gift tax exclusions or might use them more advantageously, perhaps the insurance should be left in your name alone while other assets are protected. The issue is a trade-off of the risk of the estate tax versus the risk of leaving particular assets less protected.

SUMMARY

This chapter reviewed the most common trusts and explained their consequences to lawsuit protection planning. Differences in how these common techniques can be applied to better address your asset protection goals were indicated. These planning ideas should be read in conjunction with the general trust planning ideas noted in Chapter 14.

17 DOMESTIC SELF-SETTLED ASSET PROTECTION TRUST RULES

Many Americans are extremely concerned over the potentially devastating effects of a lawsuit. These worries are not confined only to doctors worried about malpractice suits not covered by increasingly expensive malpractice insurance. All professionals, investors, business owners, and almost anyone with any significant net worth are concerned.

Although there are many asset protection techniques, trusts can offer a flexible and workable solution. This solution, however, has been subject to a major drawback. With the exceptions of Alaska, Delaware, Nevada, and Rhode Island (with perhaps some additional states to follow), you could not set up an irrevocable trust to protect your assets if you remained a potential beneficiary of the trust. If you could receive or benefit from trust assets, under the general rules, your creditors would have the right to reach the trust assets to the same extent that you could. Thus, in theory, if you could receive all trust assets, your creditors could as well. The result was that well-to-do persons who were sufficiently concerned about asset protection planning would establish offshore foreign asset protection trusts. Many people, however, are uncomfortable with the use of foreign asset protection trusts. The cost of establishing such trusts is very high. The laws of the countries involved may be different, the location is often distant, and there is often a general discomfort with the concept. IRS reporting requirements are also complex and stringent. As a result, the domestic asset protection trust offers, if it proves viable in the face of future litigation and legislation, a viable, even if somewhat less protective, alternative.

What Is a Domestic Asset Protection Trust?

Several states have enacted legislation permitting asset protection trusts to be established domestically. At present, Alaska, Delaware, Nevada, and Rhode Island have enacted such laws. Trusts organized under these laws are called *domestic asset protection trusts* (DAPT). Although asset protection is not necessarily the only motive for establishing DAPTs, it is a motive for many, and the same features that provide creditor protection planning are often necessary to achieve the desired estate tax result as well.

It was the rule in every state in the United States that you could not create a self-settled spendthrift trust. You could not transfer assets to a trust for which you are a beneficiary and then have those trust assets protected from your creditors. This has been a strong legal policy and one that, until recently, has not been strongly challenged. The Alaska, Delaware, Nevada, and Rhode Island statutes are the first to legislatively change what had been a fundamental legal principal.

The concept in a nutshell is that you can create a trust for your own benefit (retain discretionary benefits, etc.) while still removing it from your estate for tax purposes and from the reach of your creditors. These two objectives are dependent on each other. The theory is that if your creditors cannot reach the asset, it should be removed from your taxable estate as well. If your creditors can reach the assets, the gift transfer of your assets to the trust is incomplete. If you retain eligibility to receive property back, there is not a completed gift. If your creditor can attach the property given away, the transfer is incomplete for transfer tax purposes.

There had been no jurisdiction in the United States where you could make a gift that would be deemed complete for transfer tax purposes, but for which you could be a discretionary beneficiary. This concept, however, has been accepted for foreign asset protection trusts where the host country laws permit you to make a completed gift while remaining a discretionary beneficiary. Under host country statute, your creditors would not be able to reach the assets. The IRS has even informally determined that if a U.S. taxpayer transferred assets to an offshore jurisdiction where creditors cannot reach it, the transfer is a completed gift even if the taxpayer remains a discretionary beneficiary.

Domestic asset protection trusts were devised as tax planning and asset protection devices. They include a lengthy number of years in their fraudulent conveyance statutes. The key objective the proponents of these laws sought to address was to provide a mechanism for which modest to large estates could make gifts to remove assets from their taxable estates, without the fear of making a gift completely beyond their reach in case they need the money or assets back for emergencies. Taxpayers fear not having access to sufficient money if they need it when the worst-case scenario happens.

The DAPT provides a mechanism to accomplish this in lieu of using an offshore trust, which is not satisfactory to a number of people. A major reason many taxpayers are uncomfortable with foreign asset protection trusts is the fear of dealing with offshore unknown jurisdictions.

Domestic asset protection trusts are for people who are uncomfortable making gifts but should for estate tax or asset protection planning purposes. Here you can make a gift to get it out of your estate but still retain some benefit. These trusts are also a technique for those people who feel the need to protect assets but are concerned that they may need the assets in the future.

Self-Settled Domestic Trusts Generally Do Not Provide Protection

To better understand the laws in these new DAPT states, consider how a typical law in the other 48 states reads:

Creator's reserved interest in trust alienable subject to creditor's claims:

"The right of any creator of a trust to receive either the income or the principal of the trust or any part of either thereof, presently or in the future, shall be freely alienable and shall be subject to the claims of his creditors, notwithstanding any provision to the contrary in the terms of the trust."

Conveyances of personal property in trust for use of persons making them void as to creditors:

"Every deed of gift and every conveyance, transfer and assignment of goods, chattels or things in action, made in trust for the use
of the person making the same, shall be void as against creditors."

Not much asset protection benefits from funding your own trust
in a typical jurisdiction.

The law generally has provided, and in most states continues to
provide, that if you create a trust for benefit of your own support,
your creditors can reach the maximum amount that the trustee can
apply to you. This is narrower than what the laws had historically
provided for. In the past, the entire trust may have been held to be
void. Now, your creditors, in the absence of statutory change, can
get whatever could be given to you as the grantor. If the grantor
can get only income, the creditors can get only income.

Requirements for a Domestic Asset Protection Trust

If you meet the necessary requirements, you can create a self-settled
trust and transfer assets. And even if you, as the transferor, are the
sole beneficiary or one of several beneficiaries, subject to fraudulent conveyance rules, these assets should not be available to claims
of your creditors. If you are not residing in one of the DAPT states,
you must have sufficient connection to one of those states to support your using that state's laws for your DAPT. For example, your
trust can name as a trustee a corporate trustee having its office in
that jurisdiction or an individual residing in that jurisdiction. Trust
activities must occur in the jurisdiction. This could include administration of the trust and other functions.

People need to feel that they can get their money back. But if you
gave it too much discretion, creditors would have access. If the
grantor has unlimited access, the creditors might, also. You can set
up grantor as sole beneficiary. You can give a power to veto distributions to other beneficiaries.

Domestic Asset Protection Trust Laws Are Not
Perfect Safeguards

Statutes must have appropriate protections and exceptions. All
statutes have exceptions for domestic relations creditors. Delaware
has an exception for torts created on or before the formation of the

trust. All statutes have fraudulent transfer overlays. If you have a bad malpractice judgment and before attachment you moved assets into one of these trusts, the transfers would be characterized as fraudulent transfers and would not provide any protection. Therefore, these laws cannot easily be used to run away from valid claims.

Real estate and personal property is difficult to put into a DAPT if you live in another state. If real estate is in a jurisdiction without such a statute, the courts in those jurisdictions may try to attach real estate or personal property located within their jurisdiction. This result may even be true if the real estate is converted into personal property by transferring it to an FLP or LLC.

The key risk of these laws is the risk that another state may not recognize the protective features of Alaska, Delaware, Nevada, or Rhode Island law. The full faith and credit clause of the U.S. Constitution requires that each state give credit to a judgment in a sister state. If you have a judgment in New York, for example, but DAPT in Alaska, will the Alaska courts recognize the New York judgment? The DAPT state would, the argument goes, have to respect a sister state's judgment against the beneficiary or trustee. How much "heat" may courts in other jurisdictions put on the trustees or beneficiaries in trying to get assets? These trusts, their advocates say, should survive contract law and full faith and credit arguments, but the result is still unproven. There are significant risks and different views among experts on whether this will occur.

Does this risk mean that you should avoid using DAPTs? Probably not. Even if this becomes an issue, there may be a several-year time period to get a judgment in the jurisdiction where the action occurred. Then, you will have to go to Delaware, for example, where the trustee will seek protection, which creates another proceeding. Thus, there are a number of proceedings and time and expense in attacking such a trust even if the full-faith credit clause of the constitution were found to apply to enable the claimant to reach your trust's assets.

TAX CONSEQUENCES OF A DOMESTIC ASSET PROTECTION TRUST

Income Tax Consequences

Most DAPTs are grantor trusts for federal and state income tax purposes. This means all of the income and deductions of the DAPT are to be reported on your personal income tax return. This result occurs because you as the grantor are a permissible beneficiary of the trust.

Gift Tax Consequences

For gift tax purposes, you can gift $11,000 per person per year to any trust. However, for a gift to a DAPT to qualify for this annual gift tax benefit, your lawyer should include an annual demand power, which would enable each beneficiary to withdraw that year's gift. It is not clear that this is the desired approach for a DAPT. If not, gifts to your DAPT would use some portion of your lifetime $1 million gift tax exclusion.

If you as the grantor forming the DAPT do not have ascertainable interests (i.e., distributions can be made to you in the sole discretion of the trustee), assets transferred by you to the DAPT are treated as completed gifts for gift tax purposes. This means that the assets should not be included in your estate for estate tax purposes, but a gift tax may be due if the value of the transfer exceeds what remains of your $1 million gift tax exclusion. The exception to this result is that if your creditors can reach the assets, the gift is judged incomplete. Thus, the tax laws use a test that requires that a DAPT protect your assets from creditors.

Estate Tax Consequences

If the transfer is a completed gift, the DAPT assets should be excluded from your estate for estate tax purposes. You cannot have a right to revoke, amend, or receive the beneficial interest in the trust assets. If by incurring debt you can enable your creditors to get at the assets, it will be included in the grantor's estate. If there is a "side deal" that all income should be distributed to you, you will be deemed to have retained the entire trust and all trust assets will be included in your taxable estate. If there are no distributions to the grantor during grantor's lifetime, it should not be included. However, there is no assurance that the DAPT assets will be excluded. One planning consideration you should discuss with your attorney is whether you should provide in the DAPT trust agreement that an unrelated person (third party) be given the right to exclude you as a permissible beneficiary so that you can avoid the risk of estate inclusion. If this is done even a day before death, your estate may argue that you did not hold any impermissible rights on death.

CHARACTERISTICS OF DOMESTIC ASSET PROTECTION TRUSTS

Domestic asset protection trusts have a number of common characteristics to enable them to provide asset protection benefits.

Spendthrift Trust

In a spendthrift trust, a beneficiary cannot appoint the assets before those assets are distributed to the beneficiary. Spendthrift protection is sometimes afforded by operation of law. In many jurisdictions, a spendthrift clause must be added to the trust agreement to have spendthrift protection. However, in DAPT states, statutes provide for spendthrift protection automatically. Spendthrift trusts are generally resistant, if not immune, to the claims of your creditors. However, if you engaged in a fraudulent conveyance on forming or funding the trust, spendthrift protection is tainted.

The trust should also be immune from attacks by the creditors of the beneficiaries. Exceptions, however, are provided for the IRS, the provision of necessities, and so on (see discussion in Chapter 14).

Fraudulent Conveyance

The term *fraudulent conveyance* was explained in Chapter 8. If assets are transferred to a DAPT in a transfer intended to defraud your creditors, the transfers are deemed to be fraudulent conveyances and are not protected.

Independent Trustee

The trustee of an asset protection trust should not also be a beneficiary of the trust. To ensure protection from claimants, the person serving as trustee with a capacity to distribute assets should be independent of the trust beneficiaries. An independent trustee can be defined as any individual who:

1. Is not related or subordinate to any beneficiary of a trust or to you as the grantor.
2. Has no interest in the income and/or principal of such trust.
3. Does not have a legal obligation in his or her individual capacity to support the beneficiary of a trust to whom a discretionary payment of income and/or principal may be made by such individual.
4. Cannot appoint trust income or principal to himself or herself, his or her creditors, his or her estate, or the creditors of his or her estate.

A trust company, bank, or other financial institution is generally independent.

Nexus and Contacts with Host Jurisdiction

Some minimal level of contacts with the host jurisdiction is required to give credibility to the argument that the trust, especially if you reside in another jurisdiction and are a citizen of another jurisdiction, has sufficient contacts with the jurisdiction offering the favorable asset protection statute. The scope of contacts can vary from jurisdiction to jurisdiction, but the general rule must be that the greater the contact with the host jurisdiction, the more likely the trust can withstand a challenge that jurisdiction laws do not apply.

Contacts can include a trustee in that particular jurisdiction, assets in that jurisdiction, performance of certain key trust functions in that jurisdiction, and so on.

DYNASTY TRUST CHARACTERISTICS OF DOMESTIC ASSET PROTECTION TRUSTS

If your estate is sufficiently large that your heirs are likely to face a significant estate tax on their death, it may be advisable for you to plan your estate for them and later generations so that the overall transfer tax burden is minimized over several generations of people. This same planning can enable you to bequeath to your heirs, in addition to wealth that is tax protected, wealth that is protected from claimants and divorce. The basic approach to this type of planning is to have assets held in trust for the life of your children, their descendants, or other heirs. You allocate your generation skipping transfer (GST) tax exemption (the base exclusion of $1 million increases in future years to $3.5 million until it is repealed in 2010) to all assets transferred to the DAPT if it is to be used as a dynasty trust as well. The assets so protected can then be passed by your heirs to their heirs, free of estate, gift, or GST taxes. The estate tax savings over several generations can be significant, hence the term *multigenerational* planning is used for these dynasty trusts. Not all DAPTs are used for multigenerational planning, but it is a tremendous tool that warrants consideration. It may also serve to demonstrate that your DAPT has objectives beyond just protecting assets.

This type of planning has a number of benefits in addition to merely saving taxes and asset protection benefits for your heirs. It can provide a mechanism to control your heirs' access to assets in a manner that encourages your heirs to become and remain productive members of society—which a large inheritance received too quickly can destroy. In the event that an heir becomes incapacitated, the trust structure provides an ideal mechanism to protect assets for your heirs. As a result of all of these benefits, you will be providing greater flexibility to your heirs, not necessarily restricting or controlling them. Thus, this type of planning can be appropriate even if your estate is not sufficiently large to warrant GST planning.

If your DAPT is to continue for many generations or even indefinitely, it must be based in a state (jurisdiction) whose laws permit trusts to continue forever (in perpetuity). Each of the four states that presently permit DAPTs has laws permitting this. However, most states do not. Therefore, care must be taken if the law governing your DAPT is ever changed (see following discussion). With this planning, your DAPT, as dynasty trust, may continue for future generations until the assets are exhausted. This long-term time horizon makes the trust more complex to prepare because there are a host of additional issues to address. Who will be a trustee in 200 years? Who will be a beneficiary?

Distribution provisions in the trust must be tailored to address this long-term, perpetual time horizon. For example, instead of simply distributing money from the trust to enable a child to purchase a house, in a longer term GST or dynasty trust, the better approach may be to have the trustee loan the child or grandchild money to buy the house or even to buy the house in the trust and permit the beneficiary to use the house. The trustee, for example, could purchase artwork or a vacation home and permit the beneficiary to use these assets. Because the beneficiary has not been given title to the asset, the asset can remain in the ownership of the trust and continue to pass on to later generations without incurring additional transfer tax costs. This approach can enable these assets to continue to pass on free of any gift, estate, or GST tax costs. Once an asset is distributed from the trust, these benefits are lost.

To accomplish this, the investment provisions of the trust must exempt these types of purchases from any applicable state or other statute or regulation (e.g., the Prudent Investor Act), which would otherwise require the diversification of the trust assets and so on. The trustee powers should also include sufficient detailed powers authorizing these types of transactions, which keep the assets protected in the trust. This more comprehensive approach is rarely used for a trust that will make substantial distributions by age 30 or so.

WHAT SPECIAL ISSUES MUST YOUR DOMESTIC ASSET PROTECTION TRUST AGREEMENT CONSIDER?

Recital/Whereas Clauses

Consideration should be given to the purposes of the trust and to corroborating that no fraudulent conveyance has occurred. It is advisable to consider stating clearly that your transfer of assets to the trust is intended to be a completed gift and if your intent is that the assets not be included in your taxable estate. If you intend for the trust to continue through future generations, which is usually the case, but not always, the trust should expressly state this. Your tax advisors can explain to you the GST tax implications and filing requirements this objective creates.

Note: See Shenkman, *The Complete Book of Trusts* (3rd ed.), John Wiley & Sons, Inc., 2002, for a detailed discussion of GST tax planning.

Spendthrift Provision

This provision is key to the asset protection planning intended (see Chapter 14 for a general discussion). Each of the states with DAPT laws has special spendthrift provisions to help protect the assets you transfer to such a trust.

Example: The Delaware Qualified Dispositions in Trust Act Section 3572(b) provides that a creditor's claim shall be extinguished unless the creditor's claim arose before the qualified disposition to the trust was made and the action was brought within the Delaware statute of limitations (Section 1309 of Title 6); or the creditor's claim arose concurrent with or subsequent to the qualified disposition and the action was brought within four years after the qualified disposition to the trust was made. The creditor must prove such matters by clear and convincing evidence. Section 3573 provides exceptions for alimony and child support. An exception is also provided for certain tort creditors.

The implications of the previous example may be surprising. Your primary goal for setting up a DAPT is to protect assets. Yet, if you transfer assets to a DAPT, all transfers are identifiable (nothing is secretive about it), and if you are sued within four years, your claimant can reach the trust assets. The purpose of these rules, in contrast to some of the foreign jurisdictions seeking asset protection trust business, is not to make it easy for you to protect assets if you have claims at the time of the transfer. If you've done something that gives rise to a claim (you left the surgical clamp in the patient), the patient has four years to sue. The implication is that you should set up a DAPT now; don't wait for some future date when any potential claims might exist. It also means that you should endeavor to demonstrate no existing claims before you create your DAPT and document that you've done so.

Trust Protector

When a DAPT is intended to continue for a long period of time, uncertainty and discomfort over decisions you make today that are binding for future generations grow. Also, in most DAPTs, an institutional cotrustee is frequently named, and most people worry about what will happen if they are not responsive or don't perform. The answer, which should be considered when planning your DAPT, is to name a series of persons other than trustees, who are given specific powers to build flexibility into the trust and generally to change institutional trustees. This person or position is referred to as a *trust protector*. The trust protector role has been commonly used in many foreign situs asset protection trusts and is now making its way more commonly into domestically structured trust agreements. The trust protector is clearly a fiduciary role (position of trust), but, unfortunately, as a new function, does not have substantial case law or other authoritative literature defining its parameters, obligations, responsibilities, and so on. The trust protector is typically a very limited but powerful and important role. The role should be clearly defined in your DAPT trust document because the laws are so new and sparse. A typical approach would be to grant the protector a very limited number of powers or rights granted to the trust protector, such as changing or removing an institution or even noninstitutional cotrustee or sole trustee, changing the governing law or situs of the trust (this might be important to transfer the trust to a state where there is no restriction on the rule against perpetuities; see later discussion), changing the designated investment advisor (see later discussion), and occasionally additional limited powers as well. The ability to change governing law and situs could be important because, in addition to possibly making a rule against perpetuity restriction lapse (although some authorities do question whether this would be feasible if the state where the trust was initially formed had such a limitation), you could have estate tax ramifications that might affect investment decisions. Others prefer to give the protector only "negative" powers (e.g., to disapprove a trustee decision). This may prevent a court from ordering a protector to take a specific action.

The trust protector is typically a person named outside the family who is independent of both the trustees and the beneficiaries. However, in some instances, typically after a succession of trust protectors, a class of beneficiaries may be granted the right to nominate a person, perhaps specifically excluding, or, in some instances, even including, a member of that class to serve as the trust protector.

Some DAPTs name a succession of other persons to have powers and rights different from the trustee and different from the trust protector. These may include an *investment advisor, distribution committee,* or the like and could be used for making investment and distribution decisions, respectively.

Perpetuities

Many, if not most, DAPTs are established for a perpetual term. However, some may not be. For example, if asset protection is a key objective but the grantor anticipates needing trust assets in the future, such as for retirement, a perpetual trust may not be necessary. A perpetuities savings clause should be included in any event to ensure compliance with applicable statutes in the event any trust property becomes subject to the laws of another jurisdiction that does not permit a perpetual trust.

For this type of planning to be successful, the trust should include GST powers. These include, for example, the power to divide trusts if necessary to preserve an inclusion ratio of zero.

The trustee must also have the authority to purchase assets and to then permit the beneficiaries to use the assets, in lieu of distributing the assets directly to the beneficiaries, to preserve the perpetuities benefits.

Beneficiaries

You, as the grantor forming the trust, as well as other named persons, can be eligible beneficiaries. You preferably should not be the sole current beneficiary. Naming a group (class) of beneficiaries from which the trustee can select to make distributions to is a safer approach. It is important to name classes of persons who can be defined and identified in the future because of the duration of the trust.

Your DAPT should also address whether it will be divided into separate trusts on your death (or the death of the latter of you and your spouse) for your children (or other heirs). You might prefer that the trust continue to operate as a single "pot" of assets instead of dividing it. If you choose to divide the trust so that each child inherits his or her own separate trust, should those now separate trusts be divided for your grandchildren? What about each generation thereafter? This, however, could be problematic as future generations are added because the number of separate shares could mushroom. The distribution provisions should address what should happen if a particular generational line should cease.

Sample Clause: The trust will last until the death of the survivor of CHILDNAME-1, HUSBANDNAME, and WIFENAME. Thereafter, the trust will be divided on each generational level into trusts for the benefit of CHILDNAME-1's issue.

Distribution Provisions

A DAPT raises several special considerations in drafting distribution provisions. You should be no more than a discretionary eligible beneficiary. Although Delaware law permits you to retain certain rights to income, these rights taint the hoped-for asset protection benefits certainly as to the amounts you retain access to, perhaps more. Mandatory income or principal distribution provisions could jeopardize the asset protection benefits the trust is hoped to afford. Also, if the trust is intended to be GST–exempt, mandatory distributions would represent leakage of GST benefits back into a taxable estate, defeating that planning as well.

Should distributions be made on an incentive basis? For each dollar earned, a beneficiary receives a distribution. What about requiring distributions to charity to teach beneficiaries about philanthropy?

Trust Termination

"In perpetuity" is a long time. Some flexibility should be given to the trustee to terminate the trust and distribute trust assets if the trust is uneconomical, impractical, or otherwise inappropriate to operate. This could be especially important if the trust distribution provisions require that the trust estate be divided at each generational level into separate trusts. At some point, if the growth in trust principal does not exceed the distributions and divisions sufficiently, the trustee could end up administering scores of small and uneconomical trusts.

Trustee Selection

Trustee selection for a DAPT must consider a number of factors, which differ from those considered for a typical trust. If the trust is to exist perpetually, an institution that can exist perpetually should be named trustee. To establish nexus with the DAPT jurisdiction, an institution in that jurisdiction should be sued. For example, to demonstrate nexus, the Alaska statute requires that the trustees be Alaska-qualified persons. Thus, state requirements should be considered in selecting fiduciaries. Because the trust will continue for a long period, if not perpetually, a mechanism should be included to enable future generations to appoint successor trustees. Many DAPTs name an institutional cotrustee to work with an individual cotrustee. When the listing of persons you include in the trust document as individual cotrustees ends, perhaps the beneficiaries should be given the right to nominate by majority vote successor individual cotrustees.

Where Is Your Domestic Asset Protection Trust Based and What Law Governs?

When selecting the state (jurisdiction) to govern your DAPT, you must select from one of the four states and any future states that have enacted the laws necessary for this type of trust. There are some differences among the laws enacted by each of these states, and you should review the differences with your attorney before making a decision. Another practical, not legal, factor some people consider is how many institutions operate in each state. This could seem important if you or your heirs become unhappy with the institutional trustee named and want to replace it. Which trust companies operate in that jurisdiction? Delaware is likely to seem the winner by these criteria. If you prefer Alaska, for example, as your jurisdiction but are concerned about the limited number of trust companies there, you can address this concern by permitting the trust to be moved to another state with comparable legislation, such as Delaware, at a later date.

Consider the following (as well as any other applicable) characteristics of the available state statutes:

1. Little or no state income tax or other tax on trust assets, activities, or investments. Even a modest tax percentage, when

compounded over decades and longer, has an extremely negative impact on the value of trust assets.

2. The degree to which state law would involve itself in trust activities (i.e., except if actually requested by the beneficiaries).

3. State spendthrift statute and the attitudes of that state's courts toward spendthrift provisions in trusts.

4. General legal environment of the state toward asset protection planning, trust planning, and related legal matters and trends.

5. Status of the state's statutes governing limited liability companies (and family limited partnerships). How many members are required to form an LLC (e.g., Can a one-member LLC be valid?)? This is important if there is a goal not to involve others, a desire to support lack of marketability, minority interest discounts, and so on.

6. The state statute's asset protection benefits and, in particular, how they have been viewed by the courts governing the case.

Example: What issues does state law address? Alaska law, AS Section 12.26.035(a), for example, provides: The Alaska court has exclusive jurisdiction of proceedings initiated by interested parties concerning the internal affairs of trusts, including the new Alaska Domestic Asset Protection Trust. This includes proceedings concerning the administration of trusts, the declaration of rights, and the determination of other matters involving trustees and beneficiaries. The statute provides a nonexclusive list of items, including:

- Appoint or remove a trustee.
- Review trustee fees and interim or final accounts.
- Ascertain beneficiaries; determine questions arising in the administration or distribution of any trust, including construction issues, instruction for trustees, and the existence of any immunity, power, privilege, duty, or right.
- Release registration of a trust.

Establishing Sufficient Connection to the State Whose Law You Want to Apply

A number of provisions in the trust can be tailored to help establish sufficient legal connection (nexus) to the state whose law you want to apply. An institution based in the DAPT jurisdiction should be a trustee. The trust can require a specified portion or merely a dollar amount of assets to be invested in that jurisdiction. Specified services or actions important to the trust, such as accounting records and tax filings, can be addressed in that jurisdiction. The governing law can be stated to be the DAPT jurisdiction, and so on.

Example: A trust formed under the Alaska statute should have exclusive jurisdiction in Alaska if the various requirements of the statute (AS Section 13.36.035) are adhered to. A trust formed under the Alaska statute should not be subject to the claims of your creditors if you meet the various requirements contained in the Alaska statute. Generally, these statutory provisions seek to ensure that you cannot defraud creditors because of the long statute of limitations.

- You must have a real Alaska connection—Alaska person as trustee, assets in Alaska, or significant trust functions performed in Alaska by a trustee who is a "qualified person." This term is defined in AS Section 13.36.390 and includes an individual who is resident in Alaska. *Residence* is defined as a true and permanent home. For a trust company to qualify, it must be organized under the laws of Alaska and have its principal place of business in Alaska. For a bank, it must be organized under Alaska law.

- Your trust administration must be in Alaska. This must include the trustee's maintaining records in Alaska, the preparation of trust income tax returns in Alaska, and some administration of trust assets in Alaska.

- You cannot retain the right to revoke the trust even with the consent of an adverse party.

- You (the grantor) can have no more than the status as an eligible beneficiary of the trust. You cannot have any entitlement or right (e.g., to the income only).

- To avoid the application of laws of another state, the trust should not own real estate or tangible property in another state. You should also consider limiting all trustees to qualified Alaskan persons to avoid another state's claiming jurisdiction as a result of the nexus obtained through a trustee domiciled or operating in that state.

Change in the State Where Your Domestic Asset Protection Trust Is Based and Change in Governing Law

Once a jurisdiction is selected, circumstances could change such that it is advisable to change to another jurisdiction and governing law. These provisions are sometimes called *jurisdiction skipping provisions,* or a *flight clause* (because it enables the trust to flee to a jurisdiction with more favorable laws). This power can be given to the trust protector.

Caution should be exercised, however, before changing situs of your DAPT. If the change in situs could jeopardize an otherwise grandfathered tax benefit, it may not be advisable. Further, a change in situs from a state with a rule against perpetuities to a state without such a rule may not serve to extend or eliminate the perpetuities problem applicable to the trust involved. Undoubtedly, one of the key aspects of a change in situs, in many taxpayers' views, is the flight to an offshore asset protection jurisdiction if the assets in the DAPT are at risk. A change in situs to a jurisdiction with a lower (or no) state income taxation (or other taxes applicable to a trust) is a desired goal for many settlers and beneficiaries. It is not clear, however, that the "relocation" of a trust from one state to another will ensure that the former state will not assert long-arm jurisdiction over the trust even following the relocation.

SUMMARY

This chapter provided an overview of using a domestic asset protection trust to protect your assets from claimants. While there may be some element of protection from the risks of divorce, all state statutes provide some exclusions from their protection for certain divorce-related claims. These domestic asset protection trusts may also provide tremendous gift, estate, GST, and even income tax benefits. While the promise of these laws is tremendous, proceed with caution and competent professional advice. The laws are new, untested, and still developing.

18 FOREIGN TRUST LAWSUIT AND DIVORCE PROTECTION RULES

THE USE OF FOREIGN TRUSTS IN ASSET PROTECTION PLANNING

Foreign asset protection trusts (FAPTs) are often the first thing most people think of when the phrase *asset protection planning* is heard. A foreign situs trust (FST) is also known by other names, including, but not limited to, asset protection trust (APT), international offshore estate planning trust (IOEPT), or simply a foreign trust. The foreign trust may provide a practical means to protect the assets of a high net worth person. Although a foreign trust can provide asset protection planning benefits, the limitations of these trusts should also be addressed before proceeding. In addition, the complexity of forming such trusts, the numerous issues that can arise upon formation, and the burdensome IRS reporting requirements should be considered. Finally, foreign trusts are rarely, if ever, the sole answer to asset protection concerns. They should be used as only part of an overall program, which includes many other appropriate asset protection techniques discussed throughout this book.

Assets held in foreign trusts can provide a measure of protection in that the countries in which they are formed have enacted laws more favorable to the protection of assets from claimants than are any American laws, including the domestic asset protection trust laws discussed in Chapter 17.

Contrary to what many believe, secrecy is not a factor in using a foreign trust. Secrecy is less than you might anticipate because to avoid gift and excise tax on transferring assets to a foreign trust, the trust is a form of grantor trust so that the assets and income of the trust may be readily identified once a U.S. income tax return is obtained in a legal proceeding (discovery).

Secrecy aside, a foreign trust may inhibit actions of judgment creditors as a result of the actual or perceived costs, time delays, and difficulties of enforcing a U.S. judgment against foreign assets. Even if the assets can be reached, the judgment creditor must carefully address whether the process is worth the reward.

Persons seeking protection from perceived or future creditors must proceed with caution when using foreign trusts. The use of foreign, as compared with domestic, trusts is more suspicious and hence the availability of bankruptcy relief or the application of fraudulent conveyance issues should be expected to be harsher.

The foreign situs asset protection trust may afford you greater control possibilities under the laws of the host foreign jurisdiction than you would be permitted as a grantor under U.S. laws. Again, however, great care must be exercised. Even if a U.S. court lacks jurisdiction over your trust, it may have jurisdiction over you. If you retain powers, a U.S. court might just incarcerate you to provide you time to contemplate whether you should exercise those powers to benefit your creditors.

BENEFITS OF A FOREIGN TRUST

Several potential benefits can be afforded to you for using a FAPT, but income tax advantages and avoiding reporting to the IRS, contrary to what some promoters advertise, are not among them.

Your Lack of Control Insulates Assets

If the foreign trust is established as an irrevocable trust, the grantor may have no authority to terminate the trust or direct the distribution of its assets. Thus, if a judgment creditor is successful in a U.S. court, the court should not be successful in ordering the grantor to turn over trust assets to the creditor. However, many foreign trusts are set up as incomplete transfers so that the grantor can avoid the excise and gift taxes, which may otherwise be due on a transfer.

More Favorable Statute of Limitations Than under Applicable U.S. Law

Where the jurisdiction of the FAPT is properly selected and certain other criteria adhered to, the benefits of the laws of a foreign jurisdiction may be available. These laws may be more favorable to the protection and creditor rights than applicable U.S. law. For example, the statue of limitations for filing claims may be shorter.

The U.S. Uniform Fraudulent Transfer Act (UFTA) provides that the statute of limitations begins to run upon actual discovery of the transfer of the assets. However, this discovery rule is not applicable in many British Colony jurisdictions, which provide that the statute of limitations begins to run at the actual time of the transfer. Thus, in many instances, the statute of limitations will have already expired by the time the creditor obtains a judgment.

In some jurisdictions, in addition to a shorter statute of limitations, the local law equivalent of a fraudulent conveyance law is more favorable than the UFTA. For example, local law may preclude a fraudulent conveyance challenge by a creditor who was a future unknown creditor at the time of the transfer.

Fraudulent conveyance statutes are generally designed to be very pro-grantor in the FAPT. These rules are far harsher against the claimant than are the laws of domestic asset protection trusts, such as under the Alaska statute. This may, however, be a positive characteristic of the Alaska statute, not a negative. The use of a domestic asset protection trust may "smell" less offensive than the use of an FAPT because of this. Also, if the severity of your circumstances has reached the point that a transfer must be made to a country with no fraudulent conveyance statute (i.e., the suit against you is being walked to the courthouse), the risks you face can be significant.

National Barriers to Claims and Actions

There is a national barrier where an American claimant must file a foreign legal action to pursue and obtain recovery from the assets located in the foreign trust. The judgment creditor may first attempt to seek an order from a U.S. court to have the assets of the trust turned over to the creditor. However, the beneficiary may not have the power to revoke the trust when an irrevocable trust is used. Further, under an irrevocable FAPT, the beneficiary would not have the power to require the trustee to distribute the assets to the creditor. Therefore, the creditor's only remedy is to fight the debtor in the foreign jurisdiction.

If creditors seek to pursue the claim in a foreign jurisdiction, they must establish the grantor's personal liability again under the laws of that foreign jurisdiction. For such an action to be successful, the foreign jurisdiction where the trust is based must have jurisdiction over the grantor (personal jurisdiction) and jurisdiction over the matter being contested (subject matter jurisdiction). If claimants are successful, to reach the trust assets, they must then prove that the transfer of assets by the grantor to the trust was somehow a fraudulent transfer under the laws of that country so that those assets can be reached.

Foreign Jurisdiction Will Not Recognize a U.S. Judgment

Some foreign jurisdictions do not recognize a judgment by a U.S. court. In legal parlance, there is no comity. Therefore, a new case would have to be pursued in the foreign jurisdiction where the trust was organized. The cost and difficulties of such a trial could dissuade less than serious claimants in the United States from pursuing such claims because the creditor who still wishes to pursue the claim must retain an attorney in the foreign jurisdiction to seek execution of the judgment against the trust assets. To accomplish this goal, the creditor must prove personal liability, *de novo,* under the laws of the foreign jurisdiction. The foreign court must have sufficient personal and subject matter jurisdiction, and the alleged violation must also be a violation of the laws of the foreign jurisdiction for the creditor to assert a proper cause of action.

The goal is that the obstacles and costs created by the use of a foreign trust serve as a strong incentive to settle the claim at a substantially lower amount than if the option of a U.S. forum were open to the potential litigant.

Spendthrift Rules Are Strong

Trusts in FAPT jurisdictions are always spendthrift trusts. The statutes providing such results override the historical treatment of self-settled trusts in a manner that is more beneficial than the domestic trust laws. Foreign asset protection trust laws are more favorable in that they do not have the exceptions for alimony, child support, and certain tort claims that a domestic asset protection trust laws include.

Global Investment Opportunities Increased

The foreign trust can be a good vehicle for global investing because foreign jurisdictions often are subject to less stringent regulation then in the United States. As a result, investment products available to overseas investors are not always available to U.S.-based investors. This can be a legitimate and important nonasset protection motive for establishing a foreign situs trust.

Secondary Legal Benefits of the Foreign Trust

The foreign trust may enable you to strengthen the protection of a spendthrift provision for the trust's beneficiaries. As a U.S. trust, assets held in a foreign trust should avoid probate in the United States. The secrecy laws of foreign jurisdictions may provide more privacy than domestic trusts can offer.

Inability of Claimants to Hire Attorneys to Pursue Claims

Attorneys in the FAPT host jurisdiction are often unwilling or unable to accept a suit against the institutional trustee in their jurisdiction because of the manner in which local laws are written. In some of the smaller FAPT countries, the number is modest, and many may work for the institutions serving as FAPT trustees and thus be disqualified from representing your creditor trying to sue that institution to have them disgorge your FAPT assets. The result is few attorneys may be able or willing to even commence a suit against such an institution, so it may be nearly impossible for a creditor to obtain adequate local counsel to even pursue a claim. This situation obviously does not apply in any U.S. jurisdiction.

OPTIONS FOR STRUCTURING THE FOREIGN TRUST

Grantor/Completed Gift versus Nongrantor/ Noncompleted Gift

A threshold issue in planning the use of a foreign trust is to determine whether the foreign trust should be a grantor trust. (See later detailed discussion.)

If it is a grantor trust, the transfers of property to the trust should not be deemed completed gifts for gift tax purposes, trust income is taxable annually to the grantor, and the assets of the trust are included in the grantor's estate on his or her death. Grantor trust status is achieved by the grantor retaining sufficient powers under the provisions of the trust agreement to cause this result for federal tax purposes without retaining sufficient powers to taint the creditor protection aspects of the trust. This approach can provide two beneficial results that initially would appear contradictory: (1) Trust is deemed foreign with respect to legal and administrative issues, and (2) trust is deemed domestic with respect to tax issues.

If this is not the desired result, the trust could be structured to be a nongrantor trust. In such a situation, the transfer of assets to the trust may be a completed gift for gift tax purposes and may trigger the 35 percent excise tax, but the trust assets may be able to grow completely tax free and possibly be made available in perpetuity as a financial resource of the grantor's family without diminution by any taxes.

Foreign Trust Combined with Family Limited Partnership

Many people seeking the asset protection benefits of an FAPT may still not want to move assets offshore even with all the safeguards possible (see later discussion). Thus, a commonly used planning structure for many FAPTs, used by those not willing to move assets offshore, includes the use of a U.S. family limited partnership (FLP). Some FAPT plans include an FLP of which you as the grantor forming the FAPT serve as general partner. The family partnership could also be formed with a corporation serving as the general partner through which you could retain control but perhaps not majority ownership of the general partner.

You would then transfer your actual assets (stocks, bonds, cash, etc.) into the FLP in exchange for the partnership's issuing you limited partnership interests. Once you receive these limited partnership interests, you would then transfer most of them, perhaps constituting 99 percent of all partnership interests other than a 1 percent interest in the general partner, which you personally retain in your newly formed FAPT. This same type of planning can be done with a domestic or foreign limited liability company (LLC) in which you would serve as manager (analogous to the general partner of the FLP).

Alternatively, you could sell the limited partnership interests to the foreign trust in exchange for installment notes or a private annuity.

Your FAPT will have a foreign trustee, a trust protector, and perhaps even an investment advisor. The actual physical assets may be left in the United States. They might even be left in the same brokerage firm they had originally been in, only in a new FLP or LLC account.

The courts may likely view these controls you now have, as well as the U.S. connections, as a substantial degree of control being retained by you as the grantor. The result is that your assets, even if somewhat protected, are subject to greater risk of being attacked by a creditor.

If this structure is in place for many years and you want more protection, you can, when you feel more comfortable, unwind the U.S. connections. You could, as manager of the LLC or general partner of the FLP, direct that the physical situs of assets be moved offshore, although the assets would remain owned by the FLP or LLC. The trustee of your foreign trust may discharge you as general partner or manager if that authority was given. The result would then be that no control remains in your hands, and no U.S. person remains that the court can order to bring assets back.

This plan, however, raises issues as to whether the transfer of assets offshore and your resignation of your positions (and release of powers) are fraudulent conveyances intended to hinder your claimants. On the other hand, you arguably did not own the assets at the time of these structural changes, so you would argue that a fraudulent conveyance by you could not have been possible. However, because the trust is a self-settled trust, the court may view this as your assisting the trustee in hindering and delaying the reach of your creditors.

This approach would appear to increase the vulnerability of trust assets even if a fraudulent conveyance problem is surmounted. A transfer of assets offshore by the trustee just following the filing of a motion would appear rather suspicious.

The moral of this discussion is that your attorney can craft a plan that works to your level of comfort. The more strings you need to be comfortable, the more risks you face that your plan won't succeed.

The following steps are commonly used to implement the family limited partnership/foreign situs trust structure:

Step 1: Form a limited partnership (or LLC) by filing the appropriate certificate of limited partnership and naming yourself and perhaps your spouse (to avoid any tax consequences from the transfer of ownership interests). You could "take back" (i.e., in exchange for the transfer of the initial assets transferred) all of the general partnership interests and 99 percent of the limited partnership interests. Your spouse could "take back" 1 percent of the limited partnership interests.

Step 2: Have your attorney prepare, and you and the other partners sign, a family limited partnership agreement that includes restrictions on transfer of any partnership interests, language, and other protective steps discussed in Chapter 10.

Step 3: Transfer stock (except in S corporations), bonds, real estate (except a personal residence), and cash to the family limited partnership.

Step 4: Transfer the limited partnership interests to the FAPT. The interests in the FAPT are managed by the trustee (perhaps only foreign, or foreign and U.S. cotrustees) and the trust protector. However, because the assets of the limited partnership are managed by the general partner of the family limited partnership, it is you as the general partner (or perhaps you as president of the S corporation serving as general partner) who controls the underlying assets.

Step 5: Before an emergency, the foreign trustee/trust protector can liquidate the limited partnership into the foreign trust and remove the U.S. trustees to sever any and all ties with the United States.

Other Considerations for Structuring Foreign Trusts

In some instances, the investments are made through a corporation organized in a tax haven country, all of the stock of which is owned by the trust. Alternatively, the shares of stock could be held by the limited partnership, which interests the trust then owns. The advantage of the use of a corporation is that the corporation can be organized in a country with favorable tax and creditor protection laws, which differs from the country in which the trustee is based or the trust organized. This may serve as yet another hurdle for a potential claimant to surmount.

RULES TO MAKE FOREIGN TRUSTS SUCCEED

Foreign asset protection trusts are complex and require great care. The following sections are some of the steps you should address with your professional advisors to help ensure that your FAPT succeeds.

Selection of Trustees

You should have at least one trustee resident in the jurisdiction where you want the trust to exist. You can have a cotrustee, even someone in the United States, but doing so creates a risk that the U.S. court will have jurisdiction over the FAPT, which might undermine your planning. If you have a U.S. person involved, a mechanism to remove that person if a problem occurs is essential. However, the removal mechanism itself may create a basis for challenge by a creditor seeking the help of a U.S. court. Unlike U.S. trusts, FAPT law may permit, as does the Cook Islands, for you as the grantor to serve as a cotrustee. Again, carefully consider the amount of ties and control you have over the trust.

No U.S. Presence

To limit U.S. jurisdiction, your foreign trustee should not have presence in the United States. For example, the trust company that serves as trustee of your FAPT should not have a branch office in the United States.

Trust Protector Powers

A trust protector should be used with a variety of nonfiduciary powers to change trustees, situs, governing law, and other key trust characteristics. If your FAPT is sued, the protector can move from Turks & Cacois to the Cook Islands, for example. If the FAPT jurisdiction your trust is based in changes its laws to be less hospitable, perhaps because of strong-arming by the U.S. government, your protector can shift your FAPT to another jurisdiction that remains FAPT-friendly. Carefully, distinguish a "negative" versus "affirmative" power for your trust protector. Protector usually has negative powers so that the protector cannot be ordered by court to do something by a U.S. court. A trust protector may get only veto power over acts first taken by trustee, a negative power. This contrasts with an affirmative power, such as having the trust agreement specify that your trust protector may move the situs of your FAPT. Some experts think that protector powers can be a problem, whether negative or positive.

Distribution Rights

Your rights to distributions from your FAPT should be restricted, as should your powers over the trust. If your rights become too great, even FAPT jurisdiction law may enable your creditor to reach the assets. Your right to trust income or assets should not be more than a mere eligibility, not an entitlement.

Indirect Powers

Much of asset protection planning is a trade-off. You really cannot retain complete control over assets and have them well protected. This is a particularly acute problem when using FAPTs because many people are simply uncomfortable with having significant amounts of their wealth in a small island nation they cannot locate on a map. The danger is that you counter this worry by retaining too much control over your FAPT, directly or indirectly, so that you undermine the very asset protection benefits you wish to achieve.

You should ideally limit any other rights you have, direct or indirect. The less control, the less risk. For example, as described previously, many FAPTs are created as a two-tier structure using a family limited partnership (FLP) to hold assets invested in the United States. You serve as general partner of the FLP, retaining the considerable powers and controls the position affords (see Chapter 10). Limited partnership interests are transferred to the FAPT. While, technically, the FAPT owns most of your assets, you as the general partner remain subject to the jurisdiction of a U.S. court—not a positive. What if you name yourself or your spouse as trust protector? Perhaps you take a step further back and name independent people as trust protector but reserve the right to terminate existing protectors and name new ones. A U.S. court may endeavor to require you to exercise any powers you have retained, as general partner, trust protector, or otherwise, to benefit your creditors. You must carefully weigh with your attorney in preparing your FAPT documents and plan what powers or rights you really need. If you find yourself so worried that you are retaining so many powers and your advisors question the viability of the plan, perhaps an FAPT is just not right for you.

Perhaps additional safeguards can be built into the plan to provide you with additional comfort that your assets will not disappear. If you are concerned whether your trustee will steal your assets once they are transferred offshore, you might have the assets physically located in an institution other than the institution serving as trustee. For example, your physical accounts may be with an institution in Switzerland that does not have any U.S. branches. Your trust protector may be in Isle of Mann. The actual FAPT may be based in, and created under the laws of, the Cook Islands. The actual accounts located in Switzerland, with a Swiss institution, may be established in a manner that requires two parties to sign to withdraw, transfer, or remove funds. If the two parties who must sign are independent persons, such as your Cook Island FAPT trustee, and your Isle of Mann-based trust protector, enough checks and balances may exist for you to sleep at night.

CRITERIA TO CONSIDER IN SELECTING A LOCATION FOR THE FOREIGN TRUST

Business and Other Criteria

1. The political, economic, and social stability of the jurisdiction.
2. The jurisdiction's reputation in the world business community.
3. Whether language barriers exist.
4. Whether the jurisdiction has modern telecommunications facilities.
5. Whether the jurisdiction offers adequate legal, accounting, and financial services.

Tax Criteria

The jurisdiction selected should have no significant income, gift, or estate taxes. Note, however, that if taxes are enacted after the trust is formed, the trust protector (described later) could exercise a provision in the trust agreement to change the location of trust assets to a more favorable host country.

Legal Criteria

1. When does the statute of limitations begin to run on a particular action?
2. Does the particular jurisdiction recognize the holdings of a U.S. court in a particular case?
3. Is the jurisdiction's trust law favorable, well-defined, and protective?

4. What standard of proof must a creditor meet in attempting to show fraudulent intent on the part of the transferor?

5. To what extent may a transferor retain benefit in, and control over, a foreign trust without exposing the trust to the transferor's creditors?

6. What is the importance of the grantor's solvency following transfers to the foreign trust?

7. What recognition is to be given to judgments and orders of foreign courts that affect a foreign trust, its trustees, and its assets?

8. What conditions must be satisfied to freeze trust assets?

WHAT ASSETS TO TRANSFER TO THE FOREIGN TRUST

The assets you transfer to your FAPT should generally not be tainted by legal or other risks; for example, a business with liability claims, real estate with hazardous waste problems, and so on. To transfer a tainted asset could jeopardize the integrity of the trust and the other nontainted assets transferred to the trust.

Special Considerations Where Family Limited Partnership-Foreign Asset Protection Trust Structure Is Used

If a family limited partnership is combined with the FAPT, consideration should be given to the transfer of certain assets. If a personal residence is to be transferred to a family limited partnership, tax benefits from the rollover and tax-deferred reinvestment of sales proceeds could be lost. Similarly, the ability to exclude up to $250,000 to $500,000 of gain on the sale of your residence would be lost as would home mortgage interest and property tax deductions. Therefore, a personal residence should be transferred directly to the FAPT, which, as a grantor trust, should not jeopardize the tax benefits. If stock in an S corporation is to be transferred to a family limited partnership/FAPT structure, the tax status of the S corporation election could be jeopardized. It may be feasible to transfer the stock in the S corporation directly to the FAPT to avoid this risk (see Chapter 12). If this step is taken, caution should be exercised because the beneficiary must comply with specific IRS tax filing requirements to make the S election.

As with the use of an FAPT generally, certain assets cannot or should not generally be transferred. For example, interests in a professional corporation must be owned by a licensed professional and cannot, therefore, be transferred.

KEOGH, IRA, and pension assets should not be transferred.

MECHANICS OF ESTABLISHING A FOREIGN TRUST

Opinion of Local Counsel

You should obtain an opinion of a local attorney in the FAPT host country who addresses the validity and enforceability of the trust under local law; the inability of present and future creditors to reach trust assets (this opinion will undoubtedly be based on an assumption of no fraudulent conveyance of assets to the trust); the assurance that no local income, estate, excise, or other taxes will affect the trust; and whether local law or U.S. law applies to determine whether the transfer to the trust was bona fide.

Affidavits of No Current Litigation

The bank or other entity chosen to act as trustee often requires an affidavit stating that there are no existing judgments or claims. The attorney and other professionals involved generally requires a financial statement in addition to the affidavit because the professionals can risk personal liability if it is later found that they assisted the grantor in defrauding or hindering creditors. Creditors could view the professionals assisting in a fraudulent conveyance as being joint tort feasor.

Selecting a Trustee

The person (entity) selected as a trustee could be an international bank with a strong financial basis. Alternatively, law or accounting firms in the host countries where the trust is organized often serve in the role as trustees.

It is important that the trustee have no U.S. connections such that a U.S. court could obtain jurisdiction over the trustee. This means that the bank should have not conducted any business in the United States, nor should it have any presence in the United States. For example, if a foreign bank is selected, it should not have an un-incorporated U.S. branch operation. Such a branch would be the same legal entity as the parent bank serving as trustee and could thus expose the trustee to the jurisdiction of a U.S. court. If a creditor won a judgment against the grantor in a U.S. court, the court could then serve the parent/trustee through serving an order on the branch.

Selecting and Using a Trust Protector

In many foreign jurisdictions, it is common to employ a trust protector. The protector can be considered an intermediary between the beneficiaries and the trustee, with the primary objective of protecting the beneficiaries from, and representing them before, the trustee.

A committee of advisors or protectors is formed for the purpose of advising the trustees on matters such as trust investments, administration, and distributions. This allows the persons establishing the trust, the grantors, to maintain some level of indirect input without usurping the powers of the trustees.

The trust protector may be a person or corporation that is not a trustee or beneficiary. This could be a law firm or accounting firm in the host jurisdiction. The beneficiary should not be a protector because the power to remove the trustee (one of the key powers generally given to the protector) could cause the inclusion of the trust assets in the beneficiary's estate.

The protector may exercise certain powers alone. In some instances, the trustee must have the consent of the protector to exercise certain powers.

Powers that may be given to the trust protector include the right to change the characteristics of the trust, which could expose the trust assets to risks in the event of a change in circumstances. These include a change in the trustee, the situs of the trust assets, and the choice of law provision. If a host country's rules change, the ability to change any of these characteristics could be important to the continued protection of the trust assets. Some trusts provide the trust protector the right to add or change the beneficiaries of the trust.

An important power of the trust protector is the right to remove the trustee. Another common power is for the trust protector to change the jurisdiction of the trust to another jurisdiction, to perhaps another former British Colony. This is known as a *fight-or-flight provision*. The trust protector may wish to move the trust if the foreign jurisdiction enacts income, gift, or estate tax laws; becomes threatened by war or civil unrest; enters a treaty with the United States (which could jeopardize tax, litigation, or other benefits); or if the trust becomes threatened by litigation in the original jurisdiction.

Provisions to Include in the Trust Agreement

Irrevocable/Revocable Trust.   The trust could be revocable or irrevocable. If the grantor can revoke the trust, a U.S. court could have the power to force the grantor to repatriate the funds. Therefore, the trust agreement could specifically state that it is irrevocable.

Grantor Trust.   The trust agreement must include language sufficient to make the trust taxable, for U.S. federal income tax purposes, as a grantor trust. The tax implications of this are significant, but complex.

Secrecy and Nondisclosure Provisions.   A typical foreign trust includes secrecy and nondisclosure provisions to ensure privacy. The trustee, however, may request a waiver of this with respect to inquiries by the U.S. government or its agencies.

Antiduress Clause.   This clause permits the trustee to ignore instructions given to it under duress or coercion; for example, if a U.S. court that does not have jurisdiction makes a demand, directly or indirectly, on the trustee.

Beneficiaries.   The grantor and members of the family can be named as discretionary beneficiaries of the trust. However, neither the grantor nor any member of the family should have an actuarially ascertainable interest in the trust.

Beneficiaries' Powers.   The beneficiaries should not be granted any power to compel the trustee to distribute income or principal of the trust. This is also a major drawback to the use of a foreign trust as a planning technique. Control is sacrificed.

Selection of Trust Protector.   The trust protector should not be a beneficiary or the grantor and, according to some, should be domiciled in a location different from that where the trust is based.

Flight Clause.   Allowing the trust to be moved to another jurisdiction may also be accomplished through a *flight clause*. If a creditor is successful in gaining access to the assets of the trust through a court having jurisdiction over the trust, the trust is capable of quickly fleeing to another foreign situs. Other situations may arise that would warrant the trust protector's changing the situs of the trust. These could include enactment of unfavorable income, gift, estate, transfer, or other taxes in the host jurisdiction, war or civil unrest, or other calamities. If the host country enters into a bilateral trade or tax or other treaty with the United States, information reporting and other provisions of such a treaty could jeopardize the insulation provided by the foreign trust. A shift of the trust situs and trust assets to a jurisdiction without such a treaty could ensure retention of these benefits.

The flight clause in the trust agreement could set parameters for the countries that the trust protector could select to relocate trust assets. For example, the trust could specify that the successor countries selected must be other former British Colony jurisdictions.

Choice of Law.   The provision for choice of law contained in the trust agreement should provide a mechanism to change the choice of law in the event of unforeseen changes. This differs from a typical choice of law provision, which establishes a permanent choice of law. For example, if the laws of the host country change unfavorably, the trust protector, in connection with the trustee, could designate a new choice of law. The new choice of law could be subject to certain limitations as would the fight or flight provision described previously.

When to Fund the Trust

The safest approach is undoubtedly to fund the trust as early as possible. However, some advisers believe that with a properly structured foreign trust in place, the option to move the assets to the foreign jurisdiction at a later date may also exist. Using this approach, it is argued that it is possible to defer transferring assets overseas until a creditor actually begins to take action against you. The trustee may then move the assets to another country. Caution is in order.

LIMITATIONS, PROBLEMS, AND DIFFICULTIES OF USING FOREIGN SITUS TRUSTS

The use of FAPTs involves substantial difficulties in drawbacks, including, but limited to, the following.

Cost

Cost of the initial formation of the trust, as well as ongoing annual fees, can be significant. Annual fees can include those to file several different types of tax reports, as well as the annual tax return, annual trustee fees, fees to the trust protector, and so forth.

Loss of Control

Most effective foreign trusts require that U.S. grantors forgo any significant interest or control over trust assets. These restrictions can be severe, including your not naming a U.S. person as a trustee or cotrustee of the trust. The concern in this regard is that if a U.S. person is deemed to be a cotrustee, the U.S. courts may have jurisdiction to force that cotrustee to disburse funds by transferring trust assets back to the U.S. jurisdiction.

Risk of Foreign Trust Being Attacked as a Fraudulent Conveyance

A foreign trust may be attacked to be set aside as a fraudulent conveyance. Fraudulent conveyance law seeks to protect both present and subsequent creditors. Subsequent creditors include persons against whom the transferor harbored, at the time of the transfer, the actual intent to hinder, delay, or defraud, or persons who are injured as a result of the transferor's conducting his or her affairs with reckless disregard for the rights of others after the transfer of property has taken place. However, if there are no present creditors or claims pending, the fact that the trust was created from concern with respect to environmental or health issues should not be enough to set aside the trust as fraudulent.

U.S. Courts May Try to Reach Trust Assets and Apply U.S. Law

A U.S. court may disregard the grantor's decision as to choice of foreign law and apply domestic law to reach the assets of the trust. The ultimate safety valve is the ability of the foreign trust, as an international instrument, to invest and reinvest assets in any part of the world. The option exists for the trustees to exercise their fiduciary duty to protect trust assets by diversifying investment of the trust's assets outside any jurisdiction in which a problem may be foreseen, thereby forcing the battle over the assets into the foreign court.

SUMMARY

This chapter provided an overview of one of the most powerful asset protection techniques, the foreign asset protection trust. The rules, however, are complex and changing, and care must be taken and specialized professional advise sought when planning a foreign asset protection trust.

Index